THE FATE OF ADMIRAL KOLCHAK

Vice-Admiral Aleksandr Vasilevich Kolchak
Supreme Ruler of Russia, November 1918–January 1920

THE FATE OF
ADMIRAL KOLCHAK

Peter Fleming

HARCOURT, BRACE & WORLD, INC.
NEW YORK

Printed in Great Britain by Richard Clay and Company, Ltd., Bungay, Suffolk

THIS book tells a story of failure and defeat, and from it the forces under Admiral Kolchak's command emerge with scant credit; but there were many brave men in their ranks.

I dedicate what follows to the memory of

PIOTR SERGEIVICH BORODISHIN

a former sergeant in one of the Siberian armies.

A gallant, enduring and resourceful man, he lived for years in solitary exile beside a marsh on the north-eastern confines of Tibet. In 1935 he helped two young travellers on a difficult adventure; they last saw him 'riding back along the way we had come, hunched on his camel, eternally sucking at his long Chinese pipe, his sad loyal eyes staring across the empty lands before him.' Two years later he was murdered by bandits. I remember him with gratitude, and deep respect.

Contents

vii

CONTENTS

Illustrations

ILLUSTRATIONS

MAPS

Drawn by K. C. Jordan

Foreword

My interest in the events described in these pages dates from the autumn of 1931, when at the age of twenty-four I travelled for the first time along the Trans-Siberian Railway. I knew very little then about the Civil War which had ended a decade earlier, but, noting the scrawny skeletons of barbed-wire entanglements which still flanked most of the bridges, and the bullet-holes not yet obliterated from station buildings, I often found myself speculating about the struggle which had left these petty scars in obscure corners of a vast, empty land.

In the years that followed I spent a good deal of time in Manchuria and the outlying parts of North and North West China and heard, often from the mouths of participants, many stories about the Civil War in Siberia. What I heard implanted in the back of my mind a curiosity about the central figure in this sad affair—Admiral Kolchak. White Russians, and indeed foreigners in general, spoke of him almost invariably with respect and admiration. Why, then, had he failed so signally? Above all, what was the true story of his end? Had he been, as most people claimed, 'betrayed'? If so, by whom? And why? How did the train full of gold ingots, which featured in all versions of the story, come into it?

In 1960 something (I cannot now remember what) revived this dormant curiosity. An advertisement in the Agony Column of *The Times* placed me in contact with the Admiral's son, a small boy at the time of his father's death. I journeyed, for the fourth time, along the Trans-Siberian as far as Irkutsk, where Kolchak met his fate. I got in touch with people in England and France who had been in Siberia during the Civil War.

And I set about reading the voluminous literature which illuminates, throws sidelights on, or—in some Soviet and White Russian sources—distorts the picture of what happened to the man who for just over a year was styled Supreme Ruler of Russia. The result is this book.

The political background to the episode is complex. Siberia was only one of half a dozen Russian theatres in which the Allies intervened. Intervention was not the result of an agreed policy. It was undertaken by each of the Powers for different motives. The hopes, fears and delusions which underlay those motives were never constant for long, since the march of events outside Russia regularly overtook and rendered obsolete the assumptions—most of them unsound—on which Allied plans were based.

The effect of all this is to produce a sort of bog of history. Across this bog it is necessary to pick one's way; but when one puts a wary foot down on what looks like a fact, the fact immediately ceases to be valid and sinks under one. The bog heaves. Distracting bubbles appear elsewhere on its surface. The historian, skipping as nimbly as he may on to the next tuft of evidence, finds that this too can only momentarily support the weight of truth; and the poor fellow, who during these gymnastics has to explain the provenance of the bubbles and the significance of the heaves, arrives in an exhausted state upon Siberian *terra firma*. 'Anyone,' Mr George F. Kennan has written, 'who sets out to give in brief compass an adequate picture of the origins of the Siberian Intervention imposes on himself an almost impossible task.'

I have led the reader as expeditiously as possible across this curious morass, which other writers, and notably Mr Kennan, have charted with impressive accuracy. What was said, thought and done in the Allied capitals, by the war-makers at Versailles and, later, by the peace-makers in Paris, provides the material for a fascinating study of international behaviour; but the policies of the Allies, though they were instrumental in setting the stage in Siberia and promoting the drama that was enacted upon it, had in hard fact little influence on the manner in which the actors played their parts.

No major battles were fought in Siberia, there were none of those great scything movements by strong cavalry forces which brought success alternately to Whites and Reds in South Russia. Kolchak's campaigns are of small military interest, and I have not dwelt upon them. Nor does this book attempt to describe what happened in his adversaries' camp. Even to summarise the tribulations and achievements of the Soviet Government during the period would have overburdened and unbalanced a chronicle of events to which developments in the Kremlin were only indirectly relevant. I have not, however, neglected the activities of the 5th Red Army and the Partisans, which were of capital importance.

My main purpose is implicit in the title of this book. I wanted to establish as accurately as possible the circumstances of Kolchak's failure, of his betrayal, and of his death. I think I can claim to have done this. I am less confident that I have given a satisfactory account of Kolchak's elusive, contradictory and curiously un-Russian character. There is an almost Jekyll-and-Hyde contrast between Kolchak the man and Kolchak the dictator. The man was honest, and chivalrous to the point of quixotry; the dictator presided over a corrupt and barbarous régime. The man was born to command, the dictator incapable of dictating. The man inspired loyalty and esteem, the dictator contumely and hatred. I have done my best to resolve the problems implicit in these contradictions; but I find that I am still, as I was thirty years ago, curious about Admiral Kolchak.

Nettlebed, Oxfordshire.   PETER FLEMING
   April 1963.

Sources and Acknowledgements

A BIBLIOGRAPHY of published sources will be found on pp. 245–247. The unpublished material to which I have had access comprises the following items:

The Kolchak MSS. These consist mainly of letters written by Kolchak to his wife during the last two years of his life, but they include also a certain number of official documents, mostly pertaining to the period November 1917–November 1918. I am greatly indebted to the Admiral's son, M. Rotislav Kolchak, for placing these papers at my disposal and for furthering my researches in a variety of other ways.

The Britmis MSS. This valuable collection, from the archives of a friend who served in Siberia, consists of copies of official correspondence dealing with the affairs of the British Military Mission. Most of this correspondence is in the form of telegrams originated by or addressed to the Headquarters of the Mission. Some of these telegrams are 'internal'—i.e. messages exchanged between Headquarters at Vladivostok and officers on detachment in other parts of Siberia; others are external, being messages exchanged between the War Office and the Head of the Mission, wherever he happened to be. The great majority of them, dealing as they do with administration, situation reports from the front and other routine matters, are no longer of the slightest interest; but some are illuminating, and the series of messages referring to the *coup d'état* at Omsk make it possible to dispose of a fallacy which has long been popular with Soviet publicists. Besides the telegrams there are typescript reports and appreciations compiled by officers of the Mission; and these are usefully supplemented by similar documents from consular and naval sources, of which, it was presumably felt, the Military Mission ought to have a copy.

SOURCES AND ACKNOWLEDGEMENTS

I have read with profit the diaries of several British officers who served in Siberia. I give below the titles under which these diaries are referred to in the bibliographical notes: the names (in brackets) of the kind benefactors who allowed me to see them: and a short note explaining the diarists' status in Siberia.

Wolfe-Murray's Diary (Mrs J. G. Fyfe). The late Captain James Wolfe-Murray, DSO, RN, commanded a detachment of naval 12-pounders mounted on armoured trains which supported the Czech and White Russian forces on the Volga front; he also organised a flotilla of gunboats on the Kama River.

Howgrave-Graham's Diary (M. C. Howgrave-Graham, Esq, CBE). A very full account of his experiences by an officer of the 1st/9th Battalion, the Hampshire Regiment, who spoke some Russian.

Baring's Diary (Evelyn Baring, Esq). My friend Evelyn Baring was Adjutant of the 1st/9th Hampshires and on one of Kolchak's visits to the front commanded the British element of his bodyguard.

Cazalet's Diary (Peter Cazalet, Esq, and Mrs Thelma Cazalet-Keir). The late Victor Cazalet was ADC to General Sir Alfred Knox, head of the British Military Mission.

Over the last three years many people, in many different ways, have helped me to write this book. I owe gratitude to all, but to none more than Colonel Leo Steveni, OBE, MC, a pioneer member of the British Military Mission, whose retentive memory and shrewd judgment of Siberian affairs have been of the greatest value to me. I would also like to thank Mr Jan Gerke, who served with distinction in the Czechoslovak Legion and has given me guidance in my quest for evidence about its activities; Mr David Footman of St Antony's College, Oxford, who went out of his way to encourage a poacher on what are by right his own preserves; and members of the Faculty of History at the University of Irkutsk, as well as several citizens of that town, who helped me to understand things about Kolchak's fate that I should never have got from reading.

P. F.

CHAPTER ONE

The Incident at Chelyabinsk

In the early hours of 14 May 1918 a troop-train, coming from the east, pulled into the station at Chelyabinsk, a place of small importance where the Trans-Siberian Railway debouches from the foothills of the Urals into the great Siberian plain. The train was packed with Austrian and Hungarian prisoners of war; they were being repatriated under the Treaty of Brest Litovsk, which the newly formed Soviet Government had been constrained to sign with Germany and her allies two months previously. There were no Russian guards on the train, and no Austrian or Hungarian officers.

Also in the station at Chelyabinsk, but on the east-bound track, were—and had been for some time—several trains carrying the 3rd and most of the 6th Regiment of the First Czechoslovak Army Corps. These men were stateless, since their Bohemian homelands still formed part of the Hapsburg Empire; but they had been recognised by the Bolshevik authorities, in February, as forming an autonomous part of the Czechoslovak Army* in France, and they were on their way to Vladivostok. Thence, by a decision of the Supreme Allied War Council, they would be shipped round the world to reinforce the Western Front, then under severe German pressure.

The Czechoslovak échelons† at Chelyabinsk were one link in a

* This 'Army' amounted to roughly one brigade. Another brigade was being formed behind the Italian front. Both were in action in the last weeks of the war, which ended in November 1918.

† An échelon, in Russian railway jargon, was an 80-axle train, made up of 40 two-axle trucks or of a lesser number if it included some double-axle bogies.

discontinuous chain; strung out at wide intervals along the 5000 miles of railway between the Volga and the Pacific were some sixty or seventy Czech trains (their numbers later doubled). The leading trains had already reached Vladivostok, but the eastward movement of the rearmost, slow and erratic at the best of times, had, for reasons which will appear, been brought virtually to a halt during the latter part of April.

At Chelyabinsk no love was lost between the east-bound and the west-bound travellers. The Czechs saw in the Austrians and Hungarians an odious *Herrenvolk*, personifications of the tyranny from which they longed to be free: while to the returning prisoners the Czechs—many of whom had either deserted or surrendered at the first opportunity to the Tsar's armies—appeared as traitors. On the Czech side a more immediate cause for resentment lay in their knowledge that the prisoners, enviably homeward bound, had been given priority on the railway. Germany, perturbed by rumours that Japan intended to invade Siberia, was insisting on the immediate evacuation of prisoners of war from that region; their transit over a railway system which had been overstrained even before the Revolution and was now badly disorganised supplied one of the reasons for the Czech trains being held up. For the two bodies of men at Chelyabinsk Station, exacerbated already by delays, uncertainty and the rough usages of war, propinquity held dangers.

But the Czechoslovak temperament is not combative. Throughout the war Russia's treatment of her prisoners combined the minimum of humanity with the maximum of incompetence, and when those at Chelyabinsk complained that they were half-starved the Czechs handed over to them a quantity of rations.

In spite of this many of the newcomers were arrogant and abusive, and when in the middle of the morning the whistle blew and the prisoners piled back into their trucks, both factions were in an ugly humour. As the train began to move out of the station a man in the last truck shouted a curse which was both obscene and blasphemous (and which, being shouted in Hungarian, was understood by the Slovaks present); he then hurled a large segment of cast-iron, part of a broken stove, at a group of Czech soldiers below him. One of these fell to the ground, blood streaming from his head.

This was too much for the Czechs. Before the train could gather speed they boarded the locomotive and brought it to a stop. Then they forced the occupants of the last three trucks, seventy or eighty in number, to detrain, and demanded that they identify the culprit, of whom nobody outside the train had had a clear view. At first the Austro-Hungarians refused; but the Czechs were armed, their attitude was menacing, and the prisoners, who wanted above all else to resume their journey towards freedom, had no time for heroics. The Hungarian who had done the deed was handed over; the Czechs lynched him on the spot; and the train chugged off towards the Urals.[1]

During the spring of 1918, in one cause or another, in hot blood or in cold, many lives were violently extinguished. On the Western Front the Germans, the French, the British and the Americans were killing each other by tens of thousands. The Italian front was active. In Russia, although the Terror was yet to come, life was cheap. But in all this holocaust no single death was to have more far-reaching consequences than that of the Hungarian, swiftly battered out of God's image on a Siberian railway station; for, as one authority puts it, 'this obscure brawl . . . was the spark that ignited a blaze of civil war over a vast expanse of Russian territory.' [2]

Local Soviet officials, arriving tardily upon the scene with a detachment of Red Guards, announced that a commission of enquiry would be held into the affray; and after some disputation a number of Czechs were subpoenaed as witnesses and taken off to the town, which at that period lay about three miles from the station.[3] Two days later, no more having been heard of these men, a delegation under a Czech officer went into Chelyabinsk to demand their release, only to be arrested and imprisoned for its pains.

Bolshevik power was, as the Czechs knew, insecurely

established in the area, and although the garrison numbered some 2000 men the Chelyabinsk Soviet were unsure how staunch they would prove in a crisis. The Czech command decided to act boldly; a force of two battalions, armed as heavily as resources permitted, was marched into the town centre.

Boldness paid. The men in detention were handed over, apologies were forthcoming; but the matter, the Soviet authorities pointed out, would have to be referred to Moscow. Meanwhile the Czech trains still stood immobile in their siding. The question now was not when, but whether, they would be allowed to depart eastward. As the May sunshine strengthened, their occupants began to wish that, when they first arrived at Chelyabinsk, they had sited the latrines rather further away.

The history and the status (in 1918 the first was short and the second inchoate) of the Czechoslovak national movement will be described in a later chapter. Here it will suffice to note that by mid-May of 1918 signs were multiplying that for a number of reasons the Soviet Government regretted, and might at any moment rescind, its undertaking to allow the Czech Legion to leave Russian territory (on which a few weeks earlier it had been fighting alongside the Red Army against the Germans) and proceed via Vladivostok to the Western Front.

The decision to let the Legion go was taken in Moscow on 15 March. At that date it seemed a sensible decision. The presence on Russian soil of some 42,000 foreign troops dedicated to the prosecution of a war from which Russia herself had withdrawn was an anomaly; both as fellow-Slavs and, until recently, as comrades-in-arms who had fought hard against the common enemy, the Czechs were entitled to consideration. Moscow had every motive for facilitating their withdrawal, none for impeding it.

But in the subsequent two months the situation had changed. On the borders of Manchuria and Siberia, at the far end of the railway along which the Czechs were travelling, a Cossack freebooter called Semenov (of whom more will be heard) had raised the banner of counter-revolution; he was known to have

Allied support, and the Soviet rulers began, reasonably enough, to question the wisdom of arrangements which would result in the introduction into Semenov's theatre of a compact expeditionary force under Allied control: for that was roughly what the Czech Legion was.

These misgivings led Moscow to insist on the partial disarmament of the Czechs; they were to travel 'not as fighting units, but as groups of free citizens, who carry with them a specified number of weapons for defence against counter-revolutionary attacks.' Each train was in theory allowed 168 rifles, with 300 rounds per rifle, and one machine-gun with 1200 rounds; but in practice the Czechs, who in astuteness and resource always outpointed the Russians, had little difficulty in secreting far larger quantities of arms in their rolling-stock. Although, as the Russians pointed out, the weapons belonged to them, the process of handing some of them over generated friction, delay and mistrust. On 14 April the officers of the 1st Czech Division (comprising all the most westerly units) decided in secret that they would surrender no more arms.

By this date their prospects of evacuation had been further impaired by developments in the East. At Vladivostok (where, a little later on, the continued absence of troopships to remove the Legion from Russia was to deepen Moscow's suspicion of its true role in Imperialist strategy) there was a small concentration of Allied warships; their main duty was to invigilate, as best they could, over the huge dumps of war-material lying in and around the docks. These stores, to an estimated value of $1,000,000,000, had been supplied to Russia by the Allies whom she had deserted; not only had they not been paid for, but there was or appeared to be a danger that this material would find its way, after being transported westward, into German hands. Vladivostok, unlike the rest of Siberia, was not officially under Soviet control; but the Bolsheviks in the city, increasingly powerful and increasingly aggressive, held all the cards and were playing them defiantly. They had, among other things, begun systematically to remove the dockside stores in freight-cars.

On 4 April three Japanese civilians, said to have been clerks in a shipping office, were shot in Vladivostok by persons unknown; one of them was killed. Next day, after consulting his Consul-General, the Japanese admiral landed 200 sailors and marines, who were later reinforced; the senior British naval officer, Captain Payne, ordered fifty men ashore from HMS *Suffolk*; the American admiral, Knight, held his hand, which was tied by orders from Washington; there was no French warship in the port.

The Japanese and British actions were purely precautionary, and were taken on the initiative of the local commanders. The situation in Vladivostok was tense and uncertain; the purpose of the landing-parties was to protect foreign lives and property if things got out of hand. But for some time past Moscow had been hag-ridden by fears of a Japanese incursion into Siberia. In March 1918 *Izvestia*, reacting violently to a premature report of this development, had used words—'*patriotic* duty,' 'Soviet *fatherland*,'—which were ideologically tabu[4]; and for a people traditionally immune from racial prejudice (except against Jews) the vehemence of the revulsion with which the Russians viewed the Japanese threat is surprising. It is in marked contrast to the fatalism displayed, after Brest Litovsk, to the overrunning of yet further Russian territory by German armies. Perhaps a clue to this selective xenophobia is to be found in Trotsky's statement, in June 1918, that, if he had to choose between the Germans and the Japanese as conquerors, he would prefer the former, 'because the German is more cultured, the people are more educated, and there are more workmen, and awakening [i.e. subversion leading to revolution] is possible; while the Japanese are a foreign people, we do not know their language, the working class is less conscious.'[5]

Whatever underlay Russia's fear of Japan, a wave of indignation, tinged with panic, greeted the news of the naval landings on 5 April. 'Workers and Peasants! Honest Citizens!', proclaimed a government manifesto on that day. 'A horrible new threat is coming from the East.' Vigorous protests were made to the Allies through such few semi-diplomatic channels as remained open. And, inevitably, the slow progress of the Czech trains towards the Pacific was further decelerated. On 21 April an order went out that they should be stopped altogether.*

When news of the incident at Chelyabinsk (where the Czechs had meanwhile occupied the railway station and its environs) reached Moscow, it provoked a strong reaction. Two leading members of the Russian Section of the Czechoslovak National Council, Maxa and Čermák, were arrested on 20 May and forced to sign a telegram ordering all Czech units to hand over their arms to the Soviet authorities. On the following day Aralov, Trotsky's deputy at the Commissariat of War, issued a jejune order that the Czechs should be either reorganised into labour battalions or drafted into the Red Army. On the 23rd he followed this with harsher and more positive instructions: the Czechs were to be detained, disarmed and disbanded. Finally, on 25 May, Trotsky weighed in with a telegram to all local Soviets along the railway-line, categorically forbidding any further eastward movement of any Czech train and decreeing, among other drastic measures, that any Czechoslovak found with a weapon in his hands was to be shot out of hand; delay in executing these orders would constitute treason and entail the severest penalties.

In Russia control of a railway station meant control of, or anyhow access to, all traffic passing along the telegraph line; since the messages from Moscow were in clear, the Czechs at Chelyabinsk knew what was in the wind. At that place, it so happened, a congress of delegates from a number of other Czech units was in session and had already taken two important decisions. The first, made public in a circular telegram, was that the Legion would surrender no more arms 'until we receive a guarantee of free departure'; the second was to disregard the order that units west of Omsk should change direction and make northwards for Archangel. (This order was in

---

* This was modified ten days later. The *échelons* already east of Omsk were to be allowed to proceed; those west of Omsk were to be re-routed to Archangel and the troops in them evacuated through that port.

fact an accurate reflection of Allied strategy at the time, and the
Soviet Government's concurrence in its execution was a minor
triumph for the Allies' unofficial representatives in Moscow;
but when this was belatedly explained to the Czechs they still
saw no sense and much danger in a change of plan which would
split their forces into two completely disconnected halves.)

So the delegates at Chelyabinsk were already in an intransigent mood when they intercepted Aralov's minatory telegrams;
and on 25 May Trotsky's, which was in effect a declaration of
war, convinced them that the only way to extricate themselves
from Russia was to shoot their way out. Orders to this effect
were dispatched along the Trans-Siberian in both directions;
and at dawn on the 27th the Red garrison at Chelyabinsk was
easily overpowered and disarmed.

Elsewhere brisk and determined action by the Czechs gained
them similar successes, though sometimes only after hard
fighting. Novonikolaevsk was taken on the 26th, Penza on the
29th, Petropavlovsk and Tomsk on the 31st; Omsk fell a week
later. At Marianovka and at one or two other places the Czechs
suffered casualties in ambushes or surprise attacks; but they
always recovered from their initial disadvantages, and in no
single instance was even the weakest or most isolated unit overwhelmed.

In war it very seldom pays to place the enemy in a situation
where he has no alternative but to fight. This is what Trotsky
did to the Czechs. In May 1918 the Soviet Government was
threatened from so many sides, beset by so many weaknesses,
a prey to so many fears, that its mood was understandably one
of desperation. But if Trotsky had mastered his impulse to be
bellicose, if he had used guile instead of force, the Czechs need
never have become the 'determining factor' (as Lloyd George
among many others called them) in the Allied Intervention in
Siberia. Almost the last thing the Czechs wanted to do was to
fight the Bolsheviks; their soldiers in Siberia, their political
leaders in Washington and Paris, and their chief patrons, the
French Government, all ardently desired the same thing—to

get the Legion out of Russia. This was also a main aim of the Soviet Government. With so many and such powerful factors favouring a policy of *laissez aller*—at least until such a policy was shown to be contrary to Soviet interests—Trotsky's action in precipitating a head-on clash was at best premature, at worst a bad and unnecessary blunder.*

His off-with-their-heads order of 25 May reveals very clearly two things. First, Trotsky's belief that he had the scattered Czech *échelons* at his mercy; second, his fear that the Legion was or might become a danger to the state. His belief was mistaken. But if it had been correct—if, that is to say, the Czechs were in a trap at the end of May—they would still have been in the same trap a week or a month later; and Trotsky could either have sprung the trap if evidence came to hand that his fears were well founded or, in the absence of such evidence, he could have allowed the Czechs to continue, on his own terms, to crawl across Siberia. The flouting of Soviet authority at Chelyabinsk was, after all, a trivial matter; it had produced a situation which was not even locally explosive and which could have been ironed out by allowing the Czechs to go on their way. Tantrums were not called for. By giving way to them, Trotsky set in violent motion processes which were to result, first, in the overthrow of Bolshevik power throughout the Urals and Siberia, and, second, in the provision of a ready-made *casus belli* for Allied Intervention in that theatre.

Trotsky's belief was a fallacy; his fear, if not far-fetched, was of a remote contingency. The action he took, or tried to take, against the Czechs was deluded. It was meant to liquidate a minor, potential threat to Soviet interests. What it did was to call into being a threat to which neither of these epithets could be applied.

---

* Some Communist historiographers go so far as to suggest that Trotsky deliberately provoked the Czechs in order to further Allied interests.

CHAPTER TWO

Starter's Orders

IN 1914 France and Great Britain, when they took the field against the German and Austro-Hungarian Empires, set high hopes on their ally in the East. The 'Russian steam-roller' was soon proved to be a machine which, though undeniably ponderous, was ill-designed and unreliable; after the first few months it tended to move backwards instead of forwards, and it required a great deal of maintenance in the way of supplies which could be ill spared from the Western Front.

But as a belligerent Russia remained, for more than three and a half years, one of the walls of the arena in which a cloistral war was fought. At Joffre's headquarters, and at Haig's, there was always another map to turn to. On it the yellow and black pins might sketch a pattern even more discouraging than did the blue and red ones, nearer home; but at least there *was* a Russian front, and a very long one at that. Upon it were concentrated hundreds of thousands of the enemy's troops; to it had continuously to be dispatched—however short the enemy might be of rolling-stock, however hard-pressed his factories—regular supplies of guns and shells and cartridges, of boots and bandages and bicycles, of harness and pack-saddles, of drugs and surgical instruments, of barbed wire and field-telephones and picks and shovels, of (in short) all the impedimenta that his armies could not improvise or requisition. The Russian front, even when things were at their worst, had always imposed upon the German High Command a major diversion of effort; ever since the war began, this had been one of the basic facts of life, colouring outlooks and assumptions throughout the Western Allied camp.

It was thus with a certain incredulity, as well as with alarm and indignation, that France and Great Britain watched Russia withdraw, almost overnight, from the war. On 8 November 1917, the day after the Bolshevik seizure of power in Petrograd, Russia's *de facto* rulers—'the Workers' and Peasants' Government . . . drawing its strength from the Soviet of Workers', Soldiers' and Peasants' Deputies'—appealed to all the belligerents to 'begin at once negotiations leading to a just and democratic peace.' Within three weeks the German Government had responded favourably, within six Russia had signed an armistice with the Central Powers at Brest Litovsk and fighting upon the Eastern Front had ceased. It flared up again in mid-February when, peace negotiations having broken down, German troops resumed a virtually unopposed advance. When peace was finally signed at Brest Litovsk on 3 March 1918, Germany (who had meanwhile concluded a separate peace with the Ukraine) was in effective occupation of the Baltic States, most of White Russia, all the Ukraine and the Crimea and all Southern Russia as far east as the Don. The need to garrison and to plunder these territories continued, it is true, to involve her in a big administrative commitment; but low-category troops could be employed on these tasks, and during the winter of 1917–18 the German High Command was able to transfer roughly forty first-line divisions from the Eastern to the Western Front. With them went—a vast armoury—all the artillery, aircraft, tanks and other heavy equipment already allotted to or earmarked for the front which had ceased to exist.

The triumph of Bolshevism was a political phenomenon, of which almost every aspect was repugnant to Russia's ex-allies; but its most immediate and by far its most important consequences outside Russia were military. On 21 March 1918 the Germans launched their last and greatest offensive in the West. The British Fifth Army fell back before it. The whole Western Front buckled. Paris came under long-range bombardment. As though released by some baneful thaw, rivers of small print began once more to flood the newspapers as the mounting casualty lists were published. In these weeks of desperation the impulse to intervene was born. It would have been born if the Bolsheviks had been Buddhists, or Gladstonian Liberals, or anything else. It was bred by what looked like military necessity out of what looked like impending defeat.

Soviet historians, as Kennan points out in a scathing passage, have chosen to ignore this basic truth, suppressing, distorting or inventing evidence at need; the result is 'simply to turn the facts of history upside down and to evoke an image in which the actual occurrences of this time become wholly unintelligible.' [6] Their concern has been to portray Intervention as an Imperialist plot, at once puerile and Machiavellian, prompted by envy, greed and fear, and having as its aim the strangulation in infancy of the Soviet State. This is a recognisable caricature of what Intervention *became*; but the origins of an ill-starred policy lay—and this fact cannot be too strongly emphasised— in the Allies' urgent need to repair the seemingly fatal damage to their cause wrought by Russia's defection from it.

It is true that by the autumn of 1917, even before the Bolsheviks wrested power from the Provisional Government, the Russian armies had lost the will to fight, that in the population as a whole a bewildered fatalism had given place to apathy, that there was much open discontent, and that the leadership was bad. To argue, however, that in view of all this it made next to no difference whether Russia continued to resist or laid down her arms is to overlook two points of importance.

First, an adversary who refuses to admit defeat even when he appears to be beaten remains (as Hitler was to discover on the coast of the English Channel twenty-three years later) at the very least a nuisance; he must be eliminated, or he may become something worse. By the autumn of 1917 the Germans had gone a long way towards eliminating Russia; but so, in his day, had Napoleon. By suing for terms (which in the event were dictated by the Germans) the Soviet leaders took the only course which gave the German High Command a *completely* free hand in the East; and they took it so precipitately that the Germans had more than four months in which to effect their redispositions before the campaigning season came round again.

The second important point is that neither France nor Britain realised, or came near to realising, how far downhill things had gone in Russia during 1917. Both Governments received disturbing reports from their representatives in Petrograd and elsewhere; but it was a long time since anyone had read a report from Russia that was not disturbing, and in the year of Passchendaele and Caporetto her allies tended, and perhaps needed, to view events in Russia with a certain detachment. By now they expected little or nothing from her; but they did not expect the worst. So when the worst came, and they saw suddenly that Germany could henceforth fight them with both hands, they were not as disposed as perhaps they should have been to make allowances for the new Russia, or to reason that the old one had been on her last legs anyhow and was no great loss. Remembering the high hopes they had once pinned on Russia, the solemn treaties they had signed with her, and the prodigious amounts of financial and material aid she had received from them, they saw nothing but plain treachery in her defection; and they soon more than half convinced themselves that this unforeseen development, so auspicious from Germany's point of view, must have been brought about by German plots and bribes.

Both these assumptions were false. Lenin and Trotsky and their associates were not interested in the war. Since the conception of loyalty to the capitalist allies of an Imperialist régime had no place in their ideology, the conception of disloyalty was beyond their grasp; the imputation of it would have struck their hard, teeming minds as frivolous rather than heretical. Nor was any one of them in German pay.

But the Western Allied leaders would have been less than human if they had not formed these theories, made these deductions. From them, based on the terrible exigencies of war, was to spread a climate of opinion, a vague moral and emotional atmosphere, in which the Soviet Government was instinctively held to have only itself to blame for any inconveniences which might attend the re-erection in Russia of the anti-German front which it had wantonly destroyed.

Before it petered ingloriously out in 1920, Intervention had spread from unobtrusive beginnings in the Arctic Circle to half a dozen theatres. In each theatre the motives or the pretexts of the Allies were different, as were their respective shares of responsibility or control. They supported, and were opposed by, a bewildering variety of political and racial groups. At Baku, for instance, British troops fought side by side with Armenian revolutionaries in a vain attempt to save the city from the Turks; in the Baltic States, during 1919, German volunteer contingents were among the rabble of anti-Bolshevik forces which benefited, directly or indirectly, from Britain's interventionist policy. The only characteristic common to all these theatres is so obvious that it could easily be overlooked. It is accessibility; the Allies intervened in Russia wherever it was physically possible for them to do so.

In war stagnation is unnatural, impotence unbecoming; a combination of the two almost always stimulates the production of far-fetched, unsound plans, of which the object is to prosecute the war by indirect means. In the winter of 1917–18 the Allies were powerless to reopen with their own forces an Eastern Front against Germany; it was inevitable that they should cast about for an alternative method of achieving the same result. Within less than two months of the Bolshevik Revolution the Military Representatives of the Supreme War Council were recommending that 'all national groups [in South Russia] who are determined to continue the war must be supported by all the means in our power,' and the first twenty of many millions of pounds were on their way to the pockets of Cossack and Ukrainian leaders. Of these the most notable—perhaps fashionable would be a better word—was the Cossack Ataman Kaledin, despite the fact that his forces (estimated early in December at two companies, with the promise of three more) were reported by a British officer on the spot to be 'absolutely useless and disorganised.' [7] Kaledin was, as it happens, a man of integrity; but he was a purely local leader, interested only in securing a measure of autonomy for his Cossacks' homelands on the Don, and not in the least 'determined to continue the war.' His choice as the Allies' first champion-cum-*protégé* on Russian soil cannot be described as happy.

It is true that a nebulous project existed which envisaged the creation, somewhere in South Russia, of a sort of bastion or bridgehead, upon which would converge, or round which would coalesce, the Rumanian Army, the Ukrainians, the Transcaucasians and anyone else who might be supposed or could be induced to come under the heading of what the Military Representatives of the Supreme War Council called, rather sanguinely, 'our friends in Russia.'* In this politico-strategic fantasy the territory of the Don Cossacks was allotted a central role. But the British Government had been warned, and vehemently warned, by its representatives in Russia that no reliance was to be placed on Kaledin and his Cossacks; and the War Cabinet's decision, in December 1917, to give the Ataman † 'financial support up to any figure necessary' is symptomatic of the prevailing mood of desperation.

Throughout the Intervention there was always a discrepancy between what the policy-makers intended to be done and what actually happened. The transfer of funds to Kaledin's headquarters on the Don presented technical difficulties; and when on 11 February 1918 Kaledin, most of his Cossacks having melted away, blew his brains out, he had

---

* Characteristic of the hopes and delusions prevailing at this time is a message dispatched to the War Office by the British Military Agent in the Caucasus on 1 January 1918. By April, this officer reported, it was hoped to create a new army consisting of six corps composed of Georgians, Armenians, Russian volunteers, Assyrians and Greeks. (*History of the Great War: The Campaign in Mesopotamia.* Volume IV.)

† Save that it was an elective and not an hereditary office, the title of Ataman roughly corresponded, among the Cossacks, to the title of Sheikh among the Arabs.

not received a kopeck from London or from any of the other Allied capitals.

The decision to back Kaledin was taken in London on 3 December 1917. Three days later the British Ambassador in Tokyo transmitted to the Foreign Office an unusual request on behalf of a distinguished stranger. His Russian colleague, Sir Conyngham Greene reported, had brought to the British Embassy the former Commander-in-Chief of the Black Sea Fleet, Admiral Aleksandr Vasilevich Kolchak. Admiral Kolchak had formally placed his services 'unconditionally and in whatever capacity at the disposal of His Majesty's Government,' and had expressed a desire to 'fight if possible on the Western Front on land, and as a private soldier if so required.'

The fact that this quixotic offer was dealt with by the Foreign Secretary in person (Balfour sought the Admiralty's views on it on 12 December) is evidence that Kolchak was regarded in London as a person to be taken seriously. Unlike Kaledin, of whose character and abilities virtually nothing was known, Kolchak bore a high reputation. As a young officer he had distinguished himself in Arctic exploration; he had fought with conspicuous gallantry in the Russo-Japanese War; and in the years that followed he had taken a leading though an unobtrusive part in the reorganisation of the Admiralty in Petrograd. During the war against Germany the Russian Navy, pent up in the Baltic and the Black Sea, had had few opportunities of living down the humiliations which it had suffered, earlier in the century, at the hands of Japan; but Kolchak's outstanding merits as a commander had been recognised by his promotion to rear-admiral at the (for Russia) unprecedentedly early age of forty-three. A year later, in June 1916, he was made vice-admiral and given the Black Sea Fleet; as its commander-in-chief he combined operational dash with administrative efficiency. When at length the whole fabric of naval discipline collapsed under revolutionary stresses Kolchak—after a dramatic scene in which, at a mass meeting on the deck of his flagship, he took leave of the Fleet by throwing his sword

Theatres of Intervention

overboard—resigned his appointment and accepted an invitation from the United States Navy Department to lead a small technical mission to America. He was on his way back to Russia across the Pacific when news of the Bolshevik Revolution and of Russia's impending withdrawal from the war reached him; the telegram from the British Embassy in Tokyo conveyed his reaction to that news.

Kolchak had a strong sense of personal honour. He offered his services to the British Government because, as he afterwards explained, 'I considered it to be my duty, as one of the representatives of the former Government, to fulfil my obligation to the Allies; that the obligations which Russia had assumed to the Allies were my own obligations also . . . I therefore considered it indispensable to fulfil them to the end and desired to participate in the war even though Russia under the Bolsheviks had concluded peace.' [8]

Russian officers of the period were much given to theatrical gestures, but Kolchak's request to be allowed to serve 'on the Western Front on land,' if necessary as a private soldier, was not made for effect. As he told his interrogators two years later, 'I knew the British Navy well and knew that the British Navy, of course, did not need our help . . . What could I expect if I went into their Navy? I had been Commander of the Black Sea Fleet; I would be willing to accept any conditions, but the English themselves, who knew me well, would be in a false position. If I had been a young officer I could have been assigned to some destroyer; but as it was, the situation would have been absurd. That is why I stressed my desire to go into the army, even if it were as a common soldier.' [9] The sincerity of Kolchak's motives is beyond question.

His offer was formally accepted by the Foreign Office on 29 December, and he was informed through the British Ambassador that it would be decided at an early date where he could most usefully be employed. In Whitehall, meanwhile, the War Office (which at all stages tended to take a more active interest in Intervention than any other government agency) had assumed charge of the Admiral's destinies; and early in

C

January 1918 the Embassy in Tokyo was asked to facilitate his journey to Mesopotamia.

Exactly what employment the General Staff had in mind for Kolchak is no longer, and may never have been, clear. But in the very days when Kolchak's offer of his services was under consideration in London the decision was being taken to dispatch a Military Mission under General Dunsterville (the original of Kipling's 'Stalky') from Baghdad to the Caucasus; Dunsterforce, as it later became, was to co-operate with a small but stout-hearted Russian contingent in North Persia which had refused to recognise the Brest Litovsk armistice, and it seems highly probable that Kolchak was earmarked for some undefined role in this enterprise, of which the main purpose was to prevent the Turks from gaining control of the oil-wells round Baku and establishing on the shores of the Caspian a jumping-off-point for an advance on India.

With two of the four naval officers who had accompanied him from America, Kolchak took the first available ship from Yokohama to Shanghai. He was delayed there, waiting for an onward passage, for about three weeks, and during this interlude his affairs once more engaged the attention of the Foreign Office. In the first days of February 1918 Prince Kudashev, the Russian Ambassador to China, approached the British Minister, Sir John Jordan. He was, he said, anxious to consult Kolchak about Siberia; could the Admiral be brought to Peking? The suggestion, relayed to Kolchak in Shanghai, did not attract him. He replied that he was about to leave for Mesopotamia and could not change his plans without the authority of the British Government, under whose orders he considered himself to be. Jordan referred the matter to London.

The Foreign Office, or possibly the War Office, were still anxious to get Kolchak to Mesopotamia as quickly as possible. On 10 February a message to this effect reached him through British consular channels in Shanghai, and he sailed two days later. The Director of Military Intelligence, who at this stage was master-minding Kolchak's movements, had omitted, probably in the supposed interests of security, to notify Hongkong that a distinguished volunteer was in transit; and when his ship called there the Admiral found himself under the disagreeable necessity of reporting to the police every time he went ashore.[10]

Kolchak's next port of call was Singapore; by the time he reached it, on 11 March, the War Office had changed its mind. 'Your secret presence in Manchuria,' cabled the Director of Military Intelligence, 'is most desirable';[11] the situation in the Middle East had altered, and Prince Kudashev and the shareholders of the Chinese Eastern Railway wanted him to join the board of that concern. This message, already a week old, was handed to him when his ship docked by the G.O.C. Straits Settlements, General Ridout; it made Kolchak angry.

He had volunteered to fight for the Allies, preferably on the Western Front: not to undertake clandestine commercial activities on Chinese territory. The idea that one of Russia's most renowned war-time leaders could preserve his incognito among the large Russian colony in Manchuria was infantile; and if it really was necessary for him to go there, why could not the British have foreseen the necessity a month earlier, when Kolchak and his two companions were in Shanghai? Prince Kudashev had asked for him then; the British had turned down the request and had moved Kolchak—at his own expense—half way across Asia. The Admiral had grounds for exasperation.

But deeper than his annoyance was his distrust of the influences which (he strongly suspected) had brought about this change of plan. The Chinese Eastern Railway was a Russian concern; behind it, under the banner of the Russo-Asiatic Bank, stood an array of financiers and concessionaires of whom Kolchak had a low opinion. He guessed, from tentative approaches which had been made to him in Shanghai, that they wanted to use his name and his reputation for integrity to further enterprises remotely if at all concerned with the prosecution of the war; and he was heard to mutter something about 'swindling merchants' as he went off to talk matters over at General Ridout's headquarters.[12]

The outcome of this interview was a telegram to the War Office in which Ridout reported that if the message about Manchuria was to be regarded as an order Kolchak would conform to it, but that he would much prefer to go on to Mesopotamia. In reply the Director of Military Intelligence telegraphed that Kolchak could no longer serve any useful purpose in the Middle East; on 13 March Ridout reported that Kolchak would 'return North earliest'; and thereafter the Admiral and his two companions cooled their heels in Raffles Hotel for the best part of a fortnight, waiting for a passage back to China.

They were by this time in financial straits. In America Kolchak and his officers had been the guests of the United States Government and had drawn pay and allowances through the Imperial Russian Embassy, which was still functioning and in funds. In Tokyo Kolchak had left most of the money he had saved in America in safe keeping for eventual transfer to his wife in South Russia. More than four months had elapsed since he had offered his services to the British Government, but it does not seem to have occurred to anyone that the Admiral might need, and certainly deserved, some financial assistance on the long journeys which the Director of Military Intelligence was encouraging him to undertake. Kolchak was too proud a man to raise the matter himself; and it speaks well for his tenacity of purpose that he did not, under the stress of discouragement and inconvenience, abandon what must, in Singapore, have appeared to be a wild-goose chase of an unusually aimless and expensive kind.

He sailed for Shanghai towards the end of March, and about a month later reached the Russian Embassy in Peking. 'I have come,' he told Prince Kudashev, 'to place myself at your disposal. What mission do you plan to give me?'[13]

CHAPTER THREE

The Chess-Board

AT Versailles, in May 1918, the ornamental lakes were covered with huge sheets of material painted grass-green; this subterfuge was designed to lessen the risk that German bombers would interrupt the deliberations of the Supreme Allied War Council and their numerous advisers. The thud of the enemy's heavy guns on the Marne was plainly audible. Enormous shells were falling sporadically on Paris, where the first stages of a plan to withdraw the administrative organs of the French Government to Bordeaux had been put into action. The need to resurrect an Eastern Front acquired almost hourly a greater urgency.

Reduced to terms far simpler than those in which it was seen in the first half of 1918, the problem of striking at Germany through Russia admitted, or seemed to admit, of three solutions. These were:

I. The reactivation of the Eastern Front by forces of the Soviet Government with Allied support.

II. The dispatch of a Japanese Expeditionary Force across Siberia to attack the Germans in Eastern Europe.

III. The instigation of preventive or diversionary activities by 'loyal' Russian, Ukrainian, Caucasian or Cossack resistance movements which would hinder the Germans (and incidentally the Turks) from exploiting their enormous economic gains under the Treaty of Brest Litovsk.

Each of these three projects was incompatible with the other two; none of them represented agreed Allied policy; all three were put in hand simultaneously. It is small wonder that a situation of inextricable confusion resulted. It is now time to bring into some sort of perspective the chaotic picture of events which had emerged by the time, in mid-summer, when the consequences of the Chelyabinsk Incident became apparent.

I. *Prospects of a Renewal of Hostilities by the Russians*

The Allies were in contact with the Soviet Government through three unofficial agents. Robert Bruce Lockhart, a sanguine, thirty-year-old Scot who knew Russia well and spoke the language, represented the British Government and, though not *persona gratissima* at the Foreign Office, was in the confidence of Lloyd George and Lord Milner. Colonel Raymond Robins of the American Red Cross lacked Lockhart's quasi-diplomatic status but was in close touch with the Bolshevik leaders; an honourable but rather arrogant idealist, he provided Washington with an insight into Soviet affairs which, despite his ignorance of the language, was sometimes more realistic, and always more sympathetic, than that furnished by the American Embassy. Captain Jacques Sadoul, a Socialist lawyer attached to the French Military Mission, had close contacts with Trotsky; less influential, and much less objective, than Lockhart and Robins, he was an apostle rather than an interpreter of Soviet policy and eventually joined the Communist Party.

These three men worked closely together. All came to believe fervently (they were fervent men) in the possibility that Russia might resume hostilities against Germany and would welcome, or at worst consent to, Allied participation in military operations on Russian soil. In this belief they were for some time encouraged by the Soviet leaders, and notably by Trotsky; a stage was even reached at the end of March 1918 when proposals were being actively canvassed for the employment of cadres of French, American and Italian officers to reorganise and train the Red Army, which in those days was little better than an armed volunteer militia with vestigial discipline and a low recruiting rate.

But this vision of an Eastern Front was never more than a

mirage. It vanished, as far as the Russians were concerned, when they realised, soon after the ratification on 15 March 1918 of the Treaty of Brest Litovsk, that the Germans did not intend the destruction of the Soviet State. Save in moments of panic or despair they must—and the Allies should—have seen from the first that the whole scheme was suicidal; resistance to the Germans could only have resulted in the annihilation of the Red Army (if it could be induced to fight at all, which was doubtful) long before such inadequate forces as the Allies could spare for intervention had arrived upon the scene.

But for a variety of reasons it suited the Russians' book to keep this mirage flickering before Allied eyes; and the most cogent of these reasons was their calculation that, the longer hope lasted of Soviet co-operation with the Western Allies against Germany, the longer it would be before Japan's assistance was invoked with any urgency. By mid-May the hope was dead, and the nebulous projects which Lockhart and his colleagues had based on it were far from the realm of practicality; they had never been very near it.

II. *The Japanese Steam-Roller*

Compared with the other senior belligerents, Japan had had an easy and indeed a profitable war. She had taken over, without serious fighting, the German bridgehead in Shantung, on the China coast, and the small German islands in the North Pacific. Her navy had carried out routine duties in the Indian Ocean and the Mediterranean. Her industries, expanding under the stimulus of war, had produced a useful quantity of munitions, most of which went to Russia.

Geography was the main but not the only factor which forced on Japan the role of an *embusquée*. Her military and political leaders took, reasonably enough, no more than a polite interest in the war in Europe; their long-term purpose was to exploit both Japan's status as a belligerent and the debilitating effects of the war on her enemies and her allies in order to strengthen her economic and political position in China. Her purpose had already been foreshadowed by the promulgation of the 'Twenty-One Demands' on China; this preview of an annexationist policy had deeply shocked public opinion in the United States.

There were thus two major political obstacles to Japanese intervention against Germany across Russia. One (of which her allies were imperfectly aware) was the fact that Japan had other fish to fry and regarded such an enterprise as contrary to her best interests. The other, to which the British and French were fully alive, was that America was so strongly opposed to Japanese intervention in even the most limited form that such an undertaking stood virtually no chance of finding a place in agreed Allied strategy. The efforts of France, and more especially of Britain, to overcome, undermine or by-pass these obstacles involved the Governments concerned in prolonged and otiose bouts of shadow-boxing.

All these efforts failed to make a decisive impact on their principal target, which was the mind of President Wilson. It was only when, late in June, the full repercussions of the Chelyabinsk Incident became known to the outside world that Wilson began to change his mind and to admit that the dispatch of an Allied expeditionary force to Siberia (in which the Japanese would of necessity play a leading part) deserved serious and indeed urgent consideration. By this time the German offensive on the Western Front was petering out; the tables were turning in Europe. As the plans for intervention in Siberia began to take shape, their original purpose ceased to be valid and was soon largely forgotten.

This was perhaps as well. The political obstacles to a Japanese, or mainly Japanese, expedition via Siberia against the Germans had from the first been recognised as formidable, but at least they received anxious attention from the Western Allies. This cannot be said for the military problems involved, which were insoluble and should have been plainly so. The nearest German forces were roughly 7000 miles from Vladivostok. An army dispatched against them from Japan would be wholly dependent on the Trans-Siberian Railway. The condition of this line, already parlous, was steadily deteriorating. Even assuming goodwill towards the Japanese on the part of the railway staff and the Russian population as a whole (and there was every reason to assume the opposite) the Trans-Siberian, nourished by a single port, was quite incapable of transporting to European Russia, let alone maintaining there, anything larger than a token force.

This was obvious to the Japanese, who at all stages made it clear that, if they did go to Siberia, they would move no further west than Lake Baikal;* it was obvious, too, to the Americans, whose judgment was not clouded by desperation. How the French and British Governments, and their military advisers, retained their faith in so blatantly unpractical a project is a mystery.

It is a mystery of a type which recurs throughout the history of the Intervention. Time and again one finds serious consideration being given by Allied officers of high standing to enterprises (none, admittedly, on quite so grandiose a scale as that described above) which would have been impossible to execute and disastrous to attempt. Early in January 1918, for instance, the French Government reacted to a baseless report that the Bolsheviks had murdered their consul in Irkutsk by proposing that a punitive expedition should be mounted forthwith in Tientsin, where, ever since the Boxer Rebellion, the units which found the guards for the foreign Legations in Peking had their depots. This force, comprising French, British, American, Japanese and Chinese contingents and commanded by a French naval officer, would proceed to Irkutsk (a distance of some 2000 miles) and avenge the consul's murder, also incidentally preventing the removal of war-material from Vladivostok along the Trans-Siberian.

This ludicrous proposal may well have originated in the mind of the French Foreign Minister, M. Pichon, who had been in charge of the French Legation during the siege of the diplomatic

* In June the Japanese General Staff calculated that it would take them three years to move an adequate force as far as Chelyabinsk, whence in 1918 the most advanced German outposts in Russia were distant by 1000 miles. (Ullman.)

quarter by the Boxers in 1901 and may thereby have developed a weakness for international relief expeditions. But this is only one of many instances where it is hard to understand how obviously unsound military plans (this one was scuppered by the news, which arrived in London ahead of it, that the French consul had not been done to death[14]) found their way, at one level or another, on to the Allies' agenda.

Perhaps the answer is that, although a World War was in its fourth year, most of the fighting on land had conformed to a rigid pattern; the lessons learnt from the Western Front had had an effect upon the professional military mind which, if not exactly stultifying, had done little to limber it up for a war of movement across the vast distances of Russia. It is true that the most unrealistic plans were formulated outside Russia by men with scant knowledge of what conditions were like inside Russia; but this cannot excuse the airy neglect of elementary logistics which is their leading characteristic. At a comparable stage of the Second World War, which provided staff-officers with a more liberal education, such amateurishness would have been unthinkable.*

III. Sideshows

Neither of the abortive schemes outlined above was equivocal in conception. Both, that is to say, formed part of an anti-German strategy; it was impossible to execute the first without active Soviet co-operation, and inadvisable to attempt the second without at least tacit Soviet acquiescence. Only one of the other interventionist projects which began to take shape in the first half of 1918 had similarly unambiguous credentials.

---

* In the summer of 1919 a small British force based on Archangel advanced up the River Dvina with the object of capturing Kotlas, 300 miles from Archangel. The river was unusually low, and an operation in which everyone had great confidence had to be abandoned when the naval flotilla on which the troops relied for transport and artillery support found further progress impossible. The point at which this unexpectedly occurred was *150 miles* from Kotlas. Even allowing for bad luck with the climate, this suggests a margin of error of almost Balaclavan dimensions.

This was the establishment, upon the invitation of the local Soviet authorities and for defensive purposes, of a small British bridgehead—toehold would perhaps describe it more accurately —at Murmansk.

Before many months were past the pristine character of this enterprise had changed completely. The small bridgehead became a large one; the handful of British sailors and marines was replaced by a sizeable Allied expeditionary force; and the purpose of the whole operation became, not anti-German and defensive, but anti-Bolshevik and aggressive. Here, however, we are concerned with the origins of Intervention; and this is how it began in North Russia.

Archangel was the only port of any consequence on Russia's Arctic coast, and when the German navy sealed the Baltic at the outbreak of war it assumed great importance. But Archangel is closed by ice for six months, and sometimes more, in every year; so steps were taken to develop a subsidiary port at Murmansk, not far from the Finnish and Norwegian frontiers. Although Murmansk is a good deal further north than Archangel, the Kola Inlet, on which it stands, remains, thanks to the Gulf Stream, navigable in winter. A primitive but serviceable port was opened there early in 1917.

The Royal Navy had throughout borne the main burden of convoy-duties, mine-sweeping and so on over the sea-routes to Archangel; and in the winter of 1917 a small squadron was stationed at Murmansk, its commander, Admiral Kemp, flying his flag in the old battleship *Glory*. Murmansk was linked, precariously, with Petrograd and Archangel by newly constructed and erratic railways, all the rails for which had been brought from England; otherwise it was completely isolated, and when the Brest Litovsk negotiations broke down and the Germans resumed their advance in mid-February 1918, unfounded but not unreasonable fears were entertained that they had designs on Murmansk, which could (on paper) have been threatened by German-led or German-inspired Finnish forces; for Finland had declared her independence of Russia, civil war had broken out, and Germany was backing the

43

White Finns under Mannerheim against their pro-Bolshevik compatriots.

It is needless to follow here all the events which occurred at Murmansk or had a bearing on the situation there. The salient facts are that on 6 March, at the request of the Murmansk Soviet, Admiral Kemp put a small landing-party of marines ashore: that on the following day a British cruiser arrived to reinforce his squadron, which was later joined by, first, a French and then an American cruiser: and that the supposed German threat to Murmansk set in motion a process which was to result in the seizure of Archangel (where, as at Vladivostok, there were vast dumps of valuable war-material) and, eventually, in the creation in North Russia of an anti-Bolshevik front on which the fighting was done, not as elsewhere by White Russian forces with Allied financial, technical and moral support, but by British, American, French and other Allied units under British command, with White Russians acting as increasingly unreliable auxiliaries.*

The Archangel–Murmansk enclave was to exert a powerful though an indirect influence on strategy (or what passed for it) in Siberia. So was its counterpart in South Russia, where Allied hopes of a 'loyalist' bastion were gradually fulfilled. From small beginnings the so-called Volunteer Army, in uneasy alliance with the freedom-loving Cossacks of the Kuban, gained in bitter fighting a decisive ascendancy over the ill-led Red Army. Although at the time with which we are here concerned —mid-summer of 1918—the issue of this confused struggle was still in doubt, the foundations were being laid of an anti-Bolshevik bridgehead far larger—and far more spontaneous— than that which was simultaneously being brought into being in the North.

The Volunteer Army under Denikin—its original leader,

* In a White Paper (*The Evacuation of North Russia 1919*. Cd. 818) presented to Parliament in 1920 the White Russian forces, to whom at one time or another many grandiloquent terms had been applied on official occasions by Allied commanders, appeared in War Office returns of ration-strengths, etc., as 'locals.'

Alekseev, died in October 1918—was not, save incidentally in the early stages, concerned with resistance to the Germans. It aimed at the overthrow of Soviet power and the creation of a 'great united undivided Russia.' Until the Turks acknowledged defeat in October, thus opening the Black Sea to their conquerors, the Allies' desire to help the Whites could express itself only in terms of financial and moral support: so that intervention in South Russia, when it started in earnest in the last weeks of the war, could not, save with considerable casuistry, be justified as a measure contributing to the defeat of Germany.

Intervention in South Russia (and—a later development—in the Baltic States*) was 'naked' intervention. It was not so much a policy as a reflex action; it had, as Chamberlin has pointed out, 'a defensive as well as an offensive character. If it could not lead to the crushing of Bolshevism in Russia it might at least keep the Bolsheviks so fully occupied on the various fronts of the Civil War that the spread of their militant doctrine beyond Russia's frontiers would become less probable.'[15]

Further east, although Dunsterforce was driven out of Baku by the Turks in September 1918, the Caspian was dominated by a flotilla of improvised gunboats in which Russian crews served under British officers; and in the deserts beyond the Caspian a small British–Indian force under General Malleson continued until the spring of 1919 to be the mainstay of a ramshackle anti-Bolshevik régime based on Ashkabad. But these ventures were conceived 'not as an anti-Bolshevik measure, but as a means of stemming the threatened expansion of German arms and German influence into Russia and, in the case of Transcaspia, through Russia into British Asia.'[16] Neither enterprise was ever seen, even by the most visionary strategists, as having any relevance to the Siberian intervention.

* Here the main aim of British policy was to further the cause of Esthonian, Latvian and Lithuanian independence; but this purpose, altruistic in itself, could not be accomplished without damage to Soviet interests, and Moscow naturally regarded British activities in the area as being primarily, not secondarily, anti-Bolshevik.

The northern and the southern fronts—that is, the Arch-angel–Murmansk bridgehead and the much larger and expanding enclave under Denikin's control—did on the other hand come to have a strong influence, not on what happened in Siberia, but on what people—and especially people in London —hoped would happen there. A glance at the map facing page 30 will suggest how seductive (and up to a point how specious) was the vision of a three-pronged drive on Moscow; it was even possible, for those out of touch with the realities of a chaotic local situation, to postulate a fourth prong, stabbing Petrograd in the back from the Baltic Provinces.

Thus there came into view a chess-board solution of the Russian problem, and there was much talk of the three prongs, as they converged on Moscow, 'joining hands'; it looked so logical on the map. The administrative difficulties involved in effecting a junction between the three main interventionist armies—the great distances, the decrepitude and vulnerability of the single-track railways, the virtual impassability of all roads during the spring thaw—were not so much underestimated as overlooked. The belief, which began to be entertained early in 1919, that it was White to move, and mate in half a dozen moves, coloured much influential thinking—and notably Winston Churchill's —until it ceased, even on the map, to make any sense at all.

CHAPTER FOUR

The Freebooter

No evidence, as we have seen, survives to show what the British General Staff intended Kolchak to do in Mesopotamia; their purposes in recalling him from Singapore to Manchuria are equally unclear, but it is a safe guess that this sudden change of plan was inspired, indirectly, by a twenty-eight-year-old captain of Cossacks called Grigori Semenov.

This strange and terrible man, the son of a Russian father and a Buryat Mongol mother, had served with distinction in Poland, White Russia and the Carpathians. General Wrangel, a good judge of cavalrymen, described him as 'an exemplary officer, especially courageous when under the eye of his superior';[17] Semenov was much decorated. A tour of duty in Persia, where there were few medals to be won, gave him leisure to develop a scheme for raising levies among the Buryats. In the crisis-ridden summer of 1917 he was ordered to Petrograd to expound this project and—surprisingly, since a whole army corps of Buryats could not have solved the least of the problems facing the Provisional Government—was told to go ahead with it.

He was in Trans-Baikalia, with little or no progress to report, when the Bolsheviks seized power throughout Siberia in November 1917. Semenov evaded arrest, made the most of a still fluid situation to stir up trouble for the precarious new régime, and finally, in the last days of 1917, dodged across the Chinese frontier. His handful of companions included Baron Ungern-Sternberg, who had been a fellow-squadron-commander in the Nerchinsk Cossacks; this moody swashbuckler with red hair and a pale face was to gain a reputation for sadistic brutality which was surpassed by very few contestants on either side in the Civil War. 'In his military-administrative capacity,' Semenov wrote afterwards, 'the Baron frequently used methods which have often been criticised. But it must be remembered that the abnormal circumstances in which we were working necessitated, in certain cases, the employment of measures that would not be permissible under normal conditions.'[18] Euphemism can seldom have been more blandly brought into play.

At Manchuli, a small place just inside the Manchurian frontier, the Trans-Siberian connected with the Russian-controlled Chinese Eastern Railway which provided the most direct route to Vladivostok.* Here, by boldness and bluff, Semenov first overawed and then disarmed the pro-Bolshevik garrison, who were herded into a train and consigned back to Russian territory; they were followed, in a cattle-truck, by the members of the local Soviet, who had been beaten up. This *coup de main* secured for Semenov a base which was none the worse for being situated on foreign soil, outside Russian jurisdiction; he set about recruiting a small and heterogeneous army and in January 1918, at the head of a force of some 600 men (400 of them Mongols and Chinese), he took the offensive into Trans-Baikalia.

The Red Army units stationed in the desolate little settlements strung out sparsely along the eastern end of the Trans-Siberian Railway had no great military value and little stomach for a fight. Semenov's scallywags (as they were soon being called in the Foreign Office) made rapid progress and almost reached the important junction of Karymskaia before being routed decisively by a force (it included some useful Hungarian prisoners of war) under Lazo, a partisan leader of talent whose career ended when, about two years later, he was captured by the Japanese, handed over to the Whites, and burnt alive in the firebox of a locomotive.

Semenov extricated himself without serious loss and went to ground once more in Manchuli; the whole affair was over in ten days. But in the British and the French the little foray

* See map facing page 163.

A Czech unit handing over arms at Penza

A Czech échelon, June 1918: the days of improvisation

Ataman Semenov

Japanese officers of the 71st Regiment

aroused a feverish interest. Was it possible that in Russia the winter of their discontent was going to be made glorious summer by this vigorous *beau sabreur*? Since all sincerely hoped that this would prove to be so, there was no disposition to underestimate Semenov's potential importance.

On Captain R. B. Denny, the British Assistant Military Attaché at Peking, who was dispatched promptly to Manchuli, he made an 'extremely favourable impression.' His army now had a total strength of 750—180 Russian officers and cadets, 270 Cossacks and 300 Mongols; they were soon to be joined by 300 Serbian prisoners of war. Denny felt that Semenov deserved to be taken seriously. Long before his report reached London the British Government had arrived independently at the same conclusion; and in the first days of February Semenov was given £10,000 and told that he could expect a similar sum every month until further notice. No conditions were attached to these payments, which were made through the British Consulate in Harbin.

The French, when informed of this transaction, also began to subsidise Semenov, while the Japanese provided—in addition to funds—arms, ammunition and a number of 'volunteers' who arrived at Manchuli in mufti and, besides manning some of Semenov's field-guns, formed the flower of his infantry. (Most if not all of the volunteers were reservists of less than exemplary character; of the first 400 to join Semenov 100 had to be sent home for taking part in drunken brawls and other acts of insubordination.) Japan, alone of Semenov's three benefactors, exerted some measure of control over his activities; an energetic staff-officer, Captain Kuroki, was permanently attached to his headquarters, where Japanese influence was soon so strong that Semenov was for practical purposes a puppet.

In the first weeks of 1918 the Ataman was an exciting portent—just how exciting can be gauged by the spontaneity with which three foreign Governments hastened to underwrite him. But there was one quarter from which Semenov, however forlorn the hope he led, had every right to expect support and from which, save for some grudging financial aid, he got none. In Harbin, less than 400 miles from Manchuli, there was a considerable reservoir of Russian man-power. The large Russian community, presided over by the patriarchal figure of General Horvath, was swollen with men who had got out of Russia while the going was good. Many were officers. A few had fled for their lives, or at least had undergone in their flight adventures which lost nothing in the telling; but most had prudence to thank for their presence in Manchuria, and prudence continued to guide the conduct of all when, on the door-step of their asylum, an opportunity presented itself for striking back at the detested régime which had driven them into (as they almost all sincerely believed) a temporary exile.

In the overcrowded public rooms of the Hotel Moderne spurs continued to clink, patriotic toasts to be drunk, eyes to fill with tears. Rumours were anatomised by pundits, intrigues were carried on by knaves, fortunes were made by speculators. Salutes were exchanged, hands kissed, sword-hilts polished. But, save for a few shady and regrettable adventurers, nobody left the scene of this martial–patriotic *tableau vivant* and took a train for Manchuli.

The failure of Semenov's compatriots to rally to his cause could hardly have been foreseen in London, and for a long time it went unremarked. All the Russians anyone knew anything about were always talking about the need to fight the Bolsheviks; and since Semenov was the only Russian, at any rate in the Far East, who was actually doing this, it was tacitly assumed that he must represent some sort of 'national' movement. This was a delusion; Semenov represented nobody but himself. But it was a natural delusion and Britain continued, though more and more uneasily, to support him. A couple of days before the Director of Military Intelligence sent off the telegram which was to intercept Kolchak at Singapore, the British Minister at Peking was authorised to furnish Semenov with two five-inch howitzers from the Legation Guard's depot at Tientsin; these ancient guns, 'secretly' dispatched by rail, were held up for some days at Mukden until the Japanese railway authorities had received a suitable bribe.

Britain's involvement with Semenov was not a happy one. His status in Whitehall's eyes was at first that (in racing parlance) of a fancied outsider; and early in February Balfour, the Foreign Secretary, suggested to Colonel House, President Wilson's personal adviser, that the American Government might like to have a flutter on him, since it was 'of the greatest importance to support any purely Russian movement in Siberia.'[19] A 'purely Russian movement' inexactly described the posse of Chinese ex-bandits, Mongol cattle-rustlers, Japanese mercenaries, Serbian prisoners and Cossack adventurers based on Manchuli. Washington, though unaware of this (as indeed was Balfour when he made the suggestion), rejected the idea on a point of principle. America was still dead against intervention in Siberia, mainly because such a policy, whatever form it took, would unleash the Japanese on to the mainland.

If Semenov was hardly an asset in Washington, he was definitely a liability in Moscow, where Lockhart was striving manfully to create conditions in which Soviet Russia could, with Allied assistance, take up arms against Germany. This was then the main object of British policy, and it was in no way furthered by Britain's action in helping to finance and equip an avowedly counter-revolutionary movement; 'the French and British support to Semenov,' Kennan has pointed out, 'was one of the main sources of Soviet suspicion of Allied good faith generally.'[20]

Realising, too late, that the deeds of their right hand were incompatible with those of their left, the British Government made futile efforts to restrain Semenov. They were unwilling to cut off his subsidies for fear that they would forfeit, to the French and the Japanese, the influence over him which, they fondly supposed, their monthly payments gave them; but in April Captain Denny was instructed to warn Semenov forcibly against taking the offensive into Russian territory and forbidden to accompany an advance if one was made. Denny duly delivered this warning, of which, as might have been foreseen, the only result was to make it harder than it already was for anyone at Manchuli to take the British seriously.

This absurd situation, in which Japan and France were paying Semenov to fight the Bolsheviks and Britain was paying him not to fight them, largely regularised itself when British hopes of a working agreement with the Soviet Government disappeared in May; but by then the image of Semenov as a national liberator had also disappeared. It was becoming all too plain that the *beau sabreur* was a bandit with many of the attributes of a monster. Not only the rank and file of his small force, but the officers who were his close associates, habitually committed unspeakable atrocities. Corruption, flagrant and on a large scale, flourished wherever his writ ran. Justice was unknown, mercy unheard of. Apart from being a public scandal, Semenov was wholly subservient to the seamier side of Japanese policy in Siberia; and by the middle of 1918 he had ceased to be a charge on the British taxpayer.

With his 'enormous head, the size of which is greatly enhanced by the flat Mongol face, from which gleam two clear brilliant eyes that belong rather to an animal than to a man,'[21] his Napoleonic lock of hair and his cloudy pan-Mongolian aspirations, Semenov was an extraordinary figure, a sort of Heathcliff of the steppes. His deeds were odious, his motives base, his conduct insolently cynical; yet he somehow always contrived to produce a good impression. In April 1918, before the full depths of his turpitude had revealed themselves, he struck an experienced British officer as 'exceptionally patriotic and disinterested'; and nearly two years later the British High Commissioner in Siberia, Miles Lampson, while admitting that the harshest criticisms of Semenov's régime were justified, believed the Ataman himself to be 'personally sincere.'

A central figure in the raffish court over which he presided in, as one witness put it, 'an atmosphere of laziness, rodomontade, alcohol, lucrative requisitions, dirty money and the killing of the innocent,'[22] was Semenov's *maîtresse en tête*. Masha Sharaban was the Jewish widow of a Russian merchant;

a young British officer who saw her at Semenov's bedside (the Ataman had been wounded by a bomb in the theatre at Chita) found her 'a very pretty woman with huge black eyes.'[23] Semenov was genuinely devoted to her. On his visits to Harbin, which were invariably marked by turbulence and scandal, she was flaunted, dripping with diamonds, round the *cafés chantants*, and the amount of money he spent on her gave rise to envious criticism even among his own officers.

His wife, meanwhile, was in Japan. An American officer who met her there described her as 'a strikingly fascinating and beautiful woman, a blonde, and a typically sportsmanlike adventuress'; she was believed to possess a 'royal fortune.'[24] In September 1919 she was to rejoin her husband, who had journeyed with a large retinue to Mukden, where he hoped to improve his strained relations with the local warlord, Chang Tso-lin. The British Consul thus described the end of Semenov's visit:

> A somewhat romantic episode occurred when the Ataman was leaving his hotel for the railway station. A woman, said to be a notorious gipsy woman with whom the Ataman had for some time past been living in intimate relations, and who appears to have been discarded by him on the arrival in the Far East of his own wife, . . . suddenly ran forward and, addressing reproaches to him, swallowed some poison and immediately collapsed. She was removed to the Japanese hospital for treatment and appears to have survived.[25]

Masha not only survived but was before long reinstated. We get a last glimpse of her in January 1920, when the British liaison officer at Chita recorded: 'I had supper with Semenov and his retinue. The mistress as usual drank too much. She was so indiscreet as to sing a Yiddish song in the singing of which she showed, so far as I could judge, complete mastery of the language.'[26] The reference to 'indiscretion' is a reminder of the violently anti-Semitic tendencies which were prevalent in reactionary White circles; the fact that Semenov's long catalogue of crimes included no large-scale pogroms was almost certainly due to Masha's influence.

When, in mid-April 1918, Kolchak reported to the Russian Ambassador at Peking, they proceeded at once to a discussion of Semenov's activities. Prince Kudashev explained that his small force, which received arms and money from the Japanese, 'so far had not been especially successful'; but an influx of volunteers was hoped for and 'it was possible to expect that later on this detachment would become a large armed force.'[27] The duties proposed for Kolchak were not directly connected with Semenov's operations; he was to be the 'military member' (that is, the nominee of the Russian General Staff) on the reconstituted board of the Chinese Eastern Railway. But, said Kudashev, 'of course you will have to reach a compromise with Semenov,' and he went on to explain that he wanted Kolchak to 'assume the administration of the [foreign] funds which are now being distributed haphazard'; at present there was 'complete chaos' in this field.[28]

A day or two later General Horvath arrived from Harbin; an affable, rather sly man with a long white forked beard, he had been general manager of the Chinese Eastern Railway since 1903. With him came the industrialist Putilov and several senior representatives of the Russo-Asiatic Bank, which held most of the shares in the railway. The account in Kolchak's *Testimony* of the conference that ensued suggests that it was concerned only with the reorganisation of the Chinese Eastern Railway and the restoration of order in the railway zone. It is clear from other sources that there was more to it than this.

When he reached Peking Kolchak found waiting for him a cipher telegram, franked *Personal and Very Confidential*, from the Russian Ambassador in Washington. It was foreseen, Bakhmatiev cabled, that there would shortly be held an exploratory meeting of 'a number of Russian political personages who find themselves abroad in order to discuss the possibility of organising a Political Centre which could take the measures urgently necessary for the national restoration of Russia.' The Ambassador considered Kolchak's presence 'absolutely indispensable' and urged him to come to America 'at least for a short time without telling anyone.'[29]

Kolchak's reply, dispatched from Peking on 18 April, shows that he took seriously, and was prepared to commit himself to, the project, ostensibly concerned with the domestic economy of a railway in Manchuria, which was under discussion in Peking. 'On the invitation of Putilov and with the concurrence of the British Government I have joined the board of the Chinese Eastern Railway which is aiming, indirectly but realistically, at the same goal as you—to organize a Political Centre for the restoration of Russia.'[30] He regretted, therefore, that he could not come to America.

There is one further indication that the Peking cabal were concerned with matters that reached further than their shareholders' interests. No Allied representatives, so far as is known, were privy to their deliberations; but on 30 April Kudashev, Horvath and Kolchak called on the British Minister, Sir John Jordan, and expounded to him an ambitious plan which would result, at an unspecified date, in the liberation of Vladivostok in the east and Irkutsk in the west by a Russian force of 17,000 men based on the Chinese Eastern Railway. Sir John reported this scheme to London; the fact that nothing more was heard of it does not mean that it did not seem very real to its sponsors when they broached it.

The day after this interview Kolchak left for Harbin, travelling with Horvath in his private coach; his appointment as commander-in-chief of the Russian forces in the railway zone had been gazetted on 26 April. He was by nature a reserved and solitary man; a few months later a not very imaginative British officer, seeing him for the first time at a public function, retained the impression of 'a small, vagrant, lonely, troubled soul without a friend.'[31] He gave way easily to choler, but except when he was in a rage he seemed a proud, cold, withdrawn figure, dedicated, inscrutable, slightly inhuman. Even at the end, with death staring at him day after day over his interrogators' shoulders, no chink was discernible in his armour of aloofness.

Only one trace of his inner private life survives. As the train ran north through the fields of maize and poppy beyond the Great Wall, Kolchak wrote a letter to a woman; part of it, a pencilled draft, is among his personal papers. It tells us very little—not even who the woman was, although there can in fact be little doubt about her identity; but it helps to make a remote man a little less remote.

> A year ago [wrote Kolchak] I was returning from Petrograd to Sevastopol, and strangely enough I'm now travelling from Peking to Harbin. My carriage reminds me of the carriage in which I made my last journey as Commander-in-Chief of the Black Sea Fleet. That was a horrible journey. In Petrograd I had reached the conviction that there was nothing ahead of us except defeat and shame. I thought that you too would turn your back on me, and this made it still harder to face the fact that the war was lost, that everything was in ruins; I felt a bitter, almost an insupportable pain. That is why today I so clearly remember the Nikolaev Station, my railway carriage, my mood close to despair, even the title of the book, *The Science of Statecraft*, which I tried to read but could not understand.[32]

There is little self-revelation here; and we do not even know if the letter was finished and posted, let alone received. But it is clear that the woman to whom it was written had been important to Kolchak for at least a year; and it is safe to assume that she was the same person about whom, some twenty months later in the gaol at Irkutsk, the Chairman of the Extraordinary Investigating Commission was to ask his prisoner: 'A certain Madame Timireva has voluntarily caused herself to be arrested here. What is her relation to you?'

To which Kolchak replied: 'She is my good acquaintance of long standing ... When I came here she wished to share my fate.'[33]

CHAPTER FIVE

The Hidden Hand

IN April 1917 the German Government granted Lenin, then exiled in Switzerland, transit facilities across their territory; with thirty-one companions he returned to Russia, after travelling through Germany to Sweden in a special train which, although not—as legend has it—'sealed,' was hedged about with regulations, including one which, to the acute discomfort of the Russians, forbade smoking.[34] 'The suggestion,' Wheeler-Bennett points out, 'that Lenin in travelling through Germany to Russia was acting in any sense as a German agent is ridiculous;'[35] but it was only natural that the Allies should make the obvious deduction and should assume that Lenin was Germany's tool when in fact the opposite was nearer the truth.

Lenin's journey was a fact; it and the misinterpretations placed on it were, save for some forged documents hawked round Petrograd and finally bought by a minor American official early in 1918, virtually the only evidence the Allies had that the Bolshevik Revolution had been engineered by Germany. This fallacy however gained a firm hold on their minds. 'The Germans, as they saw it, had to be the source of all evil; nothing bad could happen that was not attributable to the German hand.'[36] Basically improbable though it was, the theory that the Bolsheviks were not only financed but to a large extent controlled from Berlin came to be widely accepted.*

* Quaintly enough, the same delusion (only the other way round) prevailed in influential German circles. C.f. 'The Russian Revolution was *engineered* by England.' (Major-General Max Hoffmann: *The War of Lost Opportunities.*)

One of the disturbing implications of this theory concerned the German, Austro-Hungarian and other prisoners of war in Russian hands. Of these there were—not counting Turks— something like a million and a half; * only about ten per cent were German; half, or perhaps rather more than half, were in Siberia. After the ratification of the Treaty of Brest Litovsk in March 1918 the men, many of whom already enjoyed a wide measure of personal liberty, ceased, technically, to be prisoners at all. But because of the chaotic state of the Russian railways their repatriation was at best a very slow business, and reports began to come in that these large bodies of marooned soldiery were being armed, or were arming themselves. It was not long before the prisoners had assumed the status of a strategic bogy.

How exactly they were expected to damage the Allied cause was never made entirely clear. It was enough that they were thought of as Germans, and—although the vast majority of them were nothing of the sort—this sufficed, against the chimerical background of a Bolshevik–German conspiracy, to invest them with mystery and menace. The British feared that those in Turkestan might form the nucleus of a threat to India. The French Ambassador to Russia spoke, in a newspaper interview on 23 April 1918, of the Germans 'trying to organize colonial centres in Siberia.'[37] Then there was the possibility that the prisoners would be instrumental in transporting valuable war-material to Germany. And, finally, there were reports that they were being recruited into the Red Army.

These reports had some foundation in fact. In general, however, Allied misgivings about the prisoners were remarkably unrealistic, for they left altogether out of account the human factor and were based, once again, on a chess-board view of the situation. Here, here and here (said the strategists) are so many hundred thousand of the enemy's soldiers, no longer

---

* The true figures may have been higher. One reputable source gives the following figures for Austrian subjects alone: Captured 2,111,146. Died of wounds, 150,000. Died of starvation, disease, etc., 530,000. Murdered, 30,000. Killed in the Civil War, 11,000. (Gustav Krist: *Prisoner in the Forbidden Land.*)

under restraint. They are pawns which, after being taken off
the board, have now regrettably been brought back into play.
How will our opponent redeploy them?

The question would have been worth asking only if men were
as immune as pawns are to homesickness, disease, malnutrition
and demoralisation. Common sense ought to have told the
Allied strategists that the prisoners of war, many of whom had
been herded together under appalling conditions for upwards of
three years, who belonged to half a dozen mutually antipathetic
races, and among whom the officers were segregated from the
men, could never be more than a negligible factor in the Russian situation. But common sense was hardly a staple ingredient
of interventionist strategy. Credence continued to be given to
proliferating reports that the prisoners of war represented a
serious threat, never mind to what; a typical example is the
statement by the British Assistant Military Attaché at Peking
on 3 July 1918 that 'there is no doubt but that German influence is rapidly increasing in Trans-Baikalia.'

This, and much else in the same vein, was nonsense. It was
however true that the Soviet authorities were doing their best to
induce the prisoners to renounce the service of their own coun-
tries and join the Red Army. These efforts were at first largely
ideological in motive. Bolshevism was going through the naïve,
almost mawkish phase when world revolution was expected to
break out at any moment; the prisoners were being given a
chance to get in on the ground floor by becoming 'Internationalists,' as those who did join up were called. Later, when
Trotsky set about reconstructing the Red Army, the need for
recruits, and especially for men already trained as soldiers, put
something of a premium on the prisoners of war. From the first
volunteers had been disappointingly scarce, but this drawback
could be, and was, overcome by restricting privileges—including, sometimes, the privilege of eating—to those who did
volunteer. By such realistic methods a sizeable force of Internationalists was built up on paper; but it seems to have represented only about five or six per cent of the total number of
prisoners;[38] very few of its members got as far as being armed,

and the Internationalists were not, except in one or two cases, allowed to form their own detachments but were distributed in dribs and drabs among Russian units.

In March Lockhart, who regarded the prisoners-of-war scare as a mare's nest but was being pestered by 'querulous' telegrams about it from the Foreign Office, raised the matter with Trotsky. Trotsky said that 'it was no use his issuing a denial'; the Allies had better go and see for themselves what was happening.[39] That night Captain Hicks, a member of Lockhart's small staff, and Major Webster of the American Red Cross left Moscow in a special train. The two observers spent six weeks in Siberia, where for a time they joined forces with the American Military Attaché from Peking, who was engaged on a similar investigation.

Their reports, and especially the Webster–Hicks report, were reassuring; with one exception—that of some Hungarians on their way to fight Semenov—they had seen or heard of no prisoners bearing arms for military purposes, though in the camps some carried rifles on guard-duty as a protection against pilferers. 'We can but add,' they wrote, 'that, after seeing the armed prisoners and the type of men they are, we feel there is no danger to the Allied cause through them.'

Their conclusions did nothing to allay anxiety in London and Washington, where the Hicks–Webster report appears to have been almost completely disregarded. Its authors' impartiality was automatically suspect, because their superiors, Lockhart and Raymond Robins, were felt in both capitals to take altogether too favourable a view of the Soviet cause; and it cannot be said that the report itself produces an overwhelming impression of objectivity. Hicks and Webster had found the Soviet authorities all along their route to be 'sincere and bright men ... they were mild-mannered, and vengeance for past wrongs does not seem to be part of their programmes.'[40] In the Foreign Office it was felt that men who would believe that would believe anything; and the report, though substantially accurate in its findings, did nothing to lessen official credulity about the terrible prisoners.

To the Internationalist recruiting drive, which was at its briskest from the middle of March to the end of May, the strongest objection was taken by the officer prisoners.[41] It evoked vehement protests from the Governments of the Central Powers, whose sole object (contrary to what the Allies believed) was to get their half-starved subjects home as soon as possible. Recruiting was stopped, and the Internationalists released from Bolshevik service, when the German and Austrian repatriation commissions began to arrive in Russia in May–June.[42] This did not however prevent the Allies from continuing to talk, and eventually from acting, as though large but unspecified tracts of Russian territory were harbouring important enemy troop-concentrations. As late as 1 September 1918—at least two months after the last bemused Magyar had returned his obsolescent Berdan rifle to the quartermaster's stores—the British Prime Minister was felicitating Dr Masaryk on the 'striking successes won by Czechoslovak forces against armies of German and Austrian troops in Siberia.'[43]

Dr Beneš, Masaryk's chief collaborator, presided over the Paris headquarters of the Czechoslovak National Council and paid frequent visits to London. Nobody in either capital, he recorded afterwards, attached the slightest importance to the Chelyabinsk Incident; the fighting which broke out as a result of it, and which gave the Czechs control of a number of key towns in the Urals and Siberia, was seen at first as a purely local affair. The French deplored a development likely to delay still further the Czechs' progress to Vladivostok or Archangel; 'I saw every day,' wrote Beneš, 'how important France felt it to be that our army should be transported to the Western Front, and not embroiled in Siberia.'[44] The handful of French liaison officers with the Legion, so far from being the interventionist *provocateurs* which Soviet historians depict them as, continued to urge the Czechs to do nothing which would jeopardise their chances of reaching the troopships.

By mid-June 1918 this, roughly, was the situation along the Trans-Siberian from the Pacific to the Volga:

At Vladivostok some 12,000 Czech troops had arrived; there were no transports awaiting them. The Amur Railway (the last 'leg' of the Trans-Siberian, skirting the North Manchurian frontier from Karymskaia to Vladivostok) was largely under Bolshevik control.

About Karymskaia were Red Army forces which had just driven Semenov back into Chinese territory.

Between Karymskaia and Irkutsk, the main Bolshevik stronghold in Siberia, there were three Czech *échelons*.

Between Irkutsk and Omsk there were eight Czech *échelons*.

Between Omsk and Penza was the whole of the 1st Czech Division, still theoretically directed on Archangel.

Confused though this situation was, it was made even more so by a breakdown in telegraphic communications, of which the causes remain obscure. At the end of May—a crucial period for the Czechs—one of their French liaison officers noted that 'cipher telegrams were not getting past Mariinsk';[45] it was not until 31 May that an *échelon* at Irkutsk learnt of the fateful decisions taken at Chelyabinsk a week earlier and of the events leading up to them; and later it was only through the arrival of a Czech courier that his compatriots at Irkutsk received news of the capture from the Bolsheviks of Samara.[46] How far-reaching were the effects of this time-lag there are no means of telling; but it and other breakdowns of the same sort almost certainly helped to blur the picture of events which filtered through to Vladivostok and—more important—to nullify the frantic efforts of the Czech political leaders there to restrain by means of urgent telegraphic orders their westernmost detachments from intervening in internal Russian politics. Repeated caveats to the most impetuous of these officers, Captain Rudolf Gajda, went unacknowledged.

On 29 June, with the full though tacit approval of the Allied naval and consular authorities, the Czechs in Vladivostok seized control of the city; a week later Ufa in the Urals was captured, leaving the Legionaries in virtually complete control of the

Trans-Siberian from Irkutsk to Penza. On this sector of the line, some 3000 miles in length, the Czech troops numbered only about 40,000, and their remarkable achievements would not have been possible without the co-operation of local counter-revolutionary forces. These emerged everywhere under the stimulus of the Czech operations, to which in some places they made decisive contributions, and by which they were automatically installed in power as successors to the ousted Bolsheviks.

Thus there came almost fortuitously into being a patchwork of regional régimes, of which the two most important were the West Siberian Commissariat (which was based on Omsk and developed reactionary tendencies) and, further west at Samara, the Government of Members of the Constituent Assembly, which was basically Socialist-Revolutionary. Omsk flew a green-and-white flag, representing the forests and snows of Siberia; Samara flew a red flag. Omsk claimed authority throughout Siberia, Samara insisted that it was—at least *in posse*—an all-Russian Government. Relations between the two were permanently strained.

At Vladivostok, meanwhile, and still more outside Russia, the situation of the westernmost Czechs was assumed, wrongly, to be as desperate as it appeared on the map. Telegraphic communications, as we have seen, were unreliable; the weakness of the Bolshevik hold on Siberia was not appreciated; and the prisoner-of-war bogy loomed more alarming every day.

'I should like,' minuted a Foreign Office official on a telegram about the Czechs in the second week of June, 'to make an eleventh-hour attempt to use these Czechoslovaks. Their intervention would almost certainly . . . set the whole thing going.' A week earlier the same hankering to 'use' the Czechs had been implicit in the decision about their future role taken by the Supreme Allied War Council and well described by Kennan as 'one of those curious and ineffective compromises to which busy Governments are addicted.'[47] Nothing was known at Versailles of the metamorphosis in the Czech position brought about by the Chelyabinsk Incident and its repercussions; but it was resolved to seek the 'approval in principle' of the Czechoslovak National Council to the retention of 'some Czech units' at Murmansk and Archangel, whither the westernmost Czechs were still, erroneously, believed to be making their way. At the same time Japan was to be invited to provide shipping to evacuate the remainder (i.e. all those west of Omsk) from Vladivostok. The Supreme Allied War Council was so wildly out of touch with the true situation in the Urals and Siberia that its decisions can have only an academic interest; this lies in the fact that both halves of the Czech problem were to be solved in a way which would make at least a part of the Legion available, at least for a time, for active service on Russian soil. Though still paramount in French official circles, the policy of moving all the Czechs as quickly as possible to the Western Front was being eroded at the highest level by the impulse to intervene.

By June 1918 the Siberian question had become 'the dominant problem of American foreign policy';[48] and American foreign policy had all along been, for the other Allies, the dominant problem in the Siberian question. The position, briefly, was this: Japan alone could provide the main sinews of armed intervention, because she alone had troops and shipping to spare and she alone was within striking distance of Siberia. But Japan was not prepared to act without American approval and support. These America was not prepared to give, mainly because she mistrusted Japan's intentions and partly because she did not want to divert any part of her war-effort from the Western Front. Everything therefore hinged on a change in the American attitude.

Upon this attitude three months of continuous French and British prodding had failed to make any decisive impact. But cracks, hardly discernible outside official circles in Washington, had begun to appear in the monolith of President Wilson's non-cooperation. The 'German' prisoners of war had disturbed him; he had come in May to wonder 'whether there is any legitimate way in which we can assist' Semenov; and at the end of that month the successful renewal of the German offensive in France underlined the urgent need somehow to relieve the pressure on the Western Front. Then there was the nagging doubt whether the President had the right to hold out indefinitely against the wishes of his allies; there was the arrival in Washington of Masaryk, with his powerful advocacy of the Czech cause; and there was an outwardly favourable development in the interminable negotiations with Japan about a possible basis for collaboration in Siberia.

These and other factors, including an impassioned appeal from Marshal Foch, the Allied Commander-in-Chief, had not altered the President's mind but they had helped to condition it for change. When, towards the end of June, circumstantial news—highly flavoured with inaccurate items about German influence and hostile prisoners of war in Siberia—opened Washington's eyes to the situation, at once promising and perilous, in which the Czechs found themselves, Wilson reversed American policy on Siberia almost overnight. A course of action which had hitherto had only expediency to recommend it (and doubtful expediency at that) was now sponsored by altruism; a dubious and ill-defined adventure had become a rescue operation with a limited and humane objective. Lansing, the Secretary of State, put the matter in a nutshell; the Czechs, he wrote, 'have materially changed the situation by introducing a sentimental element into the question of our duty.'

The American decision to send an armed force to Siberia was taken, somewhat precipitately, on 6 July. In *The Decision to Intervene* Kennan analyses the background to the decision and the curious ambiguity of the reasons officially given, in three slightly different versions, for taking it. The Czechs were to be rescued, or rather were to be helped to rescue themselves, for the American military objective was defined as 'safeguarding the rear of the Czechs operating from Vladivostok.' But from whom were the Czechs to be rescued? And against whom, for that matter, was their rear to be safeguarded? Neither point was resolved in the *Aide-Mémoire* which the President drafted, apparently without consulting anyone, on his own typewriter[49] and which was presented by the Secretary of State to the Allied Ambassadors on 17 July (though a paraphrase published a fortnight later reintroduced 'the armed German and Austrian prisoners' as the villains of the piece).

'Military action,' the *Aide-Mémoire* affirmed, 'is admissible in Russia . . . only to help the Czechoslovaks consolidate their forces and get into successful co-operation with their Slavic kinsmen and to steady any efforts at self-government or self-defence in which the Russians themselves may be willing to accept assistance.' These cloudy phrases are almost meaningless. Which Russians? Self-defence against whom? And what, above all, had enabling the Czechs to 'get into successful co-operation with their Slavic kinsmen' (against some of whom they had been engaged in desperate fighting for several weeks) got to do with winning the war against Germany?

In diplomatic communications, of which Wilson's *Aide-Mémoire* was an example, imprecision is seldom a fatal defect. Ambiguities can be clarified in later exchanges, omissions made good, inconsistencies ironed out. The woolliness with which the United States Government defined its purposes in Siberia would have done nobody any harm if a copy of the *Aide-Mémoire*, unsigned, had not been handed in a sealed envelope to the commander-designate of the American forces a fortnight after it was written. 'This,' said the Secretary for War, who gave it to him in the railway station at Kansas City, 'contains the policy of the United States in Russia which you are to follow. Watch your step.'[50]

General Graves, a conscientious officer, did his utmost to comply with these orders. But in a directive to a military commander even a very slight element of imprecision is a highly dangerous ingredient. As an attempt to rationalise America's confused but basically honourable motives for undertaking a gingerly intervention in Siberia the *Aide-Mémoire* can perhaps be allowed to pass muster; as standing orders which were straitly to control the conduct of her armed forces in a distant theatre of civil war the document was not merely valueless but harmful.

It was in this light that their hapless commander felt obliged to regard it. He was given no other directive; before he arrived in Vladivostok he had, as he wrote afterwards, 'received no information as to the military, political, social, economic or financial situation in Russia.'[51] America went into Siberia with both hands tied behind her back. There was a sort of sturdy innocence in her belief, which the *Aide-Mémoire* proclaimed, that a valid distinction could be drawn between 'military intervention in Russia' (in which her Government could neither 'take part . . . or sanction') and sending troops to Russia to support the Czechs against unidentified assailants. This was statecraft at its most academic. But the results of the American decision were the reverse of academic; for it did in fact, however involuntarily, 'sanction' action by her allies which, as the *Aide-Mémoire* quite rightly prophesied, 'would add to the present sad confusion in Russia rather than cure it, injure her rather than help her, and would be of no advantage in our main design, to win the war against Germany.'

CHAPTER SIX

The Puppet-Masters

'I RETAINED a horrible impression of Harbin,' Kolchak told his interrogators; 'I never met two people [there] who would speak well of each other.'

He arrived, early in May, to find the Russian community far gone in degradation and disunity. Horvath headed a fusty clique which had pretensions to being some sort of Government. Another Government, a splinter-group from Siberia under an Odessa Jew called Derber, lived on sufferance in some railway carriages at the station; they ruled no one, represented no one, but from time to time they sent cables to President Wilson. There were half a dozen private armies, all very small. One consisted of a large staff without any soldiers, in another the rank and file were Chinese. Each had its own counter-espionage service, whose duties were mainly concerned with private vendettas, extortion and the traffic in opium. Colonel Orlov's detachment was the least disreputable; but his relations with Semenov were so bad that the question hardly arose of his troops going to fight the Bolsheviks in Trans-Baikalia. It quickly became plain to Kolchak that the prospects of finding in 'that Harbin gutter,' as he called it, material on which to base a movement for the 'national restoration of Russia' were remote.

Throughout North Manchuria the only real power lay in Japanese hands. They controlled the supply of arms and ammunition. They had plenty of funds, and were ready to transfer them to their *protégés* with a lack of formality which suited the recipients well. (Years later, in 1927, a major political scandal was caused by allegations, made amid uproar in the Japanese Diet, about the misuse of secret military funds during the Intervention. The allegations, involving a figure of 500 million yen or roughly £50,000,000, were not refuted.)[52] Semenov, their puppet, sat astride one end of the Chinese Eastern Railway; at the other end, firmly esconced in a place called Pogranichnaia, another Cossack leader, by name Kalmykov, a lesser but in some ways a more revolting thug than Semenov, was even more dependent on his Japanese patrons.

More important than all this skulduggery, Japan concluded in mid-May a secret military agreement with China.[53] This provided for co-operation between their armed forces if 'the enemy' threatened either their own territories or 'the general peace and tranquillity in the Far East.' Since the enemy was not identified, the geographical limits of the Far East were not defined, and no interpretation was offered of what might be held to constitute a menace to its general peace and tranquillity, the treaty in effect gave Japan the right to deploy her troops on Chinese territory whenever she cared to concoct a pretext for doing so.

Thus, long before the first Japanese soldier came ashore at Vladivostok, Japan had established on the mainland a bridgehead of influence; it gave her, both before and after Intervention began, many opportunities for the sort of mischief-making which was an essential component of her continental policy.

Of all the Interventionist Powers, Japan was throughout the most realistic. Her Government was split on the question of intervention, her people were violently against it, her newspapers were for some time forbidden to mention it. But her policy was firm and consistent, her strategy cautious and sound.

Japan claimed, with partial justification, a 'special position' in Siberia. She had economic interests there which were legitimate, and political interests which were not; besides, leaving legitimacy on one side, it obviously mattered a good deal to her who controlled Vladivostok. She had therefore strong motives for intervening independently, as well as the resources necessary to do so; and the temptation to 'go it alone' was continually being reinforced by exhortations from London and Paris. ('From a military point of view,' Sir Henry Wilson, the Chief of the Imperial General Staff, wrote in his diary on 11 May, 'the Japanese Army could not intervene too soon nor go too far, and . . . I was always impressing this on my Government, and hoped that the Japanese General Staff would do the same to their Government.') [54]

But Japan stuck to her guns; she would go to Siberia only with American backing. This self-restraint paid handsomely. When the United States decided to rescue the Czechs, the President's *Aide-Mémoire* foresaw that the American troops would co-operate closely with 'a small military force like [our] own from Japan'; but this part of the plan had not been concerted in advance with the Japanese. The tables had thus been turned. Up till now, a Japanese expedition had needed American backing; now it was the other way round. Moreover the Americans had already committed themselves. On moral grounds they could not abandon their chivalrous enterprise; on military grounds they could not embark on it without the Japanese. 'Whether or not President Wilson was fully aware of it,' Kennan points out, 'the Japanese had him cornered.' [55]

They proceeded to make hay with the American project in its original form. Their own declaration—corresponding to Wilson's *Aide-Mémoire* but published a fortnight later—invited by implication the co-operation of the other Allies, whom Wilson had hoped to exclude. They refused to limit their own force to the same strength—7000 men—as the Americans'; they would dispatch in the first place one division (about 12,000 men) and reserved the right to reinforce this at need. No limit was set to the total number of Japanese troops who might become involved; and in the end it rose to roughly 72,000, more than ten times the number that the Americans had bargained for—or would have bargained for, had they not sacrificed their power to do so.

Although, however, Japan put into the field a force which, barring the Czechs, was many times larger than all the other

Allied contingents lumped together, she confined its operations to the sphere of her own immediate interests. She had always said that her troops would not go further than Irkutsk, and they never did go further than Irkutsk. After they had cleared the Amur Railway of Bolsheviks they settled down to what were basically garrison duties. In the interests of internal security they sent flying columns against the Partisans, but they never went to the front, were never in action against the main forces of the Red Army. They were the only striking-force the Allies sent to Siberia; and they never struck.

Throughout the Intervention a tug-of-war was going on between rival factions in the Japanese Government, between the Government and the General Staff, and between the General Staff and its commanders in the field; as a result the image of Japanese policy, outwardly so clear-cut, often proves on closer inspection to be slightly blurred or distorted. Japan did not intend the annexation of the Maritime Province, still less of Trans-Baikalia. She did want to consolidate her existing sphere of influence in Manchuria. She had tentative and rather clumsy designs on Mongolia. She would have liked, for strategic reasons, to neutralise Vladivostok. She was on the look-out for commercial pickings wherever they were going; and throughout the whole theatre of Intervention from the Pacific to Lake Baikal she was firmly resolved to be, as Kennan puts it, 'in the driver's seat.'[56]

Her ultimate aims were thus diametrically though unavowedly opposed to those of her allies. The very last thing Japan wanted was just what they were striving to create—a strong, stable Russian administration in Siberia. Japan had a vested interest in anarchy, or at least in the sort of warlordism which Semenov, with her help, so vividly exemplified. What happened to the Czechoslovak Legion was a matter of total indifference to Japan. Of the professed objects of the Intervention the only one with which she was concerned was the Allies' desire to 'steady any efforts at self-government or self-defence in which the Russians themselves may be willing to accept assistance'; and her concern here was to ensure that all efforts directed to this end should fail. So she lavished her help on scoundrels and thwarted the endeavours of patriots; for the Russians 'the price of British or French aid was complete unity and of Japanese aid complete disunity.'[57]

Japan's last appearance in the field of international military co-operation had been in North China during the Boxer Rebellion. The contrast between the conduct of her representatives in 1901 and in 1918–22, between the high reputation they won at Peking and the bad name with which they emerged from Siberia, shows how rapidly her national character was developing, how soon the tradition of the Samurai was to yield place to the standards of Pearl Harbour and the prison-camps. During the siege of the foreign Legations the small Japanese contingent —smaller than anybody else's—was 'the background and brains of the defence'; they were 'the only nationality of whom no criticism . . . is to be found in the copious records of the Siege,'[58] and in the International Relief Force Japanese troops bore the brunt of the fighting. They were remembered as paragons.

It was a different story in Siberia. The Japanese fought with their usual bravery when called upon to fight; but as an army of occupation they were ruthless, overbearing and extortionate. Their allies found them truculent and deceitful; it was difficult to recognise the true-blue, Hentyesque heroes of Peking in the patrons of such shoddy fiends as Semenov and Kalmykov.

None of the Powers earned any credit in Siberia; but behind all their blunders and miscalculations—in the foundations, as it were, of the folly which they built only to abandon—there lay an original intention to do good. The defeat of Germany, the rescue of the Czechs, even the 'regeneration' of Russia—these purposes, which the Allies had in common, were not in themselves dishonourable. Japan never shared them. She was out for her own ends and, having got to Siberia on the bandwagon of Intervention, proceeded to sabotage the vehicle whenever it suited her to do so.

As a wounded prisoner at the end of the Russo-Japanese War Kolchak had been treated with consideration by his captors;

he had no prejudice against the Japanese. To them, however, his appearance in Harbin was unwelcome. The qualities which had recommended him to the British—his integrity, his powers of leadership—automatically made him *persona non grata* to the Japanese; in their plans for the Far East there was no room for a Russian who commanded the general respect of his compatriots, who was incorruptible, and who might, given a chance, restore some sort of order and purpose to the flabby, bickering *demi-monde* whose leaders the Japanese found it so easy and so profitable to manipulate. They turned their thumbs down as soon as Kolchak entered the arena.

General Nakajima was head of the Japanese Military Mission in Manchuria; to the American General Graves he 'seemed to be a most important Japanese official, without any special duty.'[59] He and his Mission were part of what was to become the permanent apparatus of Japanese expansion—a small but influential politico-military organisation, subordinate to the General Staff but independent of the regular forces: rather, perhaps, on the lines of the Arab Bureau set up by the British in 1916; the most notable of his successors was probably General Doihara, 'the Lawrence of Manchuria,' who was active in the 1930's. Nakajima was a clever and, for a Japanese officer, a sophisticated man. He had been Military Attaché in Petrograd and Director of Military Intelligence; he spoke Russian and French.

Kolchak's first interview with him was not auspicious. The Admiral explained his plans for expanding and co-ordinating the small Russian forces in the Railway Zone and asked for help in arming them. Nakajima was sceptical about Kolchak's chances of achieving very much, but undertook to furnish a quantity of machine-guns and other equipment. Then, to Kolchak's surprise, he asked: 'What compensation can you offer?' Kolchak pointed out that he was not empowered to negotiate, but that the arms would assuredly be paid for by the Chinese Eastern Railway: whereupon Nakajima 'said that the money question did not interest him at all,'[60] leaving it to be inferred that his masters wanted some form of political concession. The discussion then veered away—not very happily—to the desirability of channelling all Japanese support for independent Russian detachments through a central organisation. Nakajima's reactions to this sensible idea are not on record, but they cannot conceivably have been favourable. Before they parted he asked Kolchak whether he was going to see Semenov; Kolchak said that he was.

Semenov's second petty offensive into Trans-Baikalia had been driven back across the frontier, but he still maintained his headquarters at Manchuli. At this drab and inconsiderable place Kolchak arrived in a special train on 15 May for his first—and last—meeting with a man who was to have a baneful influence on his destiny. Kolchak, or someone on his staff, had announced his coming in a telegram which is said to have been unfortunately worded. As a class White Russian leaders took umbrage very easily, and there was nobody on the platform to meet Kolchak's train.

There was nothing at Manchuli except the railway station, set in the middle of a vast, naked plain, and a little walled Chinese town round which huddled a scattering of Mongol yurts. In so small and bleak a place Semenov's failure to welcome his visitor was a deliberate act of discourtesy, particularly as he himself (it presently transpired) was in his own private coach, within a bow-shot of Kolchak's. Here Kolchak, putting his pride in his pocket, bearded him after a bootless and exasperating wait.

According to Kolchak's version of the meeting, his own attitude was reasonable and conciliatory. He had come, he said, not as Semenov's superior but in order to find out what material assistance the Ataman needed for his own forces. It was his duty to co-ordinate such matters in the zone of the Chinese Eastern Railway, and he had brought with him a contribution of 300,000 roubles from the Railway Board.

Kolchak had a violent temper and had been under grave provocation; it may be doubted whether his manner was as mild as this account suggests. But in any case no olive-branch, however tactfully proffered, stood a chance of being accepted; Nakajima had made sure of that in advance. Semenov's reply was evasive. He needed nothing; he got everything he wanted from Japan; he had no requests to make, no plans to disclose. 'I then saw,' said Kolchak, 'that there was really no use talking with him.' [61] He told Semenov, in effect, that he washed his hands of him, and the two men parted on the worst possible terms.

This unhelpful encounter was followed, a few days later in Harbin, by an interview with Nakajima at which Kolchak lost his temper ('I am very reserved, but sometimes I do explode'). [62] By now the Admiral was a spent force in Manchuria. A shrewder, more devious man might have achieved something by prostituting himself to the Japanese, by appearing to play their game, by trading worthless promises for guns and money; Harbin was full of Russians who were doing this in a small way with a certain amount of success. But guile, even in a good cause, was beyond Kolchak. 'You know,' the Russian Ambassador to Japan told him later that summer, 'you have assumed from the beginning too independent a position with regard to Japan, and they have understood it. You allow yourself to speak to them in too imperative and independent a tone . . . They have come to regard you as an enemy.' [63] There can be little doubt that Kolchak's forthright manner grated on the Japanese, that he put their backs up more than he need have done; but to say that he spoilt his chances by doing so would be misleading, because he never had any chances to spoil. In the Japanese scheme of things there was no more place for a man of integrity than there is for a fox in a fowl-run.

For a couple of months Kolchak struggled on, contending as best he could with the forces of indiscipline and intrigue which, with or without Japanese encouragement, thwarted at every step his efforts to unify the Russian armed forces in the Railway Zone. At last he recognised that the task was hopeless as long as the Japanese were against him, and early in July he handed over his command and went to Tokyo in the faint hope that the Japanese General Staff might be persuaded to see reason.

Kolchak was courteously received at the War Ministry. The Chief of the General Staff listened to his complaints and proposals, but when they were over could offer nothing more constructive than the suggestion that Kolchak should stay for a time in Japan ('we have nice places here'); he would be informed when the moment was ripe for his return to the mainland.

Kolchak saw that the game was up for the time being. He was in fact ill and suffering from overstrain; he fell in with the Chief of Staff's suggestion, sent a wire to Horvath reporting the conversation, and took up residence in a hotel.

It was seven months since he had left Tokyo, under British auspices, for Mesopotamia: seven months of frustration and failure. The outlook for Kolchak was bleak. August came, and Intervention was getting under way in earnest. But Intervention, seen from Tokyo, appeared to be an almost exclusively Japanese affair, in which there was unlikely to be a role for a senior Russian officer who had made himself objectionable to the Japanese. It was not until the end of August that Kolchak was given the opportunity which his patriotism and his personal honour insistently demanded. 'There is no doubt,' wrote the head of the British Military Mission to Siberia on 31 August, 'that he is the best Russian for our purposes in the Far East'; [64] and when, a few days later, Kolchak left Tokyo for the second time, it was once more under British auspices.

CHAPTER SEVEN

The Czechs Turn West

THE Czechoslovak Legion, whose supposed need for succour became in July 1918 the cornerstone of Allied policy towards Siberia, had by that date a strength of roughly 70,000. It bore small resemblance to the armed forces of any other nation.

There was a sizeable though scattered community of Czechs and Slovaks in Russia before the war—the Slovaks mostly living in small peasant colonies, the more sophisticated Czechs working in industry or commerce. When hostilities began many of these exiles were recruited into a *druzhina* under Russian officers. The *druzhina* was not so much a regiment as a holding unit, which supplied small specialist detachments for reconnaissance work with Russian formations. The chief military value of the Czechs and Slovaks lay, at this stage, in their command of the enemy's languages, and they were much in demand to man listening-posts and to accompany patrols; they played the same sort of role as native scouts in a colonial war.

From the first their compatriots serving in the Austro-Hungarian armies showed great readiness to desert; when this could not be arranged they allowed themselves to be captured without difficulty. For a long time, however, the Russians refused to permit these prisoners of war to enlist in the *druzhina*, which at the beginning of 1916 was still only 1500 strong. There were several reasons for the Russian attitude. It was not at all easy to distinguish between genuine Czechs or Slovaks and prisoners of other nationalities who claimed to be one or the other in order to get out of captivity. Besides (this was the main argument used by senior Russian officers) the deserters or near-deserters had already betrayed their military oath to the Emperor Franz Josef; might they not prove equally unreliable in the Russian ranks?

On the political side there was a reluctance to take any step which might prove an obstacle to the conclusion of a separate peace (should the opportunity offer) with Austria-Hungary; and perhaps there was also an instinctive feeling, natural in an Empire whose boundaries enclosed so many subject races, that it was a mistake to encourage anything which smacked, as the *druzhina* did, of self-determination and which appeared to recognise the right of an oppressed minority to fight for its freedom. In any case, the *druzhina* remained a token force, and the Czechoslovak prisoners continued to languish in their camps, though a few skilled workers managed to get taken on in munition factories.

In spite of many petitions and much string-pulling, this state of affairs prevailed until the Tsar's abdication in March 1917. The attitude of the Provisional Government under Kerensky to the Czechoslovaks was less costive than its predecessor's. The prisoners were released and the *druzhina* expanded rapidly into an Army Corps of two divisions. It was short of equipment, and especially of artillery; the standard of training was uneven; and all the senior officers were Russian. But the Legion, as it came afterwards to be called, was a well-knit, self-contained force, with far more resource and cohesion than most of the disintegrating divisions of the Russian Army. The men wore Russian uniform, embellished with a red-and-white badge representing the lion of Bohemia. The Russian peasants, who had never heard of Bohemia and may not have been well informed about lions, took this animal for a puppy; and when, as time went on, the Czechoslovaks became unpopular, the Russians referred to them as *Tcheko-Sobaki, sobaka* being Russian for a dog.

The sudden emergence of the Czech Legion in the centre of the international stage, where it appeared to be doubling the part of St George with that of the damsel in distress, was received with mixed feelings by the founders—at that stage the would-be founders—of the Czechoslovak State. In those days nationhood, a boon which later in the century was to be had for little more than the asking, was grudgingly conferred; in the long struggle to attain it the Czech armed forces in France, Italy and Russia were, as Masaryk admitted, 'our greatest asset.'[65]

In France (12,000 men) and Italy (24,000) these forces were too small and too ill-found to win much glory; but they represented the Czechoslovak presence, they got themselves on to the agenda at conferences, and they gained useful publicity for their country's cause on ceremonial occasions such as the presentation of new colours. The Legion in Russia, though twice the size of the other two, was, so to speak, too far from the shopwindow to have any symbolical value worth speaking of. In June 1917, during Kerensky's last, futile offensive, it fought with great gallantry and considerable success at Zborov; but by that time the Russian front was in disrepute and the Czechs' deeds went virtually unnoticed in the West. A few months later the Legion was for practical purposes lost to sight in the turmoil of revolution. Masaryk and Beneš had every reason for supporting the French efforts to transfer it from Russia to the Western Front, 'the theatre where the fate of the Hapsburg Empire would be decided,'[66] and where her soldiers' services to the Allied cause would strengthen Czechoslovakia's claims to be recognised as a sovereign state.

Nothing the Czechs could have achieved in Europe would have put them so firmly on the map as their dramatic and unexpected seizure of the Trans-Siberian Railway; in America, Masaryk noted, against the dark background of news from the Western Front the Legion's exploits had 'the glamour of a fairy tale.'[67] But neither he nor Beneš, shuttling between Paris and London, liked anything about the Legion's predicament except its propaganda value. Masaryk, travelling across Russia earlier in the year, had come to the conclusion—he was the first person of consequence to reach it—that the Bolsheviks would triumph in the end. Beneš, equally astute, saw the dangers of Intervention on an inadequate scale and with no clearly defined purpose; 'I feared that our soldiers would be the first victims.' [68] As a result, official Czech policy strictly forbade the Legion to interfere in internal Russian politics and envisaged a resumption of its move to Europe as soon as conditions permitted.

For three months after the Chelyabinsk Incident the overriding need of the Czechs was to regroup their forces, scattered widely along 5000 miles of railway, into a unified and self-supporting whole. During this phase it is misleading to visualise the Legion as a single armed force, directed by a central staff towards a defined objective. There were really three main groups, all facing different problems, all associated with different counter-revolutionary agencies, all deriving their impressions of Allied policy from different sources, and all in consequence taking different views of the situation in which they found themselves.

First, there were the Czechs in Vladivostok. Their seizure of that city on 29 June produced 'in the explosive Far Eastern situation an effect comparable to the removal of a pin from a hand-grenade,' [69] and almost immediately afterwards their commander, a capable Russian general of Czech descent called Dieterichs, informed the British naval authorities that they would not be needing the ships which were on their way to carry them across the Pacific *en route* for the Western Front, since they were embarking on operations towards Irkutsk. [70] The Vladivostok Czechs perhaps entertained graver fears than they need have for the comrades whom they unhesitatingly set out to relieve; but they were better informed than the groups in the interior on two important points. One was the apparent reluctance of the Allies to provide shipping for the Legion at Vladivostok (where many of them had now spent more than two months without meeting an embarkation officer). The other was the prospects for Allied intervention; Vladivostok had always tended to see these in a rosy light, and the Czechs' own

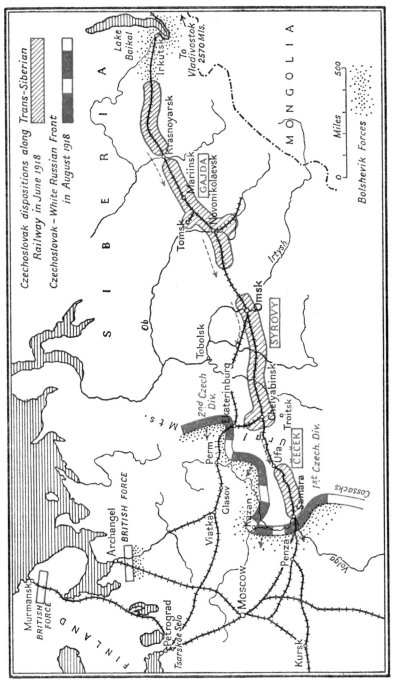

Dispositions of the 1st Czechoslovak Army Corps, June 1918

achievement in wresting control of the port from the Bolsheviks had obviously improved them greatly.

The middle group—in Central Siberia, west of Lake Baikal—were mainly concerned with reducing the Soviet strongholds, like Irkutsk and Krasnoyarsk, which continued until mid-July to break the continuity of their control over the railway. They then had to secure the forty tunnels through which the Trans-Siberian ran along the precipitous southern shore of Lake Baikal, demolition of which would have blocked the route to Vladivostok for weeks, if not for months; they were captured virtually intact by forces under the fiery Gajda in a series of highly creditable operations. On the political side the Czechs in Central Siberia found themselves collaborating with the West Siberian Commissariat at Omsk, which was no more immune from specious optimism than any other White administration in its early days.

An enterprising officer called Čeček was the leading spirit in the third and most westerly group of Czechs, which comprised most of the 1st Division. Many of these troops were still in the area of Penza, on the wrong side of the Volga, at the time of the Chelyabinsk Incident, and were thus—on paper—in greater peril than any other part of the Legion. But Čeček, fighting his way steadily eastward, established contact with the central group early in July. At an early stage of his operations the capture of Samara led to the emergence of the Socialist-Revolutionary Government of the Constituent Assembly, to which reference was made in Chapter Five; this régime evoked in the Czechs, most of whom were socialists by temperament and tradition, far greater sympathy than did the reactionaries at Omsk, and their close association with it inevitably coloured their outlook. The ease with which they had overcome Bolshevik resistance, and the enthusiasm with which they were welcomed as liberators, had made a deep impression on them. The aspirations of the Samara Government, whose own military forces appeared to be growing in strength, presented the Czechs with an alternative course of action to that on which they were engaged.

THE FATE OF ADMIRAL KOLCHAK

From almost every point of view between the extremes of altruism and self-interest there was much to be said for exchanging an eastward withdrawal for a westward crusade. Vladivostok was 5000 difficult miles away; even if there were ships waiting when they got there—and there was scepticism about this throughout the *échelons*—they would still face a journey across two oceans (one of them infested by U-boats) and the North American continent before being privileged to take part, under foreign command, in trench warfare on the Western Front against the German Army. The alternative was to stay where they were, on the Volga, and to participate, initially at any rate as the senior military partner, in operations of a type with which they were familiar, against an enemy of whom they had the measure, for a purpose which all understood and most approved. In war occasions are rare when, in an army confronted with two possibilities for its future employment, the fire-eater and the shirker, Hotspur and Falstaff, incline to the same choice. This was such an occasion.

There were several subsidiary factors which influenced the Czechs towards all-out involvement in the Civil War. Their Russian officers, whom in general they respected, were vehemently anti-Bolshevik and eager to support the pretensions of Omsk and Samara. Attempts to subvert the loyalty of the Legion by propaganda and by the use of Czech communists had caused resentment in its ranks; and there was furthermore—especially after the arrival of Count Mirbach as German Ambassador in Moscow at the end of April—a widespread belief that Germany was behind all the delays and provocations they were suffering, and that by striking back at the Soviets they were saving Siberia, not for the Whites from the Reds, but for the Allies from the Central Powers.

In addition to all this, the Czechs were convinced that help was on the way, that the Allies contemplated a speedy and massive intervention, and that they would shortly find themselves in the van of a great army moving on Moscow. This conviction was not founded merely on wishful thinking. During the latter part of June two seemingly authoritative messages from senior Allied diplomatic representatives conveyed to the Czechs the clear impression that the Allies were about to intervene in strength, and that it was the Legion's duty to hold fast to the territory it had gained. One of these messages, from the American Consul in Moscow, went to Samara and reached the most westerly group; the other, in which the French Ambassador spoke of intervention 'at the end of June' and of the Czechs forming 'the advance guard of the Allied Army,' was sent to Chelyabinsk and thus made its first impact on the central group. Kennan [71] has unravelled with great skill the skein of misunderstanding and false assumptions in which both these messages—despatched in good faith—had their origins; but the Czechs had no reason to question their validity, and the news they brought acted as a powerful stimulant on troops whose situation was peculiarly forlorn.*

Such, broadly, were the considerations which led 'the Executive Committee of the Penza group of armies' (the most westerly group, who up to then had been the rearguard) to order Lieutenant Čeček, on 7 July, 'to change the objective; instead of continuing to move eastwards, the Penza group is to stand fast and act as the advance guard of the Allies with a view to forming a new Eastern Front against the Germans.' [72] These orders disregarded the directives of the Czech political leaders in Europe and at Vladivostok. They were based on four beliefs:

(a) that strong Allied forces would shortly appear on the Volga,

(b) that the Germans were the nigger in the Soviet woodpile,

* One of the French liaison officers with the Legion, Major Guinet, seems to have encouraged the Czechs to pitch their hopes of Allied aid too high. In November, when Czech enthusiasm for the Civil War had evaporated, General Knox, head of the British Military Mission, wrote that 'Gajda, like everyone else, blamed Major Guinet of the French Mission, who for the past four months had constantly promised immediate and ample help from the Allies.' (Britmis MSS.) Guinet was a sanguine, self-important man.

(c) that the Whites would prove staunch and capable
    allies,
(d) that the Red Army need not be taken seriously.

All these beliefs were fallacious.

The last of them, however, continued for some weeks to be
borne out by developments on the 'new Eastern Front.' Thanks
partly to the enterprise of two young and unusually aggressive
White Russian commanders, Kappel and Voitzekhovski, the
Czechs and the forces of the Samara Government not only
consolidated but enlarged the territory under their control
along the Volga. On the other side of the Urals the central
group, with headquarters at Chelyabinsk, was equally successful. To the south-west contact was established with the Orenburg Cossacks, who under their Ataman, a plump, spaniel-
eyed, ineffective little man called Dutov, were adding to the
confusion of a civil war on whose outcome they were destined
to have a negligible effect. To the northward Czechs and
White Russians captured the important industrial town of
Ekaterinburg and in so doing were the unwitting instigators
of an outrage which shocked the world and—especially, perhaps, in Britain—deepened still further the detestation in which
the Soviet régime was held in right-wing circles.

The Emperor Nicholas II and his family had been brought to
Ekaterinburg under a strong guard in May. It was their third
place of detention. At Tsarskoe Selo, on the outskirts of Petrograd, the Provisional Government had treated them with
consideration; the restraints placed on them amounted to no
more than a form of palace-arrest. But in July 1917 disturbances in the capital led to their clandestine transfer, as a precaution, to Tobolsk in the heart of Siberia.

The conditions under which they were housed, fed and
guarded in this remote place deteriorated rapidly after the
Bolshevik Revolution. Their increasingly ill-disciplined guards
inflicted on them a series of minor humiliations and de-
privations; they were forbidden to go to church, 'luxuries'

like butter and coffee were eliminated from their diet, most of their servants were dismissed. The screws were being tightened.

They fared still worse after the move to Ekaterinburg, where they were accommodated under Spartan conditions in a squat, two-storey house which had formerly belonged to a merchant called Ipatiev. They were bullied and insulted. Their guards, who were often drunk, allowed them no privacy; when the young Grand Duchesses went to the lavatory the men followed them and lounged outside, shouting obscenities and drawing dirty pictures on the walls; they were badly fed and there were not enough beds to go round.

The original Soviet plan had envisaged a public trial of the Tsar and Tsarina; it was to have taken place in Moscow with Trotsky as prosecutor. But events had overtaken this plan. Ekaterinburg, which in April had seemed (for reasons that remain obscure) a safer depository for Imperial prisoners than Tobolsk, found itself three months later menaced by counter-revolutionary forces. There are three possible explanations of the Soviet authorities' failure to do the obvious thing, which was to remove the Romanovs before the military threat to Ekaterinburg became acute.

One is that Moscow welcomed the suddenly-discerned opportunity of liquidating the whole family under the pretext of revolutionary necessity in an exceptional crisis. From a severely practical point of view this course had many advantages over a public trial, which might make martyrs of the Tsar and Tsarina, and at which their children, aged between ten and nineteen, could hardly be arraigned. Although none of the counter-revolutionary movements aimed at the restoration of the monarchy, the survival of any of its representatives must, in the confused uncertain summer of 1918, have appeared contrary to Soviet interests. The possibility cannot be rejected that reasoning on these lines played some part in the fate of the prisoners.

A second explanation, which may also have been contributory, is that in the fluid, changing and obscure situation prevailing in the Urals it was felt to be imprudent to move the Imperial family, for fear that attempts would be made to rescue them *en route*. But the third and far the most probable reason for what happened is that the problem of their disposal was overlooked until events had reached a stage where a barbaric solution was the only safe one.

The Ural Soviet took their decision on 12 July, having first obtained clearance from the President of the Soviet Executive Committee in Moscow, Sverdlov, after whom Ekaterinburg was subsequently renamed; the town was expected to fall in a matter of days.[73] A Jew called Yurovski was put in charge of the operation. At midnight on the 16th the Tsar, his family and the members of the household were awakened. They were told that disturbances impended in the town; for fear of stray bullets they had better seek shelter in the basement.

The captives took their time about dressing and descended, unsuspecting, to the basement, taking pillows and cushions with them. The Tsar carried his invalid son, aged ten, in his arms and set him down in a chair. Besides the Tsarina and the four Grand Duchesses there were present the family doctor, a cook, a waiter and a chambermaid. When they were assembled, Yurovski brought in his assistants—seven Letts and two Russians from the Tcheka. He told the Tsar that he was going to be executed. 'What?' said the Tsar, who had not heard properly. Yurovski shot him down out of hand. The whole squad, firing at point-blank range, mowed down the others. After the first shots the fumes of cordite obscured their view and this, added to the fact that they were half-drunk, made for clumsy marksmanship. It was some time before the last screams died down, as the Letts, their revolvers empty, moved round the writhing bodies with bayonets.

The night's work was not yet done. The far-sighted members of the Ural Soviet had recognised that, among a superstitious peasantry, Imperial bones might acquire a counter-revolutionary *mystique*, and Yurovski's orders had included the destruction of the corpses. These were piled into a lorry and taken to a disused mine-shaft thirteen miles away which had been cordoned off by Red guards. Here they were stripped, dismembered with axes, drenched with petrol and sulphuric acid, and burnt on two enormous fires. Their clothing was rifled (the girls and their mother had a quantity of jewelry sewn into their corsets) and burnt with them. The ashes, together with a miscellany of objects including Anastasia's Pekinese, were then thrown down the water-logged mine-shaft. By the Bolsheviks, as by most revolutionaries, pity was regarded as an unbecoming if not an ignoble emotion; but it does seem as if the Soviet leaders felt a certain embarrassment about the slaughter of the Tsarina and her children. In an official announcement on 19 July the Government 'recognised as correct the decisions of the Ural Territorial Soviet,' which it had taken as a result of 'the approach of the Czechoslovakian bands' and the discovery of 'a new plot of counter-revolutionists, which had as its objective the taking of the Imperial hangman out of the hands of the Soviet Government'; but the announcement mentioned only 'Nicholas Romanov' as having been shot, and specifically stated that his wife and son 'were sent to a safe place.' This strangely odious prevarication was dictated by expediency. On the same night that the Tsar was murdered, the Tsarina's sister, the Grand Duchess Elizabeth, was also done to death; together with her husband, the Grand Duke Serge, and several other members of the Imperial family she was thrown, living, down a mine-shaft at a place called Alapaievsk.

Now both ladies, grand-daughters of Queen Victoria, were of German birth (their father was the Prince of Hesse) and the Soviet Government was using them as pawns, almost as hostages, in some delicate negotiations with the German Government. On June 14 Count Mirbach, the German Ambassador to Moscow, had been assassinated in his study, and Berlin was demanding the right to send a battalion of infantry to the Russian capital to ensure the protection of the Embassy. The Soviet rulers, objecting strongly to so humiliating a proposition, had managed to involve the Germans in a sort of informal bargain; if they would abandon their project for stationing a battalion in Moscow, the Russians would guarantee the safety, and perhaps even repatriate, the German-born princesses.

These negotiations were in full swing when both the ladies concerned were murdered (Radek discussed the matter with the German Chargé d'Affaires on 20 July, Tchicherin on the 23rd) and it was therefore essential to sustain the pretence that the Tsarina and her sister * were still alive.[73a]

A fortnight later the Legion was involved in another event which, unlike the death of the Tsar, was to have in a round-about way a considerable influence on their destinies. In operations which ended on 6 August they helped to take the great Tartar city of Kazan, and thus secured for their White Russian allies possession of the main gold reserves of the old Imperial Government. This vast hoard of bullion, valued at more than 650,000,000 roubles (about £80,000,000 or $330,000,000), had been evacuated from Petrograd to Samara to avoid the danger of its capture by the Germans. When Samara was threatened by the Czechs, the Bolsheviks shifted it up-river in barges to Kazan; and at Kazan the Czechs caught up with it.

This treasure was to have an effect on developments in Siberia comparable to the introduction of a joker into a game of cards which has hitherto been played without one. None of the various White régimes had any financial resources worth speaking of, so that whichever of them owned the gold materially strengthened its chances of being recognised as paramount by the others. The Samara Government—the Government of the Constituent Assembly—was soon replaced by a body known as the Directory, on whose orders (for the Red Army's threat to Samara was becoming acute) the gold was evacuated by rail to Chelyabinsk. While a safe place for its storage was being sought, the trains containing it were abstracted from the station and driven to Omsk by representa-

* The Soviet authorities did not, as with the Tsarina, claim in so many words that the Grand Duchess Elizabeth was safe; but her name was not mentioned in the communiqué purporting to deal with the fate of her husband and the other Grand Dukes. This alleged that they had been carried off, after a gun-fight, by unidentified bandits; the public was meant to infer that they had been rescued by the Whites.

tives of the West Siberian Commissariat (also shortly to disappear as such) [74]; and at Omsk the dazzling prize remained, more or less intact, until it was moved once more, trundling still further east and turning, as great riches sometimes do, from an asset into a liability to its owners.

CHAPTER EIGHT

The Race

'THE only thing on which everybody agrees,' Balfour, the British Foreign Secretary, had telegraphed to Lockhart on 11 June, 'is that without the active participation of America nothing effective can be accomplished through Siberia.' [75] For weeks no diplomatic effort was spared by the Allies to induce America to commit herself. Yet when, early in July, they learnt that she was going to do what they had long been urging her to do, they were seriously put out.

This was President Wilson's fault. If a young lady, after consistently rejecting the advances of a suitor, suddenly sends an announcement of their engagement to the newspapers without informing him, her swain, even though his heart's desire has been granted, is likely to take umbrage at her action. That, *mutatis mutandis*, was what happened in Washington. Not only were the Western Allies not consulted about the sudden change in American policy, but they were not even told of the change until a day after Wilson's decision had been communicated to the Japanese. They would have been less than human if they had not been piqued by what appeared to be, and indeed was, a grossly discourteous transaction; and they would have been very short-sighted if they had not discerned grave dangers in the American initiative, by which all the Allies were bound to be affected, yet which America had not taken the precaution of concerting even with her main collaborator, Japan. 'Cagey' is possibly the epithet which most fairly describes the President's conduct in this matter; but harsher terms were applied to it by Allied statesmen, and they can hardly be blamed.

THE RACE

Only a few days earlier the Supreme War Council—of whose competence in matters of strategy the Wilsonian deviation took no note—had concluded that Allied intervention in Russia and Siberia was, mainly because of the Czechs, 'an urgent and imperative necessity.' Lloyd George, reacting vigorously to the new American plan, told the British Ambassador in Washington that in Siberia it was 'now really a race between the Germans and ourselves. . . . We have only a few months before Russian harbours freeze and if we are to save Russia from becoming a German province we must have firmly established ourselves before the winter arrives.'[76] He found a 'total inadequacy' in the President's proposals; he wanted full-scale Allied intervention, not a mere 14,000 men from America and Japan. The French (of whose army, it will be remembered, the Czechoslovak Legion technically formed a part) were equally eager for the fray, equally ruffled by Wilson's obvious desire to dispense with their services.

And so a race, of a sort, began. It was not a race with the Germans, who were thousands of miles from the course, and on the point, in any case, of scratching. It was not a race with winter, for Vladivostok, unlike Archangel, is never closed by ice. It was a race between the Allies. There were few rules, and these—like the prizes understood to be at stake—tended to change from time to time. It was, in short, an unusual race, and not the least unusual thing about it was that nobody won; everybody lost.

From the terms in which Lloyd George fulminated against the proposed American–Japanese expedition—he called its small scale and limited objectives 'really preposterous'; the situation demanded that 'we should send a force which can . . . definitely secure Siberia to the Urals against German–Bolshevist attack'[77]—the obvious inference is that Wilson's puny project was standing in the way of some more substantial and rewarding enterprise. This was not so. At no stage were any of the Allies except Japan in a position to send more than a few hundred troops to Siberia; before the German armistice they were inhibited from doing so by military exigencies, after it they were deterred by domestic political considerations. Although the Americans put into the field only one tenth as many men as Japan, their 7000-strong contingent was larger than the British, French and Italian contingents added together.

As far as policy-making was concerned, the President's abrupt and unilateral decision had gained for America a head-start over the other Allies; but British troops were the first to arrive upon the scene of action.

The 25th Battalion, the Middlesex Regiment, was ordered from Hongkong to Vladivostok within a day or two of the American proposals reaching London; its dispatch was in effect a tart though feeble riposte to the American Government. Composed of men graded B1 (i.e. unfit for active service in a theatre of war), this Imperialist spearhead was affectionately known to other British personnel in Siberia as the 'Hernia Battalion;' 'Poor old men, they ought never to have been sent here,' a British officer of another regiment wrote in his diary later that year; 'they were mostly unfit when they came and are absolutely useless now.' [78] The battalion was not equipped with tents or—a more serious omission—mosquito nets; the fur coats and hats which formed the main items in its winter wardrobe were jet-black, not the happiest of choices for troops who expected to have to fight in snow.* The battalion was commanded by Colonel John Ward, Labour Member of Parliament for Stoke-on-Trent and a pioneer of the Trade Union Movement. A young officer on the staff of the British Military Mission dismissed him as 'a gas-bag';[79] there may have been an element of truth in this, but Ward, who had been a regular soldier before the war, was a sturdy, forthright, John Bullish individual. He published a bluff but valuable account of his Siberian experiences, in which Omsk is almost the only proper name correctly spelled.

* Regimental history came near to repeating itself in 1950, when the 1st Battalion, the Middlesex Regiment, was hastily dispatched from Hongkong to Korea with nothing but tropical kit to wear; shorts and bush-shirts proved wholly unsuitable for mountain warfare in a climate which had become severe by the time the men were in action.

THE RACE

The Middlesex, wearing topees, disembarked at Vladivostok on 3 August, and were given a rapturous public welcome by everyone except the dour Japanese, elements of whose 12th Division began to come ashore soon afterwards. The French—a colonial battalion from Indo-China, 1150 strong—were hard on the heels of the British. The 27th United States Infantry arrived from the Philippines on 16 August, the 31st Infantry a few days later. Japanese landings, watched from Washington with impotent alarm, went on continuously. By 21 August Japan, invoking her Military Agreement with China, had brought the whole of the Chinese Eastern Railway under her control; this precautionary measure, she insisted, was 'entirely different in nature from the present joint intervention in Vladivostok.' The United States Government, gravely distressed to find itself in Frankenstein's position and painfully aware that protests to the monster might only make things worse, took its seat firmly upon a non-existent fence, cabling to its Ambassador in Japan that it did 'not intend to approve or disapprove' Japan's action in Manchuria.[80]

Except for General Otani, who commanded the Japanese and was for some time rather vaguely regarded as commanding everybody else as well, the senior military representatives of the Allies arrived late upon the scene. General W. S. Graves, from America, was the first. Two days before he disembarked (2 September) the Czech relief force from Vladivostok joined hands in Trans-Baikalia with the main body of the Legion; the chief task, and almost the only specifically military duty, assigned to him in the President's *Aide-mémoire*—that of 'safeguarding the rear of the Czechoslovaks operating from Vladivostok'—had thus ceased to exist.

In view of this, Graves wrote afterwards, 'there was nothing left for United States troops to do but to help carry out the part of my instructions which stated: "the only legitimate object for which American or Allied troops can be employed is to guard military stores which may subsequently be needed by Russian forces".' But which Russian forces? The General received no guidance on this point. 'I could not,' he complained, 'give a Russian a shirt without being subjected to the charge of trying to help the side to which the recipient of the shirt belonged.'[81]

This awkward dilemma Graves tried to resolve by applying to a confused situation the most rigid principles of non-intervention. On one occasion, for instance, he insisted that American troops guarding the railway were not entitled to open fire unless the persons fired on had actually begun to destroy railway property. Although in practice his junior commanders took a less academic view of their responsibilities, General Graves's self-righteous neutrality, which made it virtually impossible for him to co-operate with anyone in anything, earned him universal unpopularity; and this, combined as it was with a deep mistrust of all Allies, all Russians and most of his own consular body, brought on in time a mild form of persecution mania. The predicament of this honourable and conscientious officer is a reminder that soldiers ought never to receive their orders direct from politicians.

Major-General Alfred Knox, the head of the British Military Mission, reached Vladivostok a few days after General Graves. It would have been difficult to find, in all the forces of all the Allies, an officer who knew less about Russia than Graves, or one who knew more about Russia than Knox. He had been Military Attaché in Petrograd in 1910, and, returning to Russia in the same capacity in 1914, had followed the fortunes of the Imperial Armies from the Battle of Tannenberg to the Bolshevik Revolution. An able officer with an incisive manner and a trenchant style, he had from the first been an advocate, and a very influential one, of Intervention. He had a good command of the Russian language.

The hatred and contempt in which he held the Soviet régime were natural products of his experience; it had destroyed an army with which he had to some extent identified himself, it had murdered many men, and some women, who were his friends. His views, though widely shared throughout the British and French armed services, had somehow gained for him in Washington the name of an arch-reactionary, whose presence in Siberia might impose a Monarchist orientation on the conduct of Allied policy; and Knox was instructed to travel through America as unobtrusively as possible. He did however see Colonel House, and the interview apparently went well. ('If all Americans were like House they would not be difficult to deal with,' Knox wrote on 18 July.) [82] Yet on the same day Victor Cazalet, in Tokyo, recorded in his diary: 'The Americans think Knox is the sole antagonist in Russia.' I have found it impossible to trace the origin of the widespread American prejudice against Knox.

It was in Tokyo that Knox found Kolchak, whom he already knew slightly and respected. Beneš (who did not know Kolchak) had for some reason revived London's interest in him in mid-August. In answer to enquiries the British Ambassador in Tokyo reported that the Admiral was 'honest and capable but bad-tempered. If he is going to quarrel with the Japanese I doubt whether his presence would help matters.' A report on similarly discouraging lines reached the Foreign Office from Vladivostok.

But Knox was immediately impressed by Kolchak. 'He possesses,' he wrote several months later, 'two characteristics uncommon in a Russian—a quick temper which inspires a useful awe among his subordinates, and a disinclination to talk merely for talking's sake.' [83] Knox himself was cordially received by the Japanese General Staff and seized a favourable moment to broach the question (which he knew to be a delicate one) of Kolchak's employment in Siberia, where, as he cabled to the War Office, 'there is no doubt he is the best Russian for our purpose.' [84]

The Japanese raised no objections, but Knox advised Kolchak to stay where he was until he (Knox) had tested the atmosphere in Vladivostok. Here an obstacle loomed up in the shape of Kolchak's old enemy Nakajima, and the Admiral, on Knox's advice, further delayed his departure from Tokyo. But by mid-September the coast was clear; Kolchak crossed the Sea of Japan and stood once more, after a year's absence, on Russian soil. He had no official appointment, no definite plans and very little money. A fortnight earlier he had told the British Ambassador that he thought of going to Archangel; now he decided, or perhaps half-decided, to make for the White enclave in South Russia, where his wife and nine-year-old son were—as far as he knew—living under an alias near Odessa. On 21 September he set off along the Trans-Siberian, sharing a private coach with Rudolf Gajda, the impetuous young commander who was already emerging as something of a stormy petrel in the Czechoslovak Legion.

So durable was the figment of large-scale German activities in Siberia that, on the day Kolchak left Vladivostok, the British Consul-General there was still describing the Czechs as 'turning their whole attention to defeating the Germans.' [85] The real as opposed to the imaginary Germans had acknowledged defeat five days before the last of the Allied military leaders disembarked at Vladivostok on 16 November.

There was more than a trace of self-importance about General Maurice Janin, and this minor defect, which caused him to break his journey, first in Washington and then in Tokyo, in order to see everyone who mattered, including President Wilson and the Emperor of Japan, was a main cause of his late arrival in Siberia; he had received his orders in Paris only a few days after Knox received his in London.

Janin was to the French Army roughly what Knox was to the British Army—its leading authority on Russia. As long ago as 1893 he had been attached to a Russian Mission which was visiting France, and since then had done several tours of duty in Russia, including one in 1912 as an instructor at the St Petersburg Military Academy. At the beginning of the war he fought as a brigade-commander on the Marne and the Yser, then went to the staff and in 1916 became head of the French Military Mission in Russia; he was fond of claiming, rather loosely, that he had twenty-six years' experience of Russia, and not above contrasting this record with Knox's total of eight. Janin was plump, dapper, intelligent and ambitious.

Tsar Nicholas II with the Tsarevitch, the Grand Duchess Tatiana (his second daughter) and Prince Nikita (a cousin) in confinement at Tsarskoe Selo

The Dom Ipatiev, where the Imperial Family were butchered

Major-General Alfred Knox

His role was an extremely important one on paper, for he had been designated by the Czech National Council to command the Czechoslovak Legion 'in accordance with the general directives of the Japanese Supreme Commander'; he was concurrently in charge of the French Military Mission; and he had also been given some sort of loosely defined jurisdiction over the various Polish, Yugoslav, Rumanian and other groups of Allied personnel who, with the breakdown of Russian control over the prisoner-of-war camps, had formed themselves into military units from motives mainly of self-preservation.

It may be as well to pause here, and to examine in outline the bizarre pattern formed by the channels of command and responsibility within the Allied and the White Russian forces in Siberia.

1. It had been agreed at Versailles that supreme command of the whole enterprise was to be in Japanese hands, *but*

2. The Japanese were not going west of Irkutsk, and could hardly conduct operations on the Volga front from a distance of 2000 miles; *and in any case*

3. The Americans did not regard themselves as being under Japanese command.

4. The senior French and British officers, Janin and Knox, though not technically in command of the French and British contingents, were bound to demand a say in their employment.

5. The White Russian Government (Omsk and Samara had formed a precarious coalition, known as the Directory) had its own Ministry of War—and indeed of Marine as well—and not unnaturally regarded itself as responsible for all military affairs throughout Siberia.

6. The Czechs, who had done virtually all the fighting so far, felt no need, and had no wish, to be subordinated to an alien hierarchy.

By comparison with these complex, untidy and unworkable military arrangements, the means by which the Allies sought to assert their political influence were relatively simple and straightforward. France, Britain and Japan were represented by High Commissioners. America, for a variety of bad reasons, was not; the State Department at first relied on its Consul-General in Vladivostok to represent its views at inter-Allied councils, and later dispatched the American Ambassador in Tokyo on a special mission to Siberia. The interests of the Czechoslovak Republic (France first recognised it as such on 15 October 1919; the other Allies followed suit) were in the hands of a small junta of youthful politicians who seldom saw eye to eye with each other.

This sketch leaves out of account such awkward but important anomalies as the intransigent Semenov, who recognised no one's authority, and the existence of two rival American organisations (a Railway Corps and an Advisory Commission) charged with the rehabilitation of the Trans-Siberian system, on which ultimately everything depended. But enough has been said to suggest that, even if there had been a general agreement among the Allies about what they were trying to achieve in Siberia, the machinery for achieving it was so ill designed that all their efforts were doomed from the start. Fiasco was the only possible outcome. The failure to perceive, the failure even to suspect, this was due in large part to events which occurred at Omsk in mid-November and which appeared to throw a new and a more hopeful light on the prospects for Intervention not only in Siberia but in the other theatres as well. These developments will be described in Chapter Ten.

CHAPTER NINE

A Long Way to Tipperary

KOLCHAK reached Omsk from Vladivostok on 13 October 1918 after a slow journey. He found the atmosphere 'extremely tense.' Four days earlier the Directory had arrived in Omsk. This was a sort of steering committee of five men, which had been invested with supreme governmental power in an attempt to unite the right-wing Siberian Government with their left-wing neighbours of Samara. The Directory, sandwiched like the Dormouse between the Mad Hatter and the March Hare, had the confidence of neither of the factions it was supposed to represent. Composed of moderate men and devoid of executive power, it was a constitutional folly, a structure far too fragile to stand for long in the tempestuous climate of a civil war. It was accommodated (always a bad omen) in railway carriages.

Kolchak knew none of the leading figures in Omsk, but there was something about him—'something kingly,' a romantic British professor called it [86]—which made men eager to place authority in his hands. There were enough contenders for power in Omsk already, and Kolchak belonged to none of the rival cliques; yet within a few days he had been persuaded into accepting, under protest, the Ministries of War and of the Navy.* General Boldyrev, the Commander-in-Chief and a member of the Directory, was his principal sponsor. On 9 November, thoroughly unhappy about the political situation

---

* Except for a few improvised gunboats on the larger rivers and some warships at Vladivostok there was of course no Russian navy in Siberia; but there were a good many naval officers drifting about, and some central authority was needed to register them and to deal with their pay and general administration.

in Omsk, he left for a tour of the front. Two days later the Germans were granted an armistice, and the war in the west came to an end.

At the front winter was closing in on a situation which had much deteriorated in the last two months. Kazan had fallen to the Reds on 10 September, Samara a month later. The People's Army, raised by the Socialist-Revolutionary Government which had been formed at Samara, was ill-organised and timorous; Omsk's Siberian Army was not yet in the field. But the gravest development concerned the Czechs. The Legion— 'wearying somewhat of well doing,' as Churchill put it[87]— was opting out of the Civil War.

As early as 16 September Knox reported that the Czechs were 'at their last gasp'; three weeks later a British liaison officer at Chelyabinsk spoke of them as 'absolutely worn out . . . with morale declining.'[88] Towards the end of October a regiment of the 1st Czech Division refused to obey an order to entrain for the front, and the newly-appointed divisional commander, a brave man called Sveč, committed suicide. On 2 November General Syrový, the Czech Commander-in-Chief, cabled to Janin in Japan a disquieting report on the state of both his divisions; they needed to be taken out of the line, rested and purged of agitators.[89]

For this failure of the Czech spirit there were a number of reasons. The Legion was a small force and it had been continuously engaged in operations of one sort or another since the end of May. Most of its fighting had consisted of skirmishes rather than battles, but the men had seldom been able to count themselves out of danger, and they could draw on no reinforcements to replace their casualties. The troops on the Volga front had had the hardest time. Under the daemonic direction of Trotsky the Red Army was growing rapidly in numbers, slowly but surely in skill at arms. By early September it had 550,000 men in its ranks—almost twice as many as at the time of the Chelyabinsk Incident.[90]

If the front-line Czech units were over-tired and under strength, so were those that hurried west to reinforce them after the Trans-Siberian Railway had been cleared. Many of these men had already fought their way from the Urals to Trans-Baikalia; to retrace their steps, to bury themselves once more in the heart of Russia, and to face the prospect of a winter campaign for which they were not equipped—this was a lot to demand of the staunchest troops. 'We experienced little enthusiasm for the coming fighting,' wrote a young officer of the 6th Regiment, which after struggling from Chelyabinsk to the Outer Mongolian border now found itself back in Ekaterinburg. When they went into action he realised that 'this was very different fighting from that we had experienced in the east. . . . We were not immune from the feelings of depression and ill-usage which were gradually taking possession of the Legion.' [91]

The Czechs felt very strongly that they had been let down; disillusionment gave place to rancour as they brooded on their wrongs. The Allies had never promised them in so many words that help was on its way, but this is what the Czechs had been allowed, and sometimes encouraged, to infer. No help had reached them. They were indeed to be vouchsafed—on 10 November at Ekaterinburg—a glimpse of the regimental band of the 25th Battalion, the Middlesex Regiment; but by that time their feelings towards the Allies were past being mollified by selections from Gilbert and Sullivan. Those feelings, though not entirely just, were entirely natural.

Above all, the Czechs were sick of the Russians. Much has been made of the ideological differences between the democratic Czechs and the increasingly reactionary régime at Omsk, and their refusal to continue fighting has been portrayed as a direct consequence of Kolchak's assumption of supreme power in circumstances to be described below. But their indifference to the Civil War had begun to manifest itself, and their withdrawal from the fighting was already in progress, some weeks before this event took place; Gajda, who in mid-September was back in Vladivostok and spent several days on board HMS *Suffolk* as the guest of Commodore Payne, spoke of the Legion's situation as critical and described the troops as exhausted.

Although their sincerity need not be questioned, the various public protests which the *coup d'état* evoked from the Czechs (such as that issued by their National Council on 22 November) cannot escape all suspicion of having been partly inspired by opportunism. The Czechs had decided to fight no more in Russia; and the violent overthrow of the régime under whose banner (or under one of whose two banners) they had been serving gave them the chance to justify their decision on a point of political principle.

The Czechs had never, after all, had close affinities even with the Samara Government, to whom they were bound by no formal ties of allegiance and whom experience had revealed as a group of wordy, bickering and ineffectual doctrinaires. It was mainly the troops of this Government, the red-flagged People's Army, who were put in jeopardy by the Czech withdrawal; and, although it is probable that the Czechs' aversion from Kolchak's régime strengthened their resolve (if it needed strengthening) not to *return* to the front, the theory that this aversion caused them to *leave* the front will not hold water.

The plain fact of the matter was that the Czechs had had enough of their 'Slavic kinsmen' as comrades-in-arms, no matter what the political beliefs of these Wilsonian relatives. They had seen too much of *embusqués* officers, splendidly caparisoned and enviably womaned, clinking their spurs,* speculating and intriguing in towns far behind the front. They had heard too much about Semenov and Kalmykov; 'these men are wanted at the front, we have a right to ask for them,' the official Czech newspaper insisted. They had suffered too often from delays, from broken undertakings, from the general deliquescence of responsibility which was endemic in the period. On their ranks the total lack of reinforcements imposed a steady but not a dishonourable drain. The forces of their Russian ally, with huge reserves of man-power behind them, were constantly eroded by desertion; 3000 men of the Samara Rifle Division deserted in the month before the city fell.[92] A few gallant

---

* 'The jingle made by the Russian spur,' wrote a British officer, 'is as noisy as a vigorously shaken tobacco tin with a marble inside it.' (L. E. Vining: *Held by the Bolsheviks.*)

Russian officers—Ushakov, Kappel and Voitzekhovski among them—were trusted, followed and admired; but the main lesson the Czechs had learned since the Chelyabinsk Incident at the end of May was that in the Civil War you could rely on nobody, depend on nothing. They were serious people; they wanted no more part in a bloody farce.

Apart from all this, the Czech outlook was powerfully affected by events in Europe. The Austro-Hungarian Empire had collapsed; a bloodless revolution in Prague on 28 October established the authority of the new Czechoslovak Republic over the ancient capital of Bohemia. The Legion was no longer composed of stateless men, soldiers of fortune, renegades who would face a firing-squad if they returned to their native land. What they had fought for had been achieved. They had been eager enough to get out of Russia when their destination was a blood-bath on the Western Front; now the incentives were a hundred times stronger. They saw themselves being left behind, far behind, by men who had deserved less well of the Republic, in the scramble for jobs, for land, for opportunities. They wanted to go home as soon as possible.

During their journey from Vladivostok together, Kolchak had been given by Gajda an account of the situation in the Legion which, though slightly out of date (since Gajda had been away from the front for the best part of a month), was generally accurate and far from encouraging; Kolchak thought of the Legion already as a spent force, and made no allowance for the stresses that had made it one. In Omsk (where Boldyrev, the Commander-in-Chief, confirmed that the Legion was throwing in its hand) he found that two of its political representatives were demanding the exclusion from the Siberian Government of certain candidates for office to whose views the Czechs objected; they threatened that if their demands were not met 'the Czech troops would leave the front.' [93]

Kolchak knew that the Czech troops were already leaving the front and suspected that nothing would induce them to return to it; he formed, reasonably enough, the opinion that their representatives 'were playing some kind of game'[94]—were, in other words, manufacturing a political excuse for a military development which they were neither able nor willing to arrest. He objected strongly to this use of a threat (and a hollow one at that) in an attempt to interfere in Russian domestic affairs. So did everyone else; and the candidates were duly installed in office.

It was thus with his mind hardened against the Czechs that on 9 November Kolchak left Omsk for the front, where his first official duty was to attend a ceremonial parade by four regiments of the Legion at Ekaterinburg. New colours were consecrated, a number of British decorations were presented to the Czechs, and in the evening there was a banquet at which Kolchak made the principal speech. All went well enough on the surface, but Kolchak found considerable animus against the Legion among senior Russian officers.

These men in fact had only themselves and their political leaders to blame for what was happening, since it was their failure to raise adequate forces to support and eventually to relieve the hard-pressed Czechs that was primarily responsible for the Legion's disengaging itself. A man of broader vision and more balanced judgment than Kolchak possessed would have realised this, would have given the Czechs the credit that was due to them; but Kolchak allowed prejudice to infect him, and ever thereafter retained, to his grave disadvantage, a petty resentful attitude towards the Legion. 'I was struck,' the British High Commissioner, Sir Charles Eliot, reported to the Foreign Office a few months later, 'by the harsh and ungrateful manner in which Kolchak spoke of the Czechoslovaks. He said they were no good and the sooner they cleared out the better.'[95] To General Janin Kolchak expressed himself in even more vehement terms. This unreasoning antipathy, of which the Czechs were well aware, was in the end to cost him dear.

Colonel Ward, with a hundred picked men of his battalion and the regimental band, accompanied Kolchak to Ekaterinburg for the Czech celebrations. When he landed at Vladivostok Ward's orders included one to the effect that the Middlesex were 'not to engage in operations beyond the close vicinity of the port without reference to the War Office'; but they were hardly ashore when—War Office sanction having been obtained—more than half the battalion was moved up the railway north of Vladivostok to take part in a confused but successful action at a place called Kraevsk. Here the British— like the Czechs, some French and Kalmykov's Cossacks— fought under Japanese command. The Japanese aim, as far as anyone understood it, was to reserve all the glory for their own troops, and they had more than 600 casualties; the Middlesex, though they suffered severely from mosquitoes and heat-prostration, lost no one to the enemy's copious but erratic fire.

They were never in action again, and it was to show the flag, not to fight, that they had been moved to Omsk. From Ekaterinburg Ward's detachment, still escorting Kolchak, made a brief appearance in, or just behind, the front line near Khungur, in 'a temperature' (as their colonel put it) 'quite impossible for British military operations.' Here, protected by a railway cutting, the band gave renderings of 'Colonel Bogey' and 'Tipperary', calling down a hail of shells from the Red artillery. All these, according to Ward, 'exploded harmlessly among the forest trees,' but it may be doubted whether the band's inane performance was appreciated by the troops holding the sector, whose reactions were thus described by a Czech officer:

> Smartly the British detachment marched back to the station, smartly they entrained, and as smartly the engine whistled and drew them out of the danger-zone, leaving the Bolsheviks in a thoroughly nasty frame of mind which they proceeded to vent upon us. The demonstration was over, and all it had done was to supply our pessimists with ample matter for their many and none too complimentary remarks.[96]

In the early days of Intervention there was much talk in Whitehall and even in Vladivostok of the 'steadying' effect which the appearance of small Allied units would have on the situation in Siberia; each of the Allies believed that her national prestige was enhanced in Russian eyes every time a detachment of her troops, trim and well accoutred, marched down a Russian street. This was nonsense. Cheers echoed, indeed, and handkerchiefs waved as the first foreign soldiers clattered down the gang-planks on to the Vladivostok quays. But when it became known—as it quickly did—that these troops had not come to fight, they ceased to be glamorous and became, instead, the objects of ridicule and contempt. The excellence of their equipment, the smartness of their uniforms and their high rates of pay inspired not awe but envy. They were fodder not for cannons but for cartoons.

'The Americans here,' wrote a British official in Vladivostok on 6 October, 'are making themselves ridiculous now that their limited objectives are known.'[97] This was true enough; but it is better to earn ridicule in the rear than opprobrium at the front. This, as we shall see, was the unlucky lot of the British troops in Siberia who, when the distant cities in which they were stationed were threatened by a Red advance, were withdrawn with an alacrity which had equally disastrous effects on British prestige and on Russian morale.

The function of a soldier is to fight. To send soldiers to a theatre of war on terms which virtually preclude them from discharging that function is to place them, and ultimately the Government that sent them, in a false position from which no good result can issue. America was the first Power to decide on the dispatch of troops to Siberia; their orders were to fight as little as possible, and if possible not at all. If America had held her hand, it is on the cards that no formed bodies of foreign soldiers would have gone to lose their names and confuse the issue in Siberia: that the Western Allies would have confined themselves, as they did in Denikin's South Russian enclave, to the dispatch of missions and a few technical experts: and that Japan would have relied on her Nakajimas, her puppets and her 'volunteers.'

But once one Allied contingent was known to be on the way,

all the other Allies had to follow suit. By some people in London and Paris it was hoped that these derisory units would be the spearheads of a massive expedition; others saw only folly and danger in this idea. Nobody quite knew what they were doing, why they were doing it, or what it might lead to. Almost anything was possible.

Only one course of action was out of the question, and that would, as it turned out, have been the wisest: to send no troops at all. But how, in July 1918, could anyone have known that this was the wisest course? And how, even if its wisdom had been evident, could any of the leading Powers have followed it?

To do so would have been to proclaim a callous indifference to the fate of the Czechs. Then supposing the rescue of the Czechs led, indirectly, to the regeneration of Russia? How would that great nation, resurgent and transfigured, view an ally whose flag had been absent from the battlefield on which the Germans and the Bolsheviks met defeat? '*Messieurs*,' the high-minded American President had, without realising it, called, '*faites vos jeux.*'

None of them, except Japan, could afford the stakes; but none of them could afford not to play, and they all joined in.

CHAPTER TEN

Coup d'État

KOLCHAK returned to Omsk on the evening of 16 November. His train, in which Colonel Ward and the Middlesex detachment were travelling, was stopped at Petropavlovsk to await the arrival of Boldyrev, the bear-like Commander-in-Chief, who was on his way up to the front. The two men had a conference lasting five hours. From the guarded remarks which Kolchak let fall when it was over, Ward deduced that there had been a dispute over the Admiral's powers and functions as Minister of War. 'I had my suspicions,' Ward wrote afterwards, 'that the two groups of the Government had come to grips, and that each had decided to destroy the other.' [98] He thought Kolchak's life might be in danger and ordered his men to load their rifles.

The Omsk abscess was in fact about to burst. The Directory had exchanged its railway-carriages for lodgings in the town and had been allotted a school building from which to steer the ship of state; [99] but it had as much voice in affairs as a cuckoo-clock on the wall of a rowdy saloon. Even its use as a rubber stamp by the right-wing Council of Ministers had become increasingly perfunctory and infrequent. Nothing worked, nobody knew where they were, the town was full of rumour and intrigue, public order was in jeopardy. Russians grow easily disgusted with themselves, and when this happens they either sink into apathy or resort to desperate measures. There was plenty of cause for self-disgust in Omsk, where it seemed that a civil war within a civil war might break out at any moment.

For some time there had been talk, especially in military circles, of a dictatorship, and during the 17th—the day after his

return from the front—Kolchak was approached by several officers from the Stavka* who told him that the Directory was on its last legs and that 'it was imperative to create a united power. When I asked about the form of this new united power, and whom they thought to put forward so as to have a single head, they said outright: "You must do it." '[100]
Kolchak refused. As a serving officer, it would be improper to lend himself to such a project. In any case he had no army behind him and he was a stranger to Siberian politics. On the same day he told the Council of Ministers that he intended to resign the Ministry of War as soon as Boldyrev returned to Omsk; thereafter he would either serve at the front or devote his energies to the Ministry of Marine.

'Every evening,' a member of the Directory had written to his Socialist-Revolutionary colleagues in Ekaterinburg a fortnight earlier, 'we sit and expect that they will come to arrest us.'[101] On the night of 17–18 November these expectations were fulfilled. The writer of the letter, Avksentiev, and Zenzinov, the second Socialist-Revolutionary representative in the Directory, were with five other members of their party in the quarters of the Assistant Minister of the Interior, Rogovski, who was also an S-R. Like all ministerial doors in those uncertain times, Rogovski's had a guard on it, but this did not prevent the abrupt intrusion of a squad of Cossacks led by Ataman Krasilnikov, a minor firebrand of the Semenov type. They arrested Avksentiev, Zenzinov, Rogovski and one other and spirited them off to the quarters of Krasilnikov's detachment, which were in the Agricultural Institute on the outskirts of Omsk.
The fact of the kidnapping, but not the fate of the kidnapped, became known to members of the Government in the early hours of the 18th, and an emergency meeting was summoned for six o'clock that morning. The town was silent as the generals and the politicians made their way through the bitter darkness to the big house near the cathedral which in Tsarist days had

* The General Staff.

been the Governor's residence. It was symptomatic of the atmosphere prevailing in Omsk, and of the general attitude there towards the Directory, that none of the assembled ministers suggested that disciplinary action should be taken against Krasilnikov and his Cossacks. 'The first opinion,' Kolchak recalled, 'was that the fact of the arrest signified nothing, especially since three members of the Directory—or a majority —still remained. . . . The second opinion was that after what had happened the Directory could not remain in power. . . . Since members of the Government had been subjected to some sort of arrest, and had proved unable to resist or avert it, they were consequently bound to resign their powers. Since they were arrested they therefore ceased to be the Government.'[102]

It would have been difficult for the *de facto* rulers of Omsk to make it clearer that they regarded their *de jure* superiors as expendable; and at this juncture one of the surviving three resigned all his offices and left the building. The five-man Directory was now—Boldyrev being absent—represented at the meeting by only one of its members, a worthy lawyer called Vologodski; in the deliberations that ensued no more was heard of its claims to supreme authority.

The liquidation of the Directory, though a popular measure, was hardly a constructive one. After two hours of talk a sense of urgency communicated itself to the Ministers. Omsk was still quiet, but all the Cossack troops were reported to be standing to their arms, and mounted patrols were riding watchfully through the streets, their horses' breath forming a haze around them in the frosty dawn. There was no telling what rumours were abroad or how the town, when it came fully to life, would react to them. 'If such an uncertain situation continued,' Kolchak said, 'some momentous and serious occurrences could be expected.'[103]

At this juncture somebody suggested that the only solution to their problems lay in a military dictatorship. There was almost unanimous support for this proposal, and it immediately became clear that most of those present regarded Kolchak as the only possible candidate. He himself urged the claims of Boldyrev, who as Commander-in-Chief had shown that he possessed the confidence of the troops and to whom there were no serious objections on political grounds. He, Kolchak, was a newcomer, an unknown quantity as far as the Army was concerned; Boldyrev, who had previously commanded an army on the German front, was a much safer bet.

Kolchak was not one to dissemble; there is no reason to doubt the sincerity of his arguments, though they were probably based less on his faith in Boldyrev than on his own reluctance to assume office. In a letter to his wife written shortly afterwards he spoke of 'the terrifying burden of Supreme Power' and of himself as 'a fighting man, reluctant to face the problems of statecraft.'[104]

When Kolchak had finished speaking, Vologodski, who presided, said that his views would be taken into account; meanwhile would he please leave the meeting, since it would be embarrassing for him to be present while a matter so nearly affecting him was discussed? Kolchak went out and sat, 'for a fairly long time,' in Vologodski's office. Eventually they came and told him that the Council of Ministers had decided to place themselves under a Supreme Ruler and to offer him the post. Kolchak returned to the meeting, where these decisions were formally read out by Vologodski. Kolchak 'then saw that there was nothing more to say, and gave my consent.'

Later that day he signed a decree. It ran:

1. On this day, by order of the Council of Ministers of the All-Russian Government, I was appointed Supreme Ruler.

2. On this day I have taken Chief Command of all the Forces of the Land and the Sea of Russia.

In a proclamation to the people he made these pledges:

I shall not go either on the road of reaction or on the fatal road of Party partisanship. I set as my main objectives the creation of an efficient army, victory over Bolshevism, and the establishment of law and order, so that the people may choose the form of government which it desires without obstruction and realise the great ideas of liberty which are now proclaimed in the whole world.

While these hopeful words were being drafted, and indeed throughout the day, the machine-guns of the Middlesex Regiment covered all approaches to the Stavka and the government buildings. The city remained quiet.

The whole truth about the *coup d'état* will never be known. For what it is worth, the fact that Krasilnikov did not shoot his prisoners out of hand—murders, political and otherwise, were of almost nightly occurrence in Omsk—suggests that there was some restraining influence behind him, that he was acting on behalf of persons less irresponsible and callous than himself. But who those persons were, and what purposes they had beyond the downfall of the Directory, there are no means of telling.

It does however seem safe to assume that Kolchak himself was neither involved in nor aware of the plot. He returned to Omsk less than 36 hours before the arrests took place. He was not by temperament a conspirator, and he had no friends or associates in Omsk to form the apparatus of conspiracy. Although there is a conflict of evidence as to the exact time at which he learned what had happened to the kidnapped men, it is clear that he was in the dark about their fate for at least several hours. He is perhaps the only member of the Council of Ministers of whom it can be said with certainty that he was not privy to Krasilnikov's *coup*.

Some interest attaches to the part played in the proceedings by the British, in view of the allegations made at the time by the French, and since repeated by the Russians, that it was they who engineered the affair.

Of these charges, the most specific came from General Janin. In a report to the French Ministry of War written in June 1920 he claimed that the British 'installed' Kolchak because they wanted 'a Government of their own' from which they could extort economic concessions in Turkestan; 'the English,' he

Vladivostok: the US Navy shows the flag

The Vladivostok crowd watches

Allied officers at Vladivostok, including American, British, Chinese, Czechoslovak, French, Italian, Japanese, Polish and Rumanian representatives. General Otani is seated in the centre, with Graves on his right; Nakajima is at extreme right of second row

went on, 'organised, with a group of Russian monarchist officers, a *coup d'état* whose consequences were the ruin of Siberia.'[105] In his memoirs, published in Czech in 1923 and in French (in a slightly different version) five years later, he said that General Knox had made the necessary arrangements when he was in Omsk at the end of October, and that one of Knox's officers, Captain Steveni, had taken part in the detailed planning of the *coup*. Similar but less circumstantial allegations appeared in books written by Noulens, the French Ambassador to Russia, and by two of Janin's staff officers. Soviet propagandists —and, to a less extent, Soviet historians—have made considerable play with this evidence.

The facts of the matter are, by chance, ascertainable. Apart from Colonel Ward, who returned from the front with Kolchak late on 16 November, and the officers of his battalion, there were two members of the staff of the Military Mission in Omsk on the eve of the *coup*: Colonel J. F. Nielson and Captain L. Steveni. They were quartered in a railway-coach in the square outside the Stavka building; in order to ease the acute shortage of accommodation this square had been connected with the station by a branch line and converted into a sort of railway dormitory.

Both Nielson and Steveni spoke Russian, the latter fluently. Their main duty was to keep themselves informed of the situation, political as well as military, and both knew what everyone else in Omsk knew—that the Directory was likely to be overthrown at any moment. But neither had close contacts with any of its numerous enemies, and it is in any case scarcely conceivable that Russian conspirators would have made confidants of, let alone been 'organised' by, foreign officers of any nationality. Even the theory that the men behind the *coup* received indirect encouragement from the British Military Mission is ruled out by the evidence; ten days earlier General Knox, on the eve of his departure from Omsk to meet Janin at Vladivostok, had reported to the War Office that 'Kolchak is being urged by right elements to effect a *coup d'état*. *I told him that any attempt of this sort would at present be fatal.*'[106]

THE FATE OF ADMIRAL KOLCHAK

News of the arrests was brought to the British Military Mission coach at 7.30 a.m. on the 18th by a young Russian officer, who had fought with conspicuous gallantry in the French Army; * Steveni dressed and walked over to the Stavka, where the news was gleefully confirmed. When the excitements of the day were over, it was announced that the Supreme Ruler would make formal calls on the senior Allied representatives, beginning with the French High Commissioner, M. Regnault, whose train stood in a siding near the station, about two miles from the centre of the town. Nielson happened to be in the Stavka when Kolchak, in British uniform with a Russian Admiral's epaulettes, was setting out. Kolchak offered him a lift, Nielson (thinking, perhaps, that a glass of champagne would not come amiss) accepted, and the French put their own interpretation on the fact that the Supreme Ruler made his first public appearance after the *coup* with an *éminence grise* in khaki at his elbow. This interpretation was made more plausible by the activities of the Middlesex outside the Stavka; but the British troops had their quarters in an adjacent building and their vigilance was in fact dictated by motives of prudence in a situation where 'momentous and serious occurrences could be expected.'

On the following day Nielson reported to General Knox at Vladivostok the main facts about Kolchak's assumption of power, which he described as 'an absolutely honest attempt to restore order';[107] a similar view was expressed by *The Times*, whose shrewd correspondent, David Fraser, was present when Kolchak, after leaving Regnault, called at Colonel Ward's headquarters.

At this stage, for reasons which have eluded research, Nielson's conduct was called in question, not by Paris, not by Moscow, but by London. On 28 November Knox forwarded from Vladivostok a War Office directive: 'On no account must British officers or British troops take any part in any operations or movements of a political character.'[108]

Five days later a direct rebuke reached Omsk. The signal read:

* He was Captain Zinovi Peshkov, a natural son of Maxim Gorki.

COUP D'ÉTAT

Following from CHIEF,* Nov. 30. 'You [i.e. Knox] should inform Colonel NIELSON that his recent activities in political matters are regarded by the Foreign Office as highly indiscreet and as tending to compromise His Majesty's Government by making it appear that they were intervening on behalf of one particular party in SIBERIA. While therefore NIELSON's zeal and energy are appreciated he must be cautioned against any further action of this nature.'

To this message Knox added his own comments: 'This is not the result of any representation made by the High Commissioner or by me. In fact you would have got it in the neck if your messages had not been expurgated.'[109]

There is a minor mystery here, for if Nielson's telegrams from Omsk reporting the *coup* were 'expurgated' in Vladivostok before being relayed to London, what caused the Foreign Office to believe that he had acted indiscreetly? The most probable explanation is that Regnault's dark suspicions had been communicated to Paris and had reached Whitehall from the British Embassy there; but even if this is what did happen it seems odd that the War Office should have been so quick to assume that their man on the spot was in the wrong.

In any event Nielson was asked to forward a written report on his activities immediately before the *coup* took place; it reached London in January 1919. In it he gave an account of his movements which has been summarised above and insisted that, although 'aware that a *coup d'état* was contemplated,' he had 'made it clear that the British would take no part.' Officialdom's verdict was that 'Nielson completely clears himself.'[110]

To those who take what has been well called a conspiratorial view of history, and who believe that the actions of fools or knaves or heroes in one part of the world were at the beginning of the twentieth century inspired and governed by a quite different sort of people in another part of the world, the fact

* Almost certainly the Chief of the Imperial General Staff, Sir Henry Wilson.

that Nielson and Steveni had no part in the *coup d'état* will hardly seem conclusive proof that the British Government was not somehow involved. Much evidence, some of it already adduced, points to the fact that in the race for Siberia Kolchak was riding in the British colours.

The Buchanesque alacrity with which Whitehall accepted his offer to serve on the Mesopotamian front might seem to proclaim a British interest in the Admiral. This impression is confirmed by a message from the Director of Military Intelligence to Steveni (who was then in Manchuria) in July 1918. The *Daily Mail* correspondent in those parts, the Director of Military Intelligence reported, had cabled to his paper an interview with Kolchak 'in which latter stated that British War Office originally ordered him to Mesopotamia and had subsequently diverted him to his present sphere. Above is substantially correct but you should explain to Admiral that it is most desirable that he should maintain silence with regard to his connection with us. Article in question censored as regards above.'[111]

When to such darkly suggestive clues is added the fact that British bayonets guarded the doors behind which Kolchak's accession to power took place, the case for British complicity looks a strong one. Its validity must however be judged by the manner in which the news of the *coup d'état* was received in Whitehall, where on the conspiratorial view it should have aroused jubilation.

It aroused the opposite. 'A thoroughly unfortunate performance. . . . Looks like a real calamity. . . . A great setback to our plans'—it was in phrases such as these that London reacted to the news from Omsk.[112] This perturbation was due in part to a fear that the emergence of a dictatorship in Siberia would have unfavourable repercussions on the White enclaves at Archangel and in South Russia; but its chief cause lay in the fact that the War Cabinet had just—on 14 November—taken the decision to recognise the Directory as the *de facto* Government of Russia.

It had not been an easy decision, or a wise one; but it had been a *decision*, taken in a field where decisions were overdue, badly needed and extremely difficult to reach. The draft telegram announcing it, now nearing completion, had involved craftsmanship of the highest order. The Foreign Office, all their labours gone for nothing, were back where they started; it is small wonder that their comments sounded a note of despondency, exasperation and alarm.

In Omsk, meanwhile, the British were intervening as hard as they could in Russian domestic politics, but neither their methods nor their motives were Machiavellian. They were trying to save the lives of the four men who had been arrested and who on current form in Siberia were due for what later became known as 'transfer to the Republic of the Irtysh'; the Irtysh is the river on which Omsk stands, and the slang phrase was applied to citizens who were done to death and stuffed through a hole in the ice.

Nielson and Ward, after pestering the authorities for information about Krasilnikov's prisoners without getting any reply, wrote direct to the Supreme Ruler on the afternoon of the 19th; 'My country,' Ward pointed out, 'would look with grave concern upon any injury inflicted without proper trial upon these prisoners of State.'[113] Ward's information was that the four men were to be bayoneted 'in the night, as shooting would attract attention.'

The affair had a happier and a quicker ending than was usual in Siberia. The prisoners were given money, and signed statements undertaking to go abroad and abstain from further political activity; telegrams were sent to Horvath to arrange for their transit through Manchuria. A detachment of sick Middlesex men under a subaltern was about to leave for Vladivostok, and to their protection the prisoners were entrusted. Kolchak himself interviewed the young British officer; 'If,' he told him, 'there should be an attempt to attack them, or on the other hand to free them, force of arms should be applied without further ado.'[114]

The episode throws a revealing light on the Siberian scene. Four prominent men had been kidnapped; two of them held positions of the highest authority. No action was taken against their captors, but it was decided to spare their lives. The only way of ensuring that while in transit they were not butchered—or, alternatively, rescued—was to confide them to the care of foreigners; the Supreme Commander of all the Forces of the Land and the Sea of Russia had to rely on a dozen invalid soldiers under a British second lieutenant to enforce his will.

The train carrying the four men into exile avoided stopping at large towns; they reached Manchuria without incident and eventually reappeared in Paris. Kolchak's rule thus began with what looked like an act of clemency, although the failure to execute four harmless politicians against whom no charge had been preferred cannot strictly be so described. There can be little doubt that the measures taken by the Supreme Ruler to ensure their survival were prompted rather by motives of expediency than by his own humanitarian feelings; 'only the protection of the foreign missions saved these traitors,' he wrote bitterly to his wife.[115] He was a vengeful man.

CHAPTER ELEVEN

The Augean Stables

KOLCHAK's assumption of power had a mixed reception in Siberia. Telegrams offering fealty and felicitations poured in to Omsk from local authorities and military commanders; but with them came heated denunciations from the Socialist-Revolutionaries in Ufa and Ekaterinburg. General Boldyrev, prudently furnishing himself with a bodyguard of fifty-two officers, returned to Omsk, expressed his disapproval in a personal interview with the Supreme Ruler, and found it advisable to leave for Japan. The Czech political leaders issued a vaguely minatory statement to the effect that they 'considered the crisis unfinished', and sulked in their tent.

Semenov, as might have been expected, weighed in with two expostulatory telegrams, in the second of which he threatened to set up an independent state in Trans-Baikalia. Kolchak riposted with a violently worded message dismissing Semenov from his command, whereupon the Ataman put a stop to telegraphic communications between Omsk and Vladivostok, and for some days all messages had to be routed via Mongolia. A project for a punitive expedition against Semenov was dropped when the Japanese let it be known that they would back their *protégé* with force if the need arose. It was several weeks before normal relations—relations, that is, of latent rather than overt hostility—were restored between Omsk and Chita, where the Ataman had his headquarters.

Meanwhile a White offensive, which had been in preparation before the *coup d'état* took place, captured Perm towards the end of December. Many prisoners and much booty were taken,

but there is force in the view that this success had an un-
balancing effect on Siberian strategy. The fall of Perm seemed
to open the road to Viatka, Kotlas and the Dvina, and thus
brought into prospect a junction with the Allied forces based on
Archangel, a possibility by which the planners in London had
long been seduced.

It was in fact only a chess-board possibility. An advance towards Kotlas would have carried the Siberian armies, already
barely able to maintain themselves in the field, into a sparsely
inhabited region where supplies were scanty, communications
appalling and the conditions for campaigning very poor;
General Ironside, commanding at Archangel, foresaw that they
would be 'destitute' by the time they joined hands with his
forces, who themselves would be in little better case. A far
sounder plan would have been for Kolchak to put his main
effort into his left wing, south of the Trans-Siberian, and drive
through relatively populous and well-found country towards
Denikin's expanding enclave. As it was, his success in the north
was soon counterbalanced by failure in the south, where the
5th Red Army occupied Ufa, and Dutov's Cossacks were driven
with disgraceful ease from Orenburg.

On balance, however, the military situation gave grounds for
hope. Weapons and equipment from the vast surpluses in Allied
arsenals were pouring into Vladivostok; their progress along
the Trans-Siberian was sluggish and erratic, and all too few of
them reached the troops who were doing the fighting, but at
least the recruits who were being conscripted by the thousand
could generally be clothed and armed. Although their withdrawal had dangerously weakened the sectors from which it
took place, the disgruntled Czechs were not a total loss, for they
accepted the duty of guarding the Trans-Siberian, a task which
was to become increasingly important as the Partisans grew
stronger and bolder.

On the political side there were fewer blessings to count.
Omsk was an Augean stables, and it soon became obvious that
Kolchak was no Hercules. Krasilnikov and his two chief asso-

ciates were brought perfunctorily to trial, acquitted and given promotion. Acts of violence continued. Private vendettas were prosecuted. Ministers enriched themselves by blatant frauds. Disastrous administrative errors went uncorrected; perhaps the most damaging to the régime was its failure to see that the railway staff got paid. Everyone recognised the Supreme Ruler's integrity, yet he seemed incapable of imposing his own high standards on others or even, more strangely, of realising that they needed to be imposed. Things could hardly have gone much worse in Siberia if Semenov had been in power.

It is true that Kolchak was seriously ill with pneumonia when the gravest of the political incidents which disfigured his Government's record occurred; but it cannot be asserted with any confidence that if he had not been ill the affair would have been less barbarously handled. On the night of 21 December there was an armed uprising in Omsk. The Stavka's counter-espionage agencies had wind of it in advance, and twenty-four hours earlier a score of the suspected ringleaders—mostly railwaymen—were rounded up and shot out of hand. This failed to avert the rising, in the course of which the insurgents seized the gaol and released all the prisoners.

In Omsk itself this was their only success, but bitter fighting continued for some hours in Kulomzino, an industrial suburb on the other side of the river, before order was restored. Courts martial were set up to give a veneer of legality to what were in fact brisk and indiscriminate reprisals; but the 166 people who received sentences of death were not the only ones killed. Thirty-five young soldiers, for instance, who had been overpowered by the insurgents while guarding the gaol were taken into a park and shot by Government forces because there was no room for them in the cells; and many other harmless citizens were summarily put to death.

What caused most scandal—Kolchak indeed maintained that it was deliberately done to discredit him—was the execution of a number of political prisoners, Socialist-Revolutionaries and others, who after being set free thought it prudent to return to the gaol. Five of these were arbitrarily condemned to death;

ten others, after being dismissed from the court martial because there were no charges against them, were shot out of hand on the orders of a Captain Bartoshevski, against whom no proceedings were subsequently taken. These nightmare deeds, and the Government's failure to punish their perpetrators, did grave damage to the Supreme Ruler's cause.

In external affairs the outlook for Omsk was reasonably encouraging. In due course Denikin and the other White leaders publicly acknowledged Kolchak's leadership. The attitude of the Allied representatives at his headquarters, including the American Consul-General Harris, was cordial and co-operative. Omsk's credit, thanks to the captured gold reserve, was good. Among the White Russian representatives in Paris were men of influence and standing and, although they were excluded from the Peace Conference, they did a lot of useful lobbying among the delegations.

None of the Allies was as yet prepared to extend diplomatic recognition to the Omsk régime, but the idea that this ought to be done at a suitable moment was very much alive in London, Paris and Washington. Meanwhile the British Foreign Office and the Royal Navy were arranging the removal of Kolchak's wife and son from South Russia to the neighbourhood of Paris, where they arrived in March 1919.[116] A second British battalion —the 1st/9th Hampshires from India—reached Omsk early in January, followed by the advance party of a Canadian brigade.* A naval detachment from HMS *Suffolk*, with two of her 12-pounders mounted on armoured trains, had won golden opinions in the winter fighting and was now organising an Anglo-Russian flotilla of gunboats on the Kama River with a

---

* The decision to dispatch a Canadian contingent of 5000 men and 1300 horses was taken in August 1918. About 700 landed at Vladivostok at the end of October, but the sailing of the remainder was cancelled and the men who had reached Russia were sent home a few weeks later. There were two reasons for the abortion of this project. One was that the discipline of the troops deteriorated dangerously after the Armistice, the other was that the authorities in Ottawa felt that they had not been consulted closely enough in the matter, and took umbrage.

base at Perm; apart from the Czechs, this handful of British sailors and marines was the only Allied unit which went into action at the front.* Training-cadres of British officers were at work under Knox's direction on stolid phalanxes of Siberian recruits. The French, too, were in evidence at Omsk and elsewhere. The Italians were at Krasnoyarsk. American experts were tirelessly trying to prevent the efficiency of the Trans-Siberian system from deteriorating any further. Colonel Ward was on a lecture-tour of industrial centres.

Men believe what it comforts them to believe, what they wish to be true. To anyone near the centre of Siberian affairs in January 1919 all these portents must have implied very clearly that the Allies had committed themselves to the crusade against Bolshevism, and this impression was borne out by the demeanour, in public and in private, of their leading representatives. The Prinkipo proposals therefore came as a bombshell, arousing first incredulity and then indignation.

Prinkipo is a small island in the Sea of Marmora, not far from Constantinople. It owes its obscure place in twentieth-century history to the fact that in December 1918 the British Government proposed to the other Allies that a truce should be arranged in the Civil War, and that representatives of the Bolshevik and the anti-Bolshevik factions should be brought to Paris to explore the possibilities of peace. The idea, nowhere well received, was rejected with such vehemence by France that when, in mid-January, it was revived by President Wilson, a rendezvous in Paris was clearly out of the question. Prinkipo was chosen partly, no doubt, because small islands have a discouraging effect on would-be assassins, but mainly because the Soviet delegates could reach Turkey by rail without too much danger on the one hand or too many detours on the other.

The Prinkipo project was an early and amateurish attempt

* "The Navy has often landed men to assist in military operations, but never before has such a party gone so far (4350 miles) from its parent ship." (Sir Henry Newbolt: *History of the Great War: Naval Operations*, Vol. V.)

at what forty years later became known as summitry. In conception it was sensible and humane. Lloyd George adumbrated 'a truce of God,' during which 'reprisals and outrages' as well as fighting would cease. So far so good. Since early November the Soviet Government had made repeated appeals to the Allies to stop Intervention and call off the blockade; their tone was conciliatory and hints were dropped that magnanimity in this matter would be rewarded in the economic field. It was thus clear that Moscow wanted, and wanted very badly, an end to hostilities.

The Allies desired the same thing with an almost equal ardour. Their armies were in the throes of demobilisation, which in the British forces was being carried out on a system so patently unfair that desertions were rife and mutinies recurrent; 'we dare not give an unpopular order to the troops,' the Chief of the Imperial General Staff told the Cabinet on 22 January, 'and discipline is a thing of the past.' Serious trouble was blowing up in Ireland. A few days later Foch told Sir Henry Wilson that the French soldiers 'won't stand it much longer, and will demobilise themselves as the Belgians are doing.' Public opinion in America was restive and querulous. Nothing, in short, would have better suited the Allies (always excepting Japan) than to see the Civil War wound up. Prinkipo appeared to offer some hope—the only hope—of bringing this about.

That anyone could have believed, even for a moment, that this hope would be realised seems incredible. Three things would have to happen at the Prinkipo Conference before anything fruitful could be achieved: the Whites would have to agree among themselves; the Reds would have to agree with the Whites; and the Great Powers (before whom the rival factions were to be arraigned in, to use Lloyd George's infelicitous words, 'the way that the Roman Empire summoned chiefs of outlying tributary states to render an account of their actions') would have to reach unanimity in their attitude to whatever the Reds and the Whites decided. When one remembers that any violation of the truce in Russia while the conference was in progress could hardly have failed to bring it to an acrimonious end, it is difficult to understand how three of the Great Powers got as far as appointing their own delegates to Prinkipo.

The invitations, drafted by President Wilson, were sent out on 22 January from a powerful wireless transmitter on top of the Eiffel Tower; but the White leaders received theirs by less impersonal methods through their representatives in Paris. They rejected them with contumely and at once. The Allied statesmen had failed altogether to take into account the emotional atmosphere engendered by a civil war. The Whites genuinely believed the Bolshevik leaders to be monsters, creatures beyond the pale, guilty of crimes so unforgivable that to treat with them —and especially to treat with them at the behest of foreigners— was completely out of the question; they spurned the Prinkipo proposals as spontaneously as a Pathan tribesman with a blood-feud on his hands would have spurned the suggestion that he ought to talk things over with the man who had killed his brother.

The categorical White refusal was received in Paris within two days. Moscow returned no answer until 4 February when, in a vaguely disingenuous statement, the Soviet Government claimed that it had learnt of the invitation 'through a radiogram which contained a review of the press'; it would be delighted to enter into negotiations, asked for further particulars, and outlined a number of tempting offers in respect of foreign debts and economic concessions which it would be prepared to make in order to facilitate an agreement.

Lloyd George was furious; the invitation to Prinkipo had been couched in altruistic terms, and he found the implied offer of bribes 'studiously insulting.' But the weakling project had been strangled at birth by the White refusal to participate, and such hopes as the Bolsheviks had of gaining a breathing-space by opening negotiations were doomed. On the White leaders the effect produced by the affair was one of bewildered and irate consternation; it was as if the Good Samaritan had interrupted his ministrations to give the object of his succour a sharp slap in the face. Many of the Allied representatives in Russia, who had been given no inkling of what was afoot, were almost

equally put out. 'Kolchak,' Knox's ADC wrote in his diary on
27 January, 'is said not to have slept a wink since he heard
about Prinkipo.'[117] The Civil War went on.

Kolchak's burdens were not lightened by the arrival of
General Janin, who reached Omsk on 13 December. The two
men had met briefly in 1916 when Kolchak paid a formal visit
to the Tsar's headquarters at Mogilev on his appointment to
command the Black Sea Fleet, but whatever impression the
Admiral then made on Janin had been obliterated by the criticisms to which, in Vladivostok and elsewhere, he lent a ready
ear. Janin believed Kolchak to be in the pocket of Knox, whom
he regarded, *ex officio*, as a rival; and he knew that Kolchak disliked and was disliked by the Czech Legion, which he had come
to Siberia to command. But these were grounds for suspecting
that the Supreme Ruler might prove difficult to deal with, not
for writing him off as a dangerous lunatic.

In July, when Janin was designated as their commander, the
situation of the Czechs appeared both desperate and dramatic.
Even allowing for the difficulties of war-time travel, his progress
towards the theatre of their operations was oddly deliberate; a
pencilled note in General Knox's copy of *Ma Mission en Sibérie*
records that the Englishman took 51 days to reach Vladivostok,
the Frenchman 77. And when he did get to Vladivostok he
spent a fortnight there before continuing his journey eastwards.
At Chita he found himself involved in the dispute between Kolchak and Semenov, who were exchanging threats and recriminations at long range, and at one stage he spoke to Kolchak by
telephone. The Supreme Ruler's attitude was imperious and
inflexible, and Janin, who saw clearly that with Japanese
bayonets backing Semenov it was no good being either of these
things, remembered that someone had told him that the
Admiral was 'too neurotic to be a statesman.'

Janin's most urgent task in Omsk, at any rate in his own
estimation, was to to get his own status defined. This was not
easy. His credentials as Commander-in-Chief of the Czechoslovak forces in Siberia were clearly set out in orders given him

both by his own Government and by the Czechoslovak National Council in Paris; these orders also required him to 'endeavour to extend fraternal support to' and to 'co-ordinate' the various Yugoslav, Polish, Rumanian and other units belonging to 'the oppressed nations.' He was to act under the general direction of the Japanese High Command.

But before these orders were drawn up the French Government had had under consideration arrangements which would have given Janin a position of much greater scope and importance. 'As commander of the Czechoslovak Army, at that time the largest in Siberia,' he was to have been entrusted with 'the command of all the Allied forces in Russia and Siberia (except the Japanese) and therefore with the conduct of all operations in Siberia.'[118] Janin did not find it easy to forget the original conception of his role. An ambitious man, he was sensitive in matters of prestige; 'it would be improper,' he felt, 'for a general of the French Army to be exposed to the risks of a fiasco.'[119]

Accompanied by Regnault, the French High Commissioner, he first broached the question to Kolchak (who was ailing and feverish) on 16 December. From Janin's own account of an interview which he described as 'tempestuous' it is clear that he began by claiming, if not the supreme command in Siberia, at any rate a wide measure of control over operations, and that this claim was supported by various telegrams from Paris. Kolchak rejected the claim flatly and hotly. He had, he said, a civil war on his hands. It would be out of the question to entrust its direction to a foreigner; politically it was essential that the supreme command should be in Russian hands. It is difficult to see how the Supreme Ruler could have reacted otherwise, but Janin found his attitude unreasonable.

Thus began a tedious wrangle which it took more than a month to settle. Throughout it one of Janin's stock arguments was that, the wider his powers, the more material support could be obtained from the Allied High Command, of whom he was the representative in Siberia; but the force of this argument was weakened by the fact that most of the material support that had come to hand or was in view came from Britain.

The Russians, nonetheless, had to take Allied susceptibilities
into account; so, for that matter, had the Czechs, who, as
Knox put it, 'want shirts and boots and not foreign generals.'[120]
In the elaborate Siberian hierarchy it was necessary to find an
acceptable niche for Janin, and by mid-January a formula had
been painfully hammered out which met the demands of an
unreal situation. Janin was to be Commander-in-Chief of all
Allied troops west of Lake Baikal; the Russian High Command
would 'regulate the conduct of operations in accordance with
the directives issued by General Janin as the representative of
the Allied High Command.' What this sentence meant, or was
supposed to mean, is far from clear; but its ambiguity produced
no ill-effects, since Janin never issued any directives.

Knox was given the title of *Chef de l'Arrière*, with wide responsibilities for the training, administration and supply of
Russian as well as Allied forces. He was thus, on paper, an
auxiliary if not a subordinate of Janin's, but the latter, he told
the War Office when it was all over, 'exercised no influence on
the operations and never gave me any instructions regarding
organisation, training or equipment.'[121] The two men did not
get on. Janin was essentially what used to be called a political
general, but he carried little weight with the Russians because
he was too preoccupied with his own or his country's prestige
to identify himself with their cause. He was devious where
Knox was direct, urbane where Knox was outspoken. Knox
did not hesitate to tell the Russians, from Kolchak downwards,
unpleasant truths; Janin softened his criticisms by garnishing
them with precedents from Russian history, in which he was
widely read.

The Russians preferred Knox, because they knew where they
were with him and they could see that he was all out to help
them. 'This quiet, energetic and exceptionally well informed
officer,' wrote a Russian diplomat, 'commanded the esteem and
admiration of the best elements of the Russian Army. He never
hesitated to tell the truth—*il n'y mettait pas des gants bleus.*'[122]
And a company-commander of the Hampshires thus summed
up his impressions of Knox after their first meeting in Siberia:

'This is a type of British officer one meets occasionally. They make one proud to belong to the same race and eager to spare no effort to work for the patriotic and unselfish ideals which evidently form the mainspring of their lives.'[123] No such unequivocal tributes to General Janin have survived.

CHAPTER TWELVE

The Kremlin Stakes

THE bursting of the *ballon d'essai*—for that is really all it was—
which bore aloft the Prinkipo proposals caused Allied policy towards Russia to relapse into its normal state of incoherence.
'The Allies in Paris,' Churchill, now at the War Office, wrote
to Lloyd George on 27 February 1919, 'have not decided
whether they wish to make war upon the Bolsheviks or to make
peace with them. They are pausing midway between these two
courses with an equal dislike of either.'[124] This dislike was
natural; and it arose in part from the fact that both courses
appeared to be equally impossible.

To make peace—to cease, that is, from intervention and to
lift the blockade—was incompatible with honour. Apart from
the Czechs, to whose rescue the Allies had pledged themselves,
there were the White Russians who, originally as an anti-
German measure, had been encouraged to take up arms and
could not with decency be abandoned. As Balfour put it in a
memorandum at the end of November 1918, 'recent events have
created obligations which last beyond the occasions which gave
them birth.' All over the former Russian Empire 'new anti-
Bolshevik administrations have grown up under the shelter of
Allied forces. We are responsible for their existence and must
endeavour to support them.' And some of these administrations, notably in the Baltic and in Transcaucasia, were not anti-
Bolshevik merely, but represented the nationalist aspirations
of oppressed minorities whose desire for autonomy the Allies,
directly or indirectly, had done much to foster. It was a situation from which a wholesale withdrawal, however expedient,
was out of the question.

But so was the alternative. To 'support' the Whites meant to support them against the Reds. It was already clear that the supply of advice which was seldom taken and of arms which often did not reach the front was not going to preserve the White cause; nothing could preserve it except the defeat of the Red Army and the overthrow of the Soviet power. This was a purpose to which no Allied Government was prepared to dedicate itself; and even if this had not been so, the armies, the very large armies, which would have been needed to attempt this purpose did not exist. With demobilisation in full swing, merely to maintain at something like full strength the small Allied forces already in Russia was all that (and soon became more than) the Interventionist Powers could do.

General Janin's experiences well illustrate the practical problems involved. The French Military Mission in Siberia comprised only a few dozen officers and men, who were exposed to no danger and very little hardship. When in mid-January his status and powers had at last been defined, Janin was eager to get to work. But this proved difficult, because his Mission was withering away. The dates on which the various categories of men were due for demobilisation had been fixed, and in order to keep to those dates many of his staff had to start their journeys back to France at once. Replacements on their way to Siberia 's'autodémobilisaient à tous les points du voyage,' some preferring to linger in San Francisco or Hawaii until they were due for repatriation. Others arrived in Siberia only to depart immediately—' "trois petits jours et puis s'en vont," comme les marionettes de la chanson.' One eccentric in this category, feeling that his honour was engaged, insisted on staying a month; 'il rendit service par son compétence en mitrailleuses.'' [125] Churchill recorded an important half-truth when he wrote: 'The Armistice proved to be the death-warrant of the Russian national cause.' [126]

After the Armistice only one attempt was made by the Allies at full-blown intervention on a relatively large scale; it proved disastrous. On 18 December an expedition under French command began to disembark at Odessa and to move inland; it comprised two French and two Greek divisions. Their role, as

they understood it, was to act as an army of occupation following the withdrawal of German troops from the Ukraine; but
they were soon involved in hostilities, for which they had no
stomach, with the Red Army, and after losing over 400 officers
and men, fell back in some disorder on Odessa.

As the Bolsheviks closed in on the port, where there was a
serious food-shortage, the strong French naval squadron covering the operations mutinied, and there was disaffection among
the troops on shore. On 2 April the French commander received orders from Paris to evacuate Odessa within three days;
the orders were carried out in an atmosphere not far removed
from panic (though the Greeks behaved stolidly enough) and
the force sailed shakily away, leaving Odessa wide open to
reprisals. If any of the Allied General Staffs still needed a warning against adventurism, this fiasco, with its aftermath of courts
martial, provided it.

There was an element of schizophrenia in the Allies' attitude
to the Civil War. They were painfully aware that their own
efforts to influence its course were largely ineffectual, extremely
expensive and increasingly unpopular. They deplored the absence of a common policy towards Russia and despaired of concerting one. They knew in their hearts that sooner or later they
would have to cut their losses.

But these comparatively realistic views were always being
pushed into the background by wishful thinking, by a blind
conviction that things would come out all right in the end.
Opinion about Russia in the Allied capitals was strongly
coloured by, and indeed largely based on, information derived
from *émigrés*. Their testimony, strikingly presented, dwelt much
upon the heroism and *panache* of the Whites, and emphasised not
only the turpitude of the Reds but their grave economic and
administrative difficulties. This strengthened the widespread
tendency for people outside Russia to make the same sort of
basic assumptions about the relative worth of the two sides that
children make about the relative worth of cowboys and Indians.

There was also—and it was far stronger than any faith in the

White cause—an almost total disbelief in the viability of the Soviet régime. It was perhaps rather a moral than an intellectual judgment. Crime, people told themselves, does not pay. Men who murdered their officers, butchered their Tsar, executed hostages, nationalised women,* deserted their allies, dishonoured their debts—men who bore so heavy a burden of guilt must surely be overwhelmed by it in the end. It was unthinkable that what Churchill in the House of Commons called 'the foul baboonery of Bolshevism' should emerge victorious from the struggle. The nightmare could not last for ever. Since most of those who had a say in the shaping of Allied policy thought (or at least felt) in this way, the defeat of Bolshevism had about it a certain aura of inevitability, and this caused the Whites' prospects of success always to appear a little rosier than in fact they were.

In the early spring of 1919 these prospects were at their brightest. The Bolsheviks' hold on Central Asia was menaced by a revolt of Socialist-Revolutionaries and Mensheviks, which was supported by a small British–Indian force on the Trans-Caspian Railway. The Caspian itself was dominated by the Royal Navy with a flotilla of ramshackle gunboats. In Trans-caucasia *de facto* recognition had been extended to the independent Republics of Georgia and Azerbaijan. Finland and the Baltic States of Esthonia, Latvia and Lithuania were convulsed by struggles which, though their progress was obscure and their outcome uncertain, seemed unlikely to end in a manner favourable to Soviet interests.

These were admittedly peripheral theatres of intervention.

---

* The legend that the Soviet Government had 'nationalised' women seems to have been based largely on a document in which the rights conferred by this measure on the male population were defined in some detail. Although it may have been a clever forgery, there are no particular reasons for doubting the document's authenticity; since however it only purported to be a proclamation issued by Anarchists in the town of Saratov, even irresponsible publicists had no excuse for claiming—as they did—that it represented the official policy of the Bolshevik Party and the Soviet Government.

But things were not going badly, either, in the three main sectors whence conjoint action against Moscow had always seemed potentially decisive. In the north the garrison of the Murmansk–Archangel conclave—some 12,000 British and 11,000 other Allied troops—were due for withdrawal during the short ice-free summer; but it was envisaged that, before they left the Arctic Circle, they could with the help of volunteer reinforcements make a swift drive south and realise the long-cherished dream of a junction with the Siberian armies.

For the first four months of 1919 the main news from South Russia was of French *débâcles*. One way and another, France put about 70,000 troops ashore on the Black Sea coast,* only to withdraw them pell-mell when it became obvious that she had bitten off more than she could chew. A few days after the evacuation of Odessa, Sebastopol was given up, and almost the whole of Kolchak's Black Sea Fleet, which was based there, was scuttled. Further east, however, Denikin was doggedly consolidating his bridgehead on the Don; in early May he broke out of it and began to make, with considerable impetus, for Moscow.

But in the race for the capital—and that is how it was widely regarded—the favourite was undoubtedly Kolchak. By the end of April his forces had advanced on a 150-mile front to a depth of 125 miles in the north and 250 miles in the centre.[127]

In March General Kappel, whose army had been withdrawn into reserve, was reported by Knox to be 'afraid of being late for the capture of Moscow';[128] but Knox's ADC thought that Kappel's 'fine Corps . . . will probably go through to Moscow when it gets going.'[129] 'It is from Siberia,' affirmed a Foreign Office memorandum on 6 June, 'that we are expecting the main blow at the Russian Soviet Government to be struck, and it is therefore to Siberia that our main efforts, financial and otherwise, should be directed.'[130]

The question of whether, and if so in what form, to recognise

* As well as Greek and Rumanian contingents they included a number of Senegalese, Algerian and other colonial units who were not affected by demobilisation.

the Omsk Government intermittently engaged the attention of the peace-makers in Paris, where the Supreme Ruler's military achievements were to some extent offset by the unsavoury ambience of his political administration. It was finally resolved to lay down a set of conditions on which the Allied and Associated Governments, some of whom were 'now being pressed to withdraw their troops and incur no further expense in Russia,' would be 'prepared to continue their assistance.'

These conditions were embodied in a dispatch signed by Clemenceau, Lloyd George, Orlando (for Italy), Woodrow Wilson and Prince Saionji (for Japan); it was telegraphed to Omsk at the end of May. The Allies were 'disposed to assist the Government of Admiral Kolchak and his Associates with munitions, supplies and food, to establish themselves as the Government of all Russia, provided they receive from them definite guarantees that their policy has the same objects in view as that of the Allies and Associated Powers.' These objects were to 'restore peace within Russia by enabling the Russian people to resume [sic] control of their own affairs through the instrumentality of a freely elected Constituent Assembly, and to restore peace along its frontiers by arranging for the settlement of disputes in regard to the boundaries of the Russian state and its relations with its neighbours through the peaceful arbitration of the League of Nations.'

Three of the eight guarantees demanded dealt with the second of those objects and were intended to safeguard the autonomy of Poland, Finland, the Baltic and Caucasian Republics, and Bessarabia. One called upon Russia to join the League of Nations. One reminded Kolchak that he had undertaken to pay Russia's national debts, which the Bolsheviks had repudiated. Two dealt with civil liberties, land reform and local elections. But perhaps the most interesting feature of a document of otherwise mainly academic importance is the optimism implicit in the wording of the first condition laid down: '*As soon as they* [*the Whites*] *reach Moscow* they will summon a Constituent Assembly.'

Kolchak replied on 4 June in terms which the Allied

statesmen found generally satisfactory, though the effect of his assurances about 're-establishing order and justice and ensuring individual security to a persecuted population' was marred by the receipt of intelligence which had been coming in for some time from Krasnoyarsk, where the Supreme Ruler's plenipotentiary, General Rozanov, was carrying on a reign of terror and, in particular, executing large numbers of hostages without trial.

If Kolchak had been—like, say, Kerensky—an upstart, his ineptitude in choosing his subordinates would have been less surprising than it is; but he had, after all, a long and distinguished record of command at sea, and his seeming inability, as Supreme Ruler, to tell a bad man from a good one is inexplicable. 'There is not one,' wrote Colonel Ward of the ministers at Osmk, 'whom I would trust to manage a whelk-stall.'[131] Kolchak had as his Chief of Staff a young colonel called Lebedev, who had come up on a mission from Denikin and who before long had more power (which he misused) than anyone else in Siberia. When Knox asked Kolchak why he continued to employ so equivocal a character in a key position, the reply was 'because I can be sure that he will not stab me in the back.' 'Kolchak forgets,' commented Knox, 'that the post requires more positive qualities.'[132]

Admittedly much of the human material available was of a poor quality. 'The company is awful,' Kolchak wrote to his wife on 22 July; 'I am surrounded by moral decay, cowardice, greed and treachery.'[133] It is true that, partly for geographical reasons, Denikin had a better class of officer at his disposal than Kolchak had. It is, nevertheless, impossible not to believe that his armies ought to have been better led than they were, that his staff ought to have been much smaller,* more honest and more efficient, and that his Ministries ought to have been conducted with less scandalous irresponsibility.

---

* Estimates of the number of officers serving on the Stavka at Omsk vary, but 4000 is a figure often quoted. Janin says that there were three Quartermaster Generals, of whom the most junior had 179 commissioned subordinates.

Of all the errors and omissions which can be laid at the door of the Siberian administration those which did the most decisive damage were concerned with military supplies. On Knox's first visit to Omsk, before the *coup d'état* took place, he had recommended among other measures that 'troops at the front should be equipped before those in the rear.'[134] The principle was accepted but was never acted on. The whole system of supply was infected by, and largely subordinated to, the demands of the black market. Prices of all luxury goods and some commodities (tobacco, for instance) were up to twenty-five times higher in Omsk than in Vladivostok. A bribe of between twenty and fifty thousand roubles sufficed to get a supernumerary truck attached to a train of war material,[135] but it was desirable that the train should be consigned to a depot where the staff were in the habit of handling such matters discreetly. It was also desirable that this depot should be at or near a place—Omsk was easily the best—where there were plenty of customers for the contraband.

At a pinch, of course, the illicit truck could have been dropped off and the train allowed to proceed to some commercially undesirable destination near the front. But this would not have suited the depot-commander at the base, since most military material (particularly clothing, medical supplies, saddles, revolvers and so on) commanded a ready market; it was rarely possible to misappropriate an entire consignment of government property, but there were plenty of opportunities for peculation on a moderate scale.

The results were inevitable. Sheer bad planning, bureaucratic inefficiency and the decrepitude of the railways would of themselves have sufficed to bedevil the administration of Omsk's advancing armies; widespread corruption, reinforcing these inherent weaknesses, reduced many of the front-line units to a state of near-destitution. 'The soldiers were dressed very badly,' wrote a Russian naval officer whose gunboat was supporting a bridgehead on the Kama in the spring of 1919; 'some were literally in rags. Only a few had boots, the majority were wearing bast shoes or had sacking wrapped around their feet. Some of them had bags sewn together in lieu of uniforms. The officers were also uniformed in tattered or washed-out khaki.'[136] Another reliable witness speaks of an Army Corps in which the only equipment issued to the officers over a period of six months was one thousand pairs of braces.[137] Promotions, which came rapidly to officers at the Stavka, were rare among the formations at the front.

The Red Army faced much the same problems as its opponents, but showed far more drive and resource in solving them. It was short of arms, for industry was almost at a standstill, but it made sure that such weapons as were available reached the men who had to do the fighting. The desertion-rate was staggeringly high, but it was reduced by intelligent and reasonably humane methods. The Red Army was short of trained leaders, but by June 1919 this deficiency had been partly made good by the recruitment of 27,000 ex-officers of the Imperial Army; most of these, though they 'responded to the call-up only because it was difficult and dangerous to avoid it, and because it provided the only available means of livelihood for themselves and for their families,'[138] performed their duties—under the eye of the Political Commissars—punctiliously though not, perhaps, with fervour.

In two respects the Red Army was immeasurably superior to its adversaries in Siberia. Trotsky had the organising ability, the grasp of affairs and the dynamism that Kolchak lacked. 'We must now,' he said in the winter of 1918, 'devote our whole attention to improving our material and to making it more efficient rather than to fantastic schemes of reorganisation. Every army unit must receive its rations regularly . . . The soldiers must learn to grease their boots.' Kolchak's armies were continually being reorganised—in fourteen months the Ministry of War changed hands ten times—but the soldiers had no boots to grease.

Finally, the Bolshevik leaders had a sense of mission which was lacking in the Whites. They subordinated their differences to a common aim; the Whites did the opposite. The Whites indulged in aimless brutalities which more often than not defeated their object; the Reds were ruthless for reasons which seemed to them good, and their ruthlessness produced the results they intended. Despite all its difficulties and all its blunders, the Red Army was a going concern; 'when things went wrong there was nearly always a Communist or a little group of Communists to take charge at the top, with a transmission belt of members right down to the firing line, to bring that modicum of discipline and resolution that made the difference between victory and defeat.'[139] No such sinews stiffened the flaccid armies of Siberia.

The document, dated 26 May 1919, in which the Allied leaders required Kolchak to—among other things—summon a Constituent Assembly 'as soon as' he reached Moscow was still being deciphered and translated in Omsk when the Red Army passed to the offensive. 'General situation is not satisfactory,' the British Consul at Omsk telegraphed to the Foreign Office on 3 June. The commander of Kolchak's Western Army had overreached himself, lost touch with his reserves and been driven back. 'Situation was aggravated by treachery of Ukrainian regiment going over to the enemy after murdering its officers. . . . Even Kappel's Corps in which with its British training complete confidence was placed became infected and eight companies went over to the enemy.' Mr Hodgson went on to summarise the problems of the Omsk régime and recommended its 'open and avowed support. . . . Fabric rests wholly upon personality of Kolchak.'[140]

Five days later the British Military Mission in Omsk reported 'severe reverses . . . at present general situation from military point of view most unsatisfactory and uncertain, largely due to panic . . . and also to quarrels between the chiefs and to reorganisation which is now taking place in rear.'[141]

The Supreme Ruler's chickens were coming home to roost. The rot had started.

CHAPTER THIRTEEN

The Beginning of the End

THE bad news from the front put an end to plans for moving the Stavka and the seat of government up to Ekaterinburg. Omsk was an uninspiring place. 'With its broad dusty avenues, small wooden houses interlarded here and there with a few modern stone and brick buildings, it was still deeply provincial in spite of its new dignity as the capital, not only of White Siberia but of the whole White Russian movement. . . . It was still very much of an overgrown steppe village.'[142] The town was grossly overcrowded; refugees, whose numbers rose as the summer wore disastrously on, were living in holes in the ground roofed with branches and straw. Concerts and *bals masqués* were however frequently held, and a Rumanian orchestra played nightly in a slatternly pleasure-garden much frequented by the rank and fashion.

The Supreme Ruler's 'Palace' was a small white stucco house on the banks of the Irtysh; the guards on duty wore British khaki with broad purple epaulettes edged with white piping. Kolchak lived austerely. To his wife in France, who had shown signs of wanting to entertain in a style befitting the consort of a Supreme Ruler, he wrote: 'I give no receptions; you need give none. Do not assume airs of protocol.'[143] But although he assured her, more than once, that he had 'no private life' he had in fact formed, or resumed, a liaison with the lady to whom he wrote, from a train in Manchuria, the letter given in Chapter Four.*

* A passage in Kolchak's last letter to his wife suggests that she knew of, and had reproached him for, the liaison. 'I beg you,' he wrote on 15

THE BEGINNING OF THE END

Anna Vasilievna Timireva, a serious, dark-haired, good-looking woman in her early thirties, was the daughter of a well-known composer and the wife of Rear-Admiral Timirev, who had served with Kolchak in the Baltic Fleet and in 1919 was the senior Russian naval officer in Vladivostok. How or when she reached Omsk is not clear, but her relations with the Supreme Ruler were common knowledge. The affair caused no scandal. General Janin and his officers, whose efforts at posthumous denigration include hints that Kolchak was addicted to cocaine, do not even mention Timireva, and this fact in itself is a tribute to her personal qualities and to the discretion with which, as the Supreme Ruler's mistress, she played what might have been, at the least, a controversial role. When Kolchak dined with the British Mission he was normally asked whether he wished Madame Timireva to be included in the invitation; if she was, a staff-car was sent to fetch her from her apartment—she did not live in the 'Palace'—and she and Kolchak arrived separately. She took an active part in welfare work.

Much of the Supreme Ruler's time was taken up with visits to the front. The words conjure up a mental picture of field-glasses, forward observation posts, and steel helmets respectfully proffered to the distinguished visitor; but in fact these tours tended to get bogged down in ceremony. There were endless banquets (one lasted $5\frac{1}{2}$ hours), interminable speeches. Something generally went wrong. At Ekaterinburg a priest, dabbing holy water with a brush on the foreheads of a cavalry regiment, caused the horses to shy and the parade to lose cohesion.[144] At one railway-station a Czech officer, promenading with his wife, fell foul of the cordon of guards surrounding the Supreme Ruler's train; he failed to understand an order in Russian and was bayoneted to death in a scuffle. The incident further embittered Kolchak's relations with the Legion.

October 1919, 'not to permit yourself to write letters which I cannot read through to the end. I destroy all letters after reading the first sentence that violates decorum. If you allow yourself to listen to tittle-tattle about me, I have no intention of allowing you to pass it on to me.'

On Kolchak's first journey to the front as Supreme Ruler arrangements were made to provide him with an escort of fifty men from the 1st/9th Hampshires. When this came to the knowledge of General Janin he raised the strongest objections, on the grounds that an all-British escort would be derogatory to French prestige. His point was wearily taken, and the principle of an Anglo-French escort accepted. Unfortunately the only French troops in Omsk, apart from the officers of the Mission, were their orderlies, their batmen and their indispensable cook, and of these stalwarts very few could be spared. So a process of levelling down took place, and the Supreme Ruler's escort was reduced to twenty—one officer and nine other ranks from the armies of each of his two principal allies.

Nobody doubted his need for an escort, and a reliable one at that. 'Don't forget,' he wrote to his wife, 'that I can cease to exist at any hour of any day.'[145] His progress was everywhere hedged about by the sort of precautions with which over the next few decades bigger and, regrettably, longer-lived dictators were to familiarise the world. 'Guards surrounded him continually, crowds were kept compact and well watched, sentries were posted along his route and all his movements were made at the greatest possible speed.'[146] The words used by a British officer to describe Kolchak's flying visit to Dutov's Cossacks at Troitsk form a stereotype which would have been serviceable, at later dates, in less remote corners of Europe.

Dictators tend to be small men; Kolchak was no exception. But he had an impressive presence. 'A very small man with a very keen eye and rather like what I have always imagined Napoleon to be like' was how one young British officer described him;[147] but unlike Semenov, who *tried* to resemble Napoleon, with his hand thrust into the front of his coat and his pendant lock of hair arranged every morning by his mistress, Kolchak was entirely without affectation. Probably because of his Turkish blood—the family came of Polovtsian stock—he emerges as the least Russian of the White Russian leaders. Frugal, humourless, taciturn, dedicated, he seems somehow not to belong to the feckless society which he ruled; we often have the feeling that we are watching a drama in which the leading part is written and acted in a style quite different from the rest of the play.

'I confess,' Knox wrote to the War Office in January 1919, 'that all my sympathy is with Kolchak, who has more grit, pluck and honest patriotism than anyone else in Siberia and whose difficult task is being made almost impossible by the selfishness of the Japanese, the vanity of the French and the indifference of the other Allies. You have to take what you can get in Russia, and if you find an honest man with the courage of a lion he should be supported although he may not appear to have the wisdom of a serpent in the opinion of Versailles.'[148] Nobody, not even Janin, ever questioned Kolchak's courage or his honesty; but several sources suggest that in some not easily definable way his character deteriorated in Siberia, that he was not the man he had been in former times.

A young Russian naval officer called Fedotoff White, who had served under Kolchak in the Baltic early in the war, chanced to be attached to the American Naval Mission which visited the Black Sea Fleet in 1917, and on the train from Sebastopol to Petrograd he acted as intermediary and interpreter at the interviews during which Kolchak's secondment to America was arranged. During the journey there was an incident in which the Admiral, suspecting an intrusive sailor to be a Bolshevik spy, was with difficulty restrained from shooting him. White commented: 'It was obvious that the strain he had been under [since the March Revolution] was beginning to tell, and he apparently was not able to control himself. . . . I could see a great difference since the days we last met in the Gulf of Riga.'[149]

White (who as a witness strikes one as sympathetic and reliable) turned up in Omsk early in 1919 after service with the Royal Navy. He was sent for by Kolchak and had an hour's talk with him. 'The Supreme Ruler,' he wrote afterwards, 'made a strange impression on me during that hour. He seemed less highly strung than when I had seen him on the train from Sebastopol and in England on his way to America. There was, however, some sort of listlessness in his demeanour. He looked aged and different from the active, energetic man he was when I knew him in the navy in the old days. There was something fatalistic about him which I had never noticed before. He did not look to me a "man of destiny," but rather one thoroughly tired of groping and struggling in an unfamiliar environment.'[150] The general accuracy of this picture is confirmed by other sources. The leading actor moves upon the stage with a heavy, doomed gait.

In international wars a lull in active campaigning is a normal occurrence, from which the armies of both sides benefit. This is not true of civil wars. In these internecine struggles the fighting and its immediate aftermath seem to be attended by more genuine hatred, more cruelty and more bitterness than are conflicts between the soldiers of one country and the soldiers of another; but when the fighting stops the pendulum swings the other way. An army on a foreign field uses the welcome pause to rest, recoup and re-equip. Men go on leave and return refreshed. The ranks are swelled by new recruits, fresh plans are made, supplies replenished, morale restored. At the end of the lull the army is stronger and more serviceable than it was before.

In a civil war the opposite tends to happen. Once the killing has stopped, the need to kill is called in question. A mood of self-doubt and revulsion sets in. Human society is so constituted that, if one nation is involved in hostilities with another, the combatants on either side believe with an equal tenacity in the justice of their country's cause; but in a civil war it is only the fanatics and the simpletons whose minds are proof against the suspicion that there may after all be something wrong in tearing one's own nation apart, killing one's compatriots and looting their houses.

In Siberia these moral misgivings were reinforced by more mundane factors. War was least unpopular when it was least practicable—in the long winter months. The villages needed the young men (and the horses) just when the Army had most use for them; even Partisan activity fell off at the times of the

White aviation

Kolchak presents colours to a newly formed Regiment

These men belonged to "one of the better-dressed Regiments", according to Grondijs: summer 1919

The summer retreat: infantry north of Ufa

spring sowing and the harvest. In both the White and the Red Armies, recruited largely from peasants, the temptation to dodge the call-up, to desert, or not to return from leave had a firm foundation in agricultural economics.

But although this tendency for regiments to become, like icicles, very large and imposing in the winter, only to melt away when spring came round, was common to both sides, the Bolsheviks not only managed to keep the rate of wastage within bounds but they were also able—unlike the Whites—to stimulate the process in their adversaries' forces by means of propaganda. Most of this was carried on either by agents who infiltrated the White lines or by Party members who were already behind them, and it was especially effective in towns and villages far from the front, whose inhabitants had never been exposed to the full rigours of Bolshevik control and remembered only the brief and relatively mild interregnum of the previous year.

Siberia was not a fertile field for Marxist revolutionary dogma. There had been no landlords, no great estates, hardly any serfs. The peasants were not cowed drudges, eking out a dull existence on cramped plots of land; they resembled, rather, pioneer settlers, and their farms, averaging a hundred acres, were ten times the size of their counterparts in European Russia. The population, healthily laced with exiles and their descendants (including a number of Poles) and with *brodyagi* or runaway criminals, had a traditionally independent outlook; a secret society aiming at autonomy for Siberia had been founded as long ago as the 1860's, and all forms of centralisation, of which the Siberians had had unfortunate experiences, were cordially mistrusted.[151]

But Bolshevik propaganda did not need to be particularly seductive to convince most people that almost anything was better than the rule of Omsk. Only twelve per cent of the population were literate. Outside the relatively sophisticated zone of the Trans-Siberian Railway, where the inhabitants knew roughly what was going on, hardly anybody had a clear idea of what the Whites were fighting for, or whom they were fighting against. The Civil War made its impact through call-ups, requisitions, taxes and decrees, and anyone who expounded the view that these inconveniences not only should but could be done away with was sure of a sympathetic hearing. An old peasant who had known the rule of both Reds and Whites was asked by Knox which side he preferred. 'The side that robs least,' he replied. 'We lived better under the law of Nicholas than we do now. They call this liberty but it is only robbery.'[152]

Accounts of Bolshevik atrocities and exactions, often authenticated by refugees from further west, tarnished the Soviet image; but in many districts a far more compelling impression was produced by the misdeeds of the Supreme Ruler's subordinates. It would be otiose to attempt a representative calendar of the crimes committed by either side. By what scale of values can one equate the 670 persons shot by Cossacks in Ufa, the 348 massacred by Semenov outside Chita,[153] with the Cheka's total bag during the Civil War, which Chamberlin, basing his estimate on published Soviet sources, puts at 'about 50,000' of both sexes?[154] All one can say is that the pot was black, and so was the kettle.

Nevertheless, some idea of the impression which the White régime must have made on responsible people in many parts of Siberia is conveyed by the document in which a senior administrator in the Urals resigned his post. Part of it runs: 'The military authorities, including quite junior officers, are the real masters in civil affairs, and take no account whatsoever of the civil authority. Executions without trial, flogging of men and even women, killing of prisoners allegedly while trying to escape, arrest on denunciation . . . have become the rule. I do not know of one single case of an officer guilty of any of the above flagrant acts being called to book.'[155]

The Whites had no effective service of propaganda (though at one stage the British Military Mission at Omsk were indenting on their base at Vladivostok for 'proclamation balloons'), and their high-sounding manifestoes made small impact on a population inured, after five years of war, to appeals to its patriotism and its sense of duty. 'It may be questioned,' wrote

Professor Pares, a warm partisan of the Omsk régime, 'whether Kolchak ever ruled Siberia at all; it was living its own life without him and apart from him.'[156]

To that life the Supreme Ruler restored one important amenity. The ban on the manufacture and sale of vodka, imposed by the Tsar soon after the outbreak of war, had been enforced with only partial success in Siberia; but it had driven distilling and drinking underground, thus causing much inconvenience. The Omsk Government rescinded the embargo and, by making the trade in liquor a state monopoly, derived a useful revenue.

The Bolsheviks, on the other hand, stuck to the Tsarist precedent; perhaps the fact that a high proportion of their leaders were Jews, who are more abstemious than Russians, had an influence on their policy in this matter. In areas occupied by the Red Army stills were demolished and stocks of vodka destroyed; and although in spite of these unpopular measures there was always a good deal of liquor to be had, drunkenness was nothing like so serious a problem in the Bolshevik ranks as it was in the White. Grondijs, a journalist of Dutch-Japanese extraction who was by far the most enterprising and experienced of the war-correspondents in Siberia, and who accompanied the spring advance of Kolchak's armies, thought that 'not a negligible factor' in their success was the non-availability of drink in the territory from which they drove the Reds.

But neither propaganda nor sobriety has ever won a war. Apart from their better leadership, their tighter discipline and their greater drive, the Soviet forces possessed important advantages over their opponents which were not apparent to the chess-board strategists in Whitehall and elsewhere. The chief of these were that their communications were shorter and that, unlike the Whites, they had no serious worries about the situation in their rear (although a peasant revolt in the Syzran district gravely embarrassed the 5th Red Army early in 1919). In May the map showed a picture which appeared to be extremely favourable to the Interventionists—Kolchak within 400 miles of Moscow, Denikin coming up fast from the south, the Archangel force exerting pressure in the north, a threat to Petrograd developing through Finland. But, as every invader of Russia discovers, it is the shaft of the spear that matters, not the head. Denikin, advancing from his Black Sea bases on a front 700 miles wide, was hopelessly over-extended; so was Kolchak, 5000 miles from Vladivostok; and conditions in the rear of both their armies were becoming increasingly inflamed and uncontrollable. Add to all this the fact that there was no effective liaison, let alone an agreed strategy, between any of the White leaders, whereas the Red Army, fighting on interior lines, could switch its forces from one front to another at need, and it will be seen that a chess-board view of the situation was, as ever, misleading, and optimism based on it misplaced.

Knox, describing the collapse of the Imperial armies in 1917, wrote: 'A higher type of human animal was required to persevere to victory through the monotony of disaster.'[157] Captain Howgrave-Graham of the Hampshires, a witness of Dutov's *débâcle* in the Orenburg sector, reflected that the Russian 'can't go doggedly on against adversity. He gives up, says it's hopeless and waits patiently for the end, drinking if he is male and weeping if female.'[158] This lack of stamina was evident throughout Siberia when things started going seriously wrong at the end of May.

There was little heavy fighting as the Bolsheviks advanced. The forces involved on both sides were small; the 27th Division,* which led the advance of the 5th Red Army as far as Mariinsk, had a strength of little over 4000 and recorded that many White 'divisions' mustered fewer than 1000 men.[159] The Reds, moreover, were hampered by the same administrative difficulties which had hamstrung the Whites. In the main the retreat was a self-perpetuating process. Occasionally we hear of a senior commander who conducted himself in an officer-like manner; Kappel, for instance, directed his rearguard actions from the saddle and shared the dangers with his men. But for the most

* This formation had an unusual Honorary Colonel in the person, or rather persons, of the Italian Communist Party.

part commands and staffs were based on their own private trains, in which they were often companioned by their own or other men's wives or by ladies who played, sometimes usefully, a role roughly corresponding to the *vivandière's*.

These arrangements came in for disapproval and derision at the time and afterwards, but as a matter of fact there was a good deal to be said for them as long as things were going well. Russian women are resourceful campaigners, and during an advance a commander's efficiency was not necessarily reduced by the fact that he and several of his officers had their wives or mistresses with them on the train. The ladies, who cooked and did the laundry and sometimes helped with typing, ciphering and so on, were by no means *bouches inutiles*. Many of them had no homes of their own in Siberia, and by following the drum they saved the men a good deal of worry and a great deal of expense. Their presence does not seem to have been resented by the rank and file, who took their officers' privileges for granted.

But when things began to go badly these mitigating circumstances ceased to apply. Anxiety for the feminine element in a commander's train often dictated its movements during a withdrawal. Not only did his headquarters retire with unnecessary expedition, but once on the move they tended to go on retiring, so as to avoid getting stranded behind one of the traffic-jams which were endemic on all lines, and in the end it often happened that the general and his staff and their loved ones, with all the maps and the code-books and the men's pay and the reserve ammunition, continued to steam prudently eastwards and vanished altogether from the zone of operations.

Affairs, needless to say, were not always so lamentably conducted, but there is no doubt that female camp-followers were a grave source of weakness in an army which at the best of times was not particularly stout-hearted; a British Military Mission report from Omsk recorded that 'all officers from the highest to the lowest had their wives or women with them and when a panic set in their attention was diverted from their troops to their womenfolk,' and went on to quote the case of a regimental commander's wife who had failed to get away and had been killed with her husband in the retreat.[160]

At the end of April Kolchak's Western Army had been threatening Kazan and Samara; further north his Siberian Army, under the Czech Gajda, took Glazov early in June and prospects for a junction with the Archangel bridgehead seemed momentarily bright. But the two Armies, ineptly controlled by the Stavka, were in no sense mutually supporting, and Gajda's advance was made in disregard of the disasters which, during May, had overtaken the forces on his left. Soon he too was in full retreat; and by mid-July the Bolsheviks had forced the Urals.

CHAPTER FOURTEEN

The Fall of Omsk

ALL over Russia the Intervention was dying on its feet. By the end of March 1919 Allied forces had been driven out of the Ukraine; by the end of April they were withdrawing from Central Asia, by the end of June from Transcaucasia, by the end of August from Baku and Archangel. A decision to recall the two British battalions from Western Siberia was reached while Kolchak's advance towards Moscow was still in full flood. Only in Eastern Siberia the Americans and the Japanese, locked in mutual suspicion, were to hold their ground until the end of the year for reasons tenuously if at all connected with the main issues of the Civil War.

As an episode in history, the Intervention suggests nothing so much as a game organised towards the end of a children's party. The small guests embark on it with enthusiasm, the small host is delighted, for a time the fun is fast and furious. But the shadows lengthen, mothers and nannies appear in French windows, one by one the players are summoned in out of the cold, warned that it is time to go home; the pleas of the disconsolate host are ignored, the game peters out. The party is over, the curtains are drawn. Night falls.

The Interventionists themselves were never popular in Russia, where in the conflict between hospitality and xenophobia the more basic but the less agreeable of these two impulses always wins in the end. The Whites took what they were given with both hands, offered profuse thanks and immediately started complaining that it was not enough, that they were being stinted and let down. Most of the material assistance they received was wasted or misused through incompetence, dishonesty or neglect; but when the Allied representatives, shocked by the wholesale squander of which they were the witnesses, tried to induce their beneficiaries to mend their ways, the Whites took umbrage. 'I am of opinion that it would be useless to send any more military assistance to Siberia unless we have some guarantee that it will be used with ordinary common sense,' Knox cabled to the War Office at the beginning of August.[161]

Nothing, perhaps, better illustrates the true nature of the relations between the Siberians and their allies than the short history of the Anglo-Russian Regiment. The project for its formation (it was originally to have been a brigade) was evolved by Knox during April and was cordially welcomed by the Stavka. Intervention, as seen from Omsk, already had a predominantly British complexion. After watching a parade of 10,000 troops in Ekaterinburg early in May, Howgrave-Graham of the Hampshires wrote in his diary:

> What struck me most, as a Briton, was the wide permeation of British influence and support. Ekaterinburg is only one of several dozen training centres and the Siberian Army is only one of several Russian armies. But it was a bit of an eye-opener to stand for an hour and see platoon after platoon, company after company, battalion after battalion march past carrying British rifles, wearing British tunics, overcoats, equipment, underclothing, puttees and boots. A British band (ours) played them past to British tunes.

It had been known for some time that the 1st/9th Hampshires were shortly due for repatriation, but from this battalion and from the training cadres controlled by the Military Mission enough good-quality volunteers were forthcoming to provide officers for the new regiment, in which all the other ranks and most of the NCOs were to be Russian. The spirit in which these British volunteers exchanged the prospects of a quiet journey home and early demobilisation for those of an indefinite sojourn in Siberia, and of fighting under difficult conditions in command of troops whose language few of them spoke, was in marked contrast to the attitude of most Russian officers who, the British High Commissioner telegraphed home in July, were characterised by all reports from the front as 'stupid, selfish, cowardly, profligate and corrupt.'[162]

Although launched with acclaim, the project for an Anglo-Russian Regiment soon ran into teething troubles of an unexpected kind. 'Either by design or accident,' wrote Howgrave-Graham on 19 May, 'the recruits we have received are almost all of frightfully poor physique.' His company had had to reject 93 out of 297—'and even then many have been allowed to stay who make you almost cry to look at them stripped.'

Three weeks later there were 'many indications that the Regiment is far from popular in the town, at any rate amongst the officer class. Our little soldiers get stopped and abused by the Russian officers for saluting them in the British style.' They were having difficulty over sanitary measures and water supplies. 'Here we are, after trekking nearly round the world to come and help these damned Russians, and they won't give us water to drink unless we send men with bayonets to take it by force.'

Another two weeks passed; the Urals front was collapsing. And yet, wrote the diarist on 14 June, 'the sensation of the last two days is an astonishing and disgusting outbreak of "soldier-beatings." Within 48 hours no less than seven of our poor little Russian soldiers have been more or less violently assaulted by Russian officers for saluting them in the English fashion. . . . What makes us boil over more than anything is the disgusting cowardliness of these actions. If they have a grievance against us, why haven't they the pluck to try their tricks on the British personnel? Instead of that they knock our poor little unarmed soldiers about merely for carrying out the orders they have received.'

The military situation was deteriorating fast, and a few days later it was decided that the Anglo-Russian Regiment (which had had less than two months' training and had not yet received its arms) would be withdrawn from Ekaterinburg to Omsk. 'One can't help doubting the wisdom of a policy which puts us in the position of having to scuttle as soon as the enemy appears 100 miles or so away.' But then came a change of plan; the men were to be given rifles and, after a short course in musketry, sent to the front under Russian officers, since it was felt, not unreasonably, that without a common language the British would be unable to control raw troops in action.

The last we hear of the Anglo-Russian Regiment is that two hundred unfit men from other units, most of them suffering from self-inflicted wounds, had been quartered in their barracks and there was 'a pretty bad spirit abroad.' The parade at which Russian officers formally took over command from the British on 7 July began eleven hours later than the appointed time.*

If—and it seems unlikely—there was anyone who hoped that a sense of impending crisis would electrify and regenerate the Omsk régime, he was disappointed.

> In the army, decay; in the Staff, ignorance and incompetence; in the Government, moral rot, disagreement and intrigues of ambitious egoists; in the country, uprising and anarchy; in public life, panic, selfishness, bribes and all sorts of scoundrelism.[163]

Baron Budberg, who was Minister of War when he made this diagnosis in his diary, was not being, to judge from other testimony, unduly harsh. 'Many of the Whites,' Kolchak wrote to his wife, 'are no better than the Bolsheviks.' Since he believed Bolsheviks to be devils incarnate he could not have worded his condemnation more strongly; and he went on to say that there was no honour, no sense of duty, no conscience—nothing but apathy, indifference, peculation and the pursuit of easy money.[164]

* At Archangel on the same day a similar but more ambitious project for the formation of a 'Slavo-British Legion' ended disastrously when two companies of Dyer's Battalion, so called after its Canadian commander, murdered five British and four Russian officers as they slept. Twelve ringleaders were publicly executed by machine-gunning.

THE FALL OF OMSK

As the White Armies fell back in growing disarray Kolchak and his advisers had recourse to a number of expedients, some designed to relieve pressure on the front, others to improve morale and stiffen the flagging will to resist throughout Siberia. In June, despite the fact that the Supreme Ruler had consistently and obtusely refused to countenance the claims of Finland and the Baltic Provinces to independence, urgent messages were sent to Yudenitch, the White commander in the Baltic theatre, and to Mannerheim, the Finnish national leader, exhorting them to make a joint advance on Petrograd; but, although at one stage cavalry-patrols reached the suburbs of the former capital, a stubborn defence, inspired by Trotsky, held and threw back an assault in which British tanks played an awe-inspiring part. Then an effort was made—on the suggestion of General Dieterichs, a deeply religious man, the walls of whose private railway-coach were plastered with ikons—to present the struggle with the Bolsheviks as a Holy War in which (the Bashkirs and other Moslem minorities were assured) Allah was no less deeply interested than the Christian God. Nothing came of this, either.

There were anxious, insincere flirtations with a high-powered Japanese mission which reached Omsk in July, but hopes of direct military support from that quarter proved vain. There was talk of a possible alliance with Germany. With a view to strengthening popular support for the régime, a series of administrative reforms, impeccably democratic in character, were introduced; 'I think all these measures are too late,' commented the British High Commissioner,[165] and he was right.

In July the wires from London hummed with a plan, of Churchillian inspiration, which envisaged the Czechs cutting their way through to Archangel and sailing thence for home. It was calculated in Whitehall that, if the Czechs bestirred themselves, they had at least a sporting chance of reaching the Arctic Ocean before its waters froze, and it seems to have been felt that the very narrowness of the margin by which—if all went well—they might hope to avoid being stranded in Archangel with winter and the Bolsheviks coming on would lend impetus to their operations. But this unpractical scheme held no interest for the Czechs, and it was soon forgotten.

The White cause in Siberia was doomed a little more than a year after the Chelyabinsk Incident brought it into being. The only hope of preserving it—or rather, perhaps, of prolonging its agony—through another winter lay in a vigorous rearguard action conducted by fresh troops. The Red Army's spearheads were weak, over-extended and largely dependent on the railways. If the retreating White armies, weary, demoralised and devoid for practical purposes of fighting value, had been withdrawn into reserve, and the enemy's main axes of advance plugged by even quite small forces under capable and aggressive commanders, the Red Army's triumphal progress could have been halted and even temporarily reversed.

Attempts were made to do something of the sort. Their success, jeopardised in any case by the inefficiency of the Stavka and the congestion on the railways, was finally ruled out by the unreliability of the 'shock' troops who were generally employed. It had become fashionable throughout the White Armies to form commando-type units and to give them designations and insignia—death's heads and so on—appropriate to exceptionally ruthless and dedicated fighters. But these distinctive trappings, although no doubt they enhanced the soldier's morale when things were going well, had the reverse effect when the other side had the upper hand; for then, if he were captured, his badges and his special equipment would proclaim him a particularly ferocious enemy of the Soviet cause, and he would be exposed to particularly ferocious treatment from his captors. The surest methods of minimising this risk were flight or desertion, and one or the other was often adopted by these picked units. One of them was dubbed the Immortal Regiment. 'If,' mused a war correspondent, 'this regiment, which withdrew without casualties from the field of honour, does not attain immortality, it will not be the fault of the officers and men; they have done everything humanly possible to that end.'[166]

The Red Army had only to press on. The continuous White withdrawal was the product less of military defeats than of moral collapse. One of Pasternak's characters in *Doctor Zhivago*, much of which is based on the author's experiences in Siberia, reflects:

> Before, there had been obligations of all kinds, sacred duties—your duty to your country, to the army, to society. But now that the war was lost (and that misfortune was at the bottom of all the rest) everything seemed to have been deposed, nothing was any longer sacred.

Religion, Denikin noted, had 'ceased to be one of the moral impulses which upheld the spirit of the Russian Army.'[167] Knox had the same impression. 'The Church is on our side,' but in it he found 'only unnerved old men or narrow reactionaries'; one divisional commander had had to dismiss all four of his regimental chaplains for drunkenness.[168] There were no ideals, no standards, no trust, no hope except the hope of survival.

The Supreme Ruler cannot escape all responsibility for the existence of this vacuum. He had accepted, however reluctantly, the duty of governing, and he governed, or allowed others to govern, execrably. Omsk was a sink of iniquity and folly. Kolchak knew this perfectly well, but he took no effective action to reform matters, he never got a grip of the situation. It was not that he was weak, or that his authority was challenged by powerful rivals. There was nothing artificial or precarious about his supremacy; he was the strongest man in Siberia, and the most respected—a lion among jackals. He had all the attributes of a dictator except the will to dictate.

As Commander-in-Chief he was never more than a remote figurehead. 'For us,' Semenov once said, 'an admiral is a kind of civilian.'[169] There can have been few members of any armed service in any age to whom the description was less applicable than it was to Kolchak; but it is pertinent to consider how incongruous his naval background was to the military problems he faced in Siberia. The opportunism of maritime warfare—

the need for quick decisions, the outlook based on good communications, on speed and flexibility in manoeuvre—was exchanged, upon the endless steppes, for slow, groping, ponderous campaigns, intermittently brought to a standstill by the climate and at all times hobbled by administrative commitments. Kolchak can be forgiven if, among his other preoccupations, his grasp of land-strategy was less than Napoleonic.

He must however bear heavy blame for his failure to control his staff or to select suitable commanders. The swollen Stavka, besides embodying all the worst technical vices of Russian military bureaucracy, was rotten to the core with dishonesty, nepotism and intrigue. At its head the disastrous Lebedev had succeeded in consolidating his position. 'Lebedev's increased power,' the British Military Mission reported at the end of July, 'has brought about a rapid turn to the extreme right which is supported by a handful of his closest associates and a few hangers-on of the Cossack officer type, who believe that men, provided they are beaten and flogged sufficiently, will fight for the present Government. The latter have learnt nothing from the Revolution and are the rottenest and most harmful element in the country.'[170]

Since the fighting troops always have a low opinion of the staff, their moral (as opposed to their material) well-being is scarcely affected if the staff really is bad. An army is, on the other hand, extremely sensitive to matters affecting its own leaders, and nothing is more calculated to undermine the soldiers' confidence than frequent changes in command. Kolchak continually made such changes; it was, indeed, almost the only way in which he influenced events at the front.

Of the many heads that rolled, the most important was Gajda's. Early in 1919, despite the fact that he was under thirty and a foreigner, the enterprising Czech captain was promoted general and placed in command of the Siberian Army, then theoretically directed on Archangel; later he was given control of the Western Army as well. But when the tide turned against the Whites he fell from grace. After a stormy interview (at which, according to Gajda, the Supreme Ruler broke an ink-pot and several pencils) he was dismissed and, with machine-guns mounted on his special train to prevent its seizure, left for Vladivostok. 'His fall,' commented the British Military Mission, 'is all the more unfortunate as it follows so soon after his nomination as Commander-in-Chief of the Siberian and Western Armies, on which occasion he received telegrams of congratulation from various civil organisations and co-operative societies in Siberia.'[171] Gajda's dismissal, and the manner of it, had upon the military and political situation the sort of unsettling effect which a prudent leader in an hour of crisis should have striven at all costs to avert.

More changes in command, more meaningless reorganisations, more reproachful appeals to the public did nothing to stem the Bolshevik advance. How little there was behind it was shown when at the end of September a half-hearted White counter-offensive under Dieterichs threw the Red Army back across the Tobol River, making gains in some sectors of almost 100 miles. The Stavka was seized by one of those moods of insane optimism which alternated with the deepest despondency; 'General opinion,' the British Military Mission told the War Office on 10 October, '[is that] Red morale is rapidly deteriorating and unless they receive warm clothing before winter their army will melt away.'[172]

But this was moonshine. The feeble White thrust soon spent itself and was pushed back. The Red Army came on. 'The Bolsheviks' direction of operations is far superior to ours now,' Knox had reported in August, 'and they have some units that fight with conviction while we have just at present none.'[173] This was becoming truer every day. The Reds' 27th Division, leading the hunt, was averaging an advance of 26 miles in every 24 hours. From a telegram dated 29 October the Foreign Office learnt that it had been decided on the previous night to evacuate government departments from Omsk to Irkutsk, and that the Gold Reserve was being loaded into railway waggons; it would not be dispatched eastwards 'as long as there is a possibility of Omsk being held.'[174] It was a measure of the Stavka's fatuity that such a possibility could be thought to exist.

Omsk stands on the left, or western, bank of the Irtysh and was therefore indefensible, at any rate by weak and demoralised forces. The winter, moreover, was late and the Irtysh had not yet frozen; this meant that a last-minute withdrawal would involve the abandonment of virtually all guns, transport and other heavy equipment allotted to the defence of the city. For these cogent reasons Dieterichs, who had replaced Gajda as Commander-in-Chief, urged that Omsk should be evacuated and an attempt made to form a defensive position on the right bank of the river.

Kolchak rejected this sensible plan. Omsk had in his eyes a symbolic value; it must be defended to the last, and he talked of dying in its streets with his loyal followers. Dieterichs accordingly resigned, to be succeeded by Sakharov, a time-serving braggart. 'This is the last straw,' one of Knox's officers wrote in his diary on 3 November. Four days later he had an interview with the new Commander-in-Chief, whom he found 'very pleased with himself . . . as usual smiling and full of self-confidence.'[175]

On 9 November there was a sudden rise in temperature. One hundred and seventy-eight guns were still on the wrong side of the Irtysh; the only bridge, which carried the railway, was impassable for horses, and the artillery would have to be loaded on to trucks in order to move across it. The Red Army was less than forty miles away. Sakharov, still debonair, admitted that Omsk would fall in between five and fifteen days. The foreign Missions had all left. A British Railway Mission, seven officers and men of the Military Mission, one Frenchman and one Japanese were the only Allied personnel still in Omsk.[176]

On the 12th and 13th it froze hard. Most of the guns were got across the ice to the right bank; most of the political prisoners were shot. Sakharov vanished. On the 14th advance-guards of the 27th Red Division entered the city. There was a little—very little—street-fighting, but no organised resistance. By nightfall Omsk was in Bolshevik hands; 10,000 prisoners were rounded up, and the booty included forty locomotives and over a thousand trucks, many of them loaded.

General Rudolf Gajda

West-bound Americans pass east-bound Czechs in Trans-Baikalia

The winter retreat: artillery leaving Omsk

THE FALL OF OMSK

It was still freezing, but the Reds set about consolidating the main crossing-places with causeways of straw and planks. Within the last three weeks the White forces threatening Petrograd had been decisively defeated; Denikin's advance-guards had been driven out of Orel, only 200 miles from Moscow, and his armies had begun, as Partisans and Red cavalry played havoc with their communications, to fall back all along the southern front. In Siberia the pursuit of Kolchak could be continued without detriment to more important sectors.

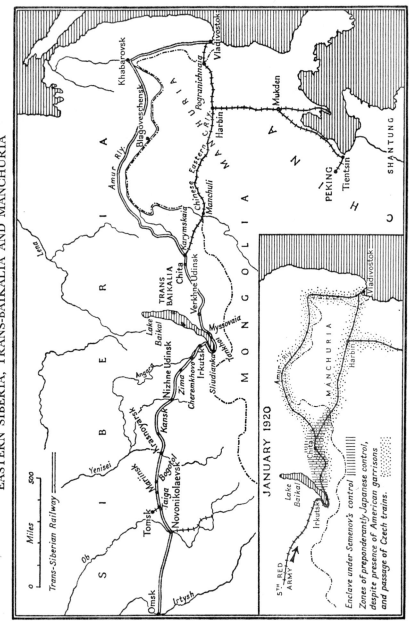

EASTERN SIBERIA, TRANS-BAIKALIA AND MANCHURIA

CHAPTER FIFTEEN

The Retreat

THE Supreme Ruler left Omsk a few hours before the Reds entered it. His Ministers, starting four days earlier, made remarkably good progress to Irkutsk but found the atmosphere there unpropitious. The Czech National Council, or at least the Russian branch of it, had just issued, in that city, a public statement proclaiming their disapproval of Kolchak's Government and their detestation of its methods. Strong Socialist-Revolutionary and Menshevik elements in the area refused to entertain the idea of a coalition which would have the Admiral at its head. The fugitive Ministers formed a makeshift cabinet; but since it had no power, no popular support and no administrative organs Siberia was in effect without a Government.[177]

Kolchak (who was accompanied by Timireva), his staff, their entourage and a picked bodyguard travelled in six trains, one of them armoured; a seventh, which formed part of the convoy, carried the Gold Reserve. This immense treasure was transported in twenty-nine freight-cars. The train commandant and officials of the State Bank occupied a passenger coach in the middle; this was connected by telephone with two *teplushki,** one at each end of the train, which were manned by the escort.

There is a conflict of evidence about the gross value of the bullion (it included platinum and silver as well as gold) at this stage of its journey, but the point is hardly an important one.

---

* A *teplushka*, the lowest form of passenger accommodation, corresponded to the French trucks labelled *hommes 40, chevaux 8.*

A small part of the State Reserve originally captured at Kazan had been shipped via Vladivostok to Hongkong and there sold in order to replenish the Omsk exchequer,* and there may well be some truth in the stories that Semenov did not allow this consignment to pass through his territory inviolate. In May 1919 the British Cabinet approved a project involving a loan of £10,000,000 to the Omsk Government by a City firm of merchant-bankers,[178] but what came of this, and how if at all it directly involved the gold, is uncertain. The significant fact is that, when Kolchak left Omsk with the Red Army on his heels, he had with him a train carrying specie to the value—at a highly conservative estimate—of £50,000,000.

The Supreme Ruler (whose own financial resources at this time consisted of 30,000 rapidly depreciating roubles) attached a talismanic significance to the Gold Reserve. As long ago as August, Knox, Janin and the High Commissioners, scenting disaster, had urged him to move it eastwards while there was still plenty of time and had offered the protection of an Allied escort. Kolchak refused. 'If,' he prophetically told Knox, 'I give the gold over to an international guard and any misfortune happens to me, you will say the gold belongs to the Russian people and give it to any new Government you may fancy.' As long as he retained control of the gold, he went on, he could continue to fight Bolshevism for three years even if the Allies deserted him.[179]

There was, of course, something in this; it was true, too, that, in view of Partisan activity and the doubtful loyalty of the railway staff, any attempt to move the gold involved serious risks, and that in any case there was nowhere in Central Siberia where it would be any safer than it was at Omsk. There was nevertheless something childish in the obstinacy with which Kolchak clung to his hoard. Except piecemeal as contraband, it had no value at all unless it could be conveyed to Vladivostok, and the only hope of getting it intact through Semenov's domain in Trans-Baikalia lay in entrusting it to the Allies. The

* Baring's Diary for 2 March 1919 has the entry: 'Toby [a brother-officer] went down the line with bullion train.'

dog-in-the-manger policy of hanging on to the gold at all costs was futile, and by making the train that carried it an integral part of his own slow-moving retinue Kolchak was merely increasing the price on his own head and reducing his chances of getting through.

The Ministers who left Omsk on 10 November reached Irkutsk, 1500 miles away, in nine days; but conditions on the railway, already appalling, were rapidly becoming catastrophic and were being aggravated by the bitterly cold weather which had set in. Two major blunders had been committed which it was now too late to rectify. One was the failure to pay the railway personnel, some of whose wages were three months in arrears. The other was the omission to build up adequate stocks of coal all along the line; on a stretch of nearly 300 miles between Taiga and Krasnoyarsk there was virtually no fuel available and trains had to wait until supplies were brought from further east or from the coal-mines near Taiga.[180]

Earlier in the year the evacuation of Ekaterinburg and other towns in the Urals had been attended by much confusion and distress. But then it had been summer. When a breakdown or some other cause immobilised a mile-long procession of trains the crowded passengers unscrambled themselves and alighted. Fires were started, tea made, news exchanged with the occupants of other trucks or coaches. Experience taught the travellers that there was little danger of being left behind. Even if the engine-driver was ill-humoured and gave no warning of departure, the train was so overloaded and the locomotive so decrepit that they could easily catch it up before it gathered speed; and it was unlikely, in any case, to go very far before being stopped again.

And so, while larks sang over the flowery plain, children played games, dogs were given a run, women changed their clothes, lovers made love, lice were hunted. With its usual buoyancy the Russian soul pushed tragedy into the background and expanded in an atmosphere of *fête champêtre*. Every now and then a train loaded with reinforcements or supplies chugged past on the west-bound track, whistling importantly and reviving in the picnickers a vague hope of ultimate victory.

But conditions were different in the winter. For one thing there was no longer any west-bound traffic. Both tracks were monopolised by the exodus from Omsk, the difference between them being that the rails which should have served the front were reserved for priority trains headed eastward. These moved slowly enough, but the great traffic-jam on the down-line hardly moved at all.

In the intense cold an engine which ran out of fuel quickly froze up, so that its pipes and boiler burst. Pumps at watering-points were put out of action by the frost and, unless an ice-free well happened to be available, the passengers had to form a human chain and fill the boiler with snow, an arduous and lengthy process. The stoves in the *teplushki* and the battered coaches consumed vast quantities of firewood, for if the heating failed the occupants faced the prospect of death from exposure. Food was scarce, sanitary arrangements non-existent.

Beside and below the *Magistral*, or permanent way, ran the *Trakt*, the old high road to Siberia, now a wide ribbon of trampled snow between two and five feet deep. Along this, in sledges, on horseback or on foot, a stream of humanity flowed sluggishly eastwards. Skeleton regiments, squadrons reduced to a score of sabres, batteries dragging their dismantled guns on sledges, groups of men without officers, parties of officers without men: the débris of an army. Intermingled with the soldiers, competing with them for shelter, fodder, food and fuel, moved straggling convoys of civilians—those who had failed to get a place on a train or whose train had already foundered, peasants driving a few scrawny cattle, children from an orphanage, lunatics, deserters.

The travellers on the *Trakt* looked up at the trains as shipwrecked men on a raft might look up at a passing liner which they know will not stop to pick them up. The people in the trains looked down on the *Trakt* with feelings which varied according to whether their train was moving or not. If it was stationary, the sight of fellow-countrymen who were still making, however painfully, progress towards safety filled them with unreasoning envy and misgivings. Remembering the wreckage of derailments they had seen, the rumours of Partisan attacks, of an outflanking movement by the Red Army, they felt trapped, abandoned, let down, and cursed themselves for putting their faith in the railway. But if they were moving, and there was plenty of firewood for the stove, they looked out on the hunched, snow-plastered pilgrims below them without any real compunction. Pity is atrophied in a *sauve qui peut*.

At the stations fresh crowds of would-be refugees waited in vain for places on trains whose numbers were being steadily reduced by breakdowns. Arguments over priorities raged all day and all night in the station-master's office. Bribes and threats were used in attempts to get defective locomotives repaired or replaced. Desperate personal calls clogged tele-phone-lines which were already inadequate to deal with the official business of the railway. A series of lurid propaganda posters, depicting Bolshevik atrocities and originally intended to stimulate recruiting, served further to lower the morale of the hapless, bewildered travellers. At most stations a sort of agony column had been started; like messages committed to the sea in bottles, notes pinned to a wall attempted to re-establish communications between castaways and the world from which they were sundered. *'Dear Masha, I have gone on by the échelon No BS408, 11 November. I will wait for you and the children in the Dom Petrov, Bolshoi Prospekt No. 12. Ivan.'* It was sympto-matic of the prevailing atmosphere of terror and mistrust that, whenever possible, the advertisers avoided giving their sur-names.

The lot of the many thousands of horses involved in the retreat was pitiful. When the cold was at its worst their nostrils had to be de-iced every few hundred yards. Fodder was scarce all along the *Trakt*, and the peasants who lived on or near the highway found it increasingly difficult to buy in fresh supplies from other villages, because the Omsk paper roubles had become almost worthless. At night shelter of any kind was so scarce that the byres and stables were filled with human beings and the horses had to spend the night outside. Almost all of them were carrying or pulling abnormally heavy loads. Inevitably they lost condition; great numbers of them collapsed and had to be abandoned.

The towns and villages were full of discarded horses. At Krasnoyarsk a British officer who fell into Bolshevik hands left this picture of their plight:

> They were as tame as pet dogs, but nobody had time to stroke their noses. They stood in the streets ruminating over the remarkable change that had taken place in their circumstances. They walked into cafés. They wandered wearily through the deep snow. Droves of them blackened the distant hills.

Since the newly-instituted Soviet authority had declared that all these horses were State property and prescribed severe penalties for their misappropriation, the cowed population 'violently resented friendly attentions from them.' In the end 5000 of them starved to death. Their meat, hides and tails were privily removed; the remainder of the State's property was left lying in the snow, to menace public health when the thaw came.[181]

Save in the rearmost *échelons*, fear of the pursuing Red Army was fitful only; the local panics started among the refugees by rumours soon died down. More permanent, more pervasive and far more acute was the fear of typhus. It is impossible even to guess how many tens of thousands died of the disease that winter; in Novonikolaevsk alone, between November and April, it claimed 60,000 victims.[182]

'It is extremely difficult to combat disease in Siberia,' wrote the authors of a treatise prepared under Foreign Office auspices during the Intervention, 'owing to the totally inadequate medical service, the unhygienic condition of the native huts, and the dirty and insanitary habits of the people.' By the winter of 1919 the medical service had completely broken down over wide areas. Personal hygiene has never been the Russian's strong suit, and on the overcrowded trains few even of the best-provided refugees were tempted to wash or change their linen. Lice, the carriers of typhus, swarmed in the wood-work of the neglected rolling-stock, in the tattered uniforms of the soldiers, in the peasants' sheepskins, in the speculator's fur coat. Soon men, women and children were dying like flies.

In the uprooted population, in the retreating army, the disease bred, as it always does, a fierce, subhuman antipathy towards its victims. 'Typhus,' wrote a British witness of the epidemic, 'develops in the healthy a deadly hatred of typhus patients, as if they were murderers who meditated an attempt on one's life.'[183] When hospital trains, or other trains known or believed to be carrying typhus cases, arrived at a station, the railway authorities did their utmost to pass them through without a halt, in total disregard of the occupants' need for succour or supplies.

Often a whole truck-load of human beings, boycotted by their fellow-travellers, perished. Nobody knew how many had been killed by the disease, how many—too weak to tend the stove—by the cold. All corpses were stripped and, being quickly frozen stiff, were piled like logs. Some British prisoners of the Red Army formed part of a crowd watching this process some-where along the line. One of them recorded that 'officers and men who had passed through the worst horrors of [the war in] France were not left unaffected by these sights, and yet the crowd did not appear to be affected by anything but curi-osity.'[184] The dead were treated with a lack of respect which seems strange in a deeply religious people. 'The only coffin I saw was in the Polish church at Novonikolaevsk, and the only shrouds I saw were those wrapped round dead children.'[185]

Ever since, thirty years earlier, the Government of Alexander III had begun work on the project of linking European Russia with East Asia and the Pacific by rail, the Trans-Siberian Railway had seemed to the outside world a symbol of menace, of aggrandisement, of conquest. To Alexander's subjects, and to his son's, it had represented, at the least, a major national achievement, a pioneering feat which could not but change for the better conditions over a vast region of the earth's surface.

Whether he regarded it with a proper pride or with (as things turned out) a needless alarm, whether he looked on it from the political, the strategic or the economic point of view, nobody could deny that the Trans-Siberian Railway had a certain greatness, a certain exotic nobility of conception, a touch, almost, of Jules Verne.

Now, less than twenty years after its completion, this main artery of progress, this symbol of Imperial vigour and vision, had lost its purpose and its dignity. The proud railway had become a *via dolorosa*, a long narrow stage on which countless tragedies were enacted. It carried at a snail's pace through the lethal winter an immeasurable load of suffering and degradation. In the strange and terrible scene, spread out across hundreds of miles of desolate country, there were no redeeming features. Misery and squalor and cowardice, pain and fear and cold, carrion and excrement—these were the ingredients of the White migration. Only the crows, perched in unusual numbers on the trees along the track, their feathers fluffed against the frost, had cause for satisfaction as they watched the trucks jolt past.

The Supreme Ruler's seven trains, each furnished with two engines, made slow progress. Although reserved for priority traffic, the up-line (as it should have been) was working only a little better than the down-line. In one respect, indeed, it was slightly worse off, for, being less cluttered with trains, it was more often used by sledges from the *Trakt*; these caused loose snow to pack on the rails, and this, particularly on gradients, induced wheel-spin and loss of momentum.

Kolchak still went through the motions of governing. On 21 November he instituted—on paper—a 'Supreme Council'; how in his estimation it would have differed from, or done better than, his own discredited but still theoretically existing Government it is bootless to surmise. On the 25th details reached him of the hostile Czech manifesto issued a fortnight earlier in Irkutsk, and he sent out orders, in cipher, that his Ministers were to break off relations with the Czechs and press the Allies for their prompt evacuation. Since prompt evacuation was already the Legion's overriding purpose, since the Allies were powerless to further its attainment, and since the Czechs were able to intercept and decode Kolchak's derogatory telegram, its despatch was worse than futile.[186]

General Janin, his private train preceding the rearmost *échelon* of the 6th Czech Regiment, left Omsk on 8 November. Before he went he had a farewell interview with Kolchak. He found him, he telegraphed to Paris, 'in a strange neurotic state. The allegations that he is a cocaine-addict are probably true.'[187] Janin reached Novonikolaevsk on the 13th and spent five days there making arrangements to expedite the eastward movement of the Czechs and of a Polish division, some 12,000 strong, who were to bring up the Legion's rear. The Poles were taking an unrealistic view of the situation. They had acquired, and proposed to take with them, 4000 horses, and they entertained hopes of coming to an arrangement with the Bolsheviks and going home by the direct route across Russia. Janin had a low opinion of them.[188]

On 18 November the gloom and confusion in Central Siberia were deepened, in so far as that was possible, by the news that Gajda had attempted a *coup d'état* in Vladivostok on the previous day. It was a botched affair, culminating in a gun-fight near the docks between Gajda's armoured train, flying the green-and-white Siberian flag, and some Russian torpedo-boats in the harbour with which the unspeakable Kalmykov, also in an armoured train, and his Japanese patrons co-operated on land. After a good deal of promiscuous shooting in torrential rain, Gajda, who was slightly wounded in one foot, surrendered and, undertaking to leave Russia for good, was put on board a ship after (it is said) being severely beaten by Russian officers. Rozanov, the military governor of Vladivostok who earlier in the year had won a name for brutality in Krasnoyarsk, embarked with his usual relish on reprisals.

On the same day (the 18th) Janin was about to leave Novonikolaevsk when he received a wire from the Supreme Ruler's train asking him to wait there until Kolchak arrived.

Janin's chief of staff replied that this was impossible; they were about to start for Irkutsk. 'He was quite right,' wrote the senior military representative of Kolchak's allies afterwards. 'After the disaster for which the Admiral and his entourage were responsible, I should have found an interview painful.'[189] It is clear, and will become clearer, that Janin had washed his hands of Kolchak.

Siberia had gone sour on the Whites. The Partisan movement, which was now a serious menace to the railway and the garrisons protecting it, was far more a manifestation of anti-Kolchak than of pro-Bolshevik feelings; and his own associates had few illusions about the Supreme Ruler's capacity to stage a recovery. In the circumstances it is surprising that no serious effort was made to depose or at least to abandon him. Even in this hour of abject defeat he still exerted some magnetism, still retained some aura of authority, was still the focus of such hopes and loyalties as vestigially survived. At Taiga, which his trains reached on 7 December, he was met by his Prime Minister, Victor Pepeliaev, coming from Irkutsk, and by Victor's brother, Anatol, commanding what was left of the Siberian Army.

They were joined by the would-be defender of Omsk, Sakharov, and during a night spent in mutual recriminations Kolchak offered to resign but was dissuaded. In the small hours his trains moved on again, and the Pepeliaevs arrested Sakharov on the grounds that he was a bad influence on the Supreme Ruler. Sakharov was released when Kappel reached Taiga next day,[190] and the main significance of this obscure and tawdry conclave lies in the fact that when it was over Kolchak, who by all the rules of White Russian politics should have been displaced, was still nominally at the head of his moribund régime.

It was at Mariinsk, on 13 December, that Fate—though no one realised it then—began the long-drawn-out process of passing sentence on Kolchak. Its humble instrument was a Second Lieutenant Schteintzel, of the Czechoslovak Army Transportation Staff. Acting on orders from Irkutsk, this officer insisted that the Supreme Ruler's trains should be switched from the up-line to the congested down-line, and told the Russian engineer in charge of them that if they attempted to go on using the up-line they would be opposed by an armoured train. Moreover the Czech staff at Mariinsk, after at first refusing to supply Kolchak's trains with any coal at all, were with great difficulty prevailed on to issue a quantity which was insufficient for their needs.

To Janin—who, like the Czech Commander-in-Chief, Sirový, was now in Irkutsk—General Zankevitch, Kolchak's Quartermaster General, addressed a telegram of protest. They had, he complained, no Czech liaison officer attached to them, and had been told that none could be appointed except on orders from the Commander-in-Chief. 'In general,' Zankevitch concluded, 'we are getting no help from the Czechs, rather indeed we meet with open ill-will and hostility. As a result we have travelled only ninety miles in the last four days.'[191]

With impotent fury the Supreme Ruler and his companions saw their seven trains relegated to the down-line; but it was said to be working reasonably well as far as Bogotol, and everyone assumed that by the time they reached Bogotol the bureaucratic solecism of which they were the victims would have been put to rights.

CHAPTER SIXTEEN

Devil Take the Hindmost

OF the Czech seizure of the Trans-Siberian Railway in the summer of 1918 Churchill wrote later that 'the pages of history recall scarcely any parallel episode at once so romantic in character and so extensive in scale.'[192] By the winter of the following year romance had ceased to be a leading characteristic of the Legion's activities.

The Czechs, withdrawn at their own insistence from the front, had taken over garrison duties along the Trans-Siberian from Omsk to Irkutsk. These they performed with great efficiency. Their intelligence service was good, and when punitive action was called for against the Partisans they were no more inclined to bring back prisoners than were the White Russian detachments with whom they co-operated; they had many atrocities, committed on their own wounded, to avenge.

But for the most part they had—and, after their exploits of the previous year, felt that they deserved—an easy time of it. They made good use of their leisure. Alongside them, all along the line of communications, the Russians were feathering their nests; but they did it untidily, and often the nests were built in trees which would shortly be felled. The Czechs made a sounder job of it. 'Throughout Siberia and the Far East a good many Russians were combining public service with private profit, and it would be unjust to expect the Czechs to do otherwise. But they were better businessmen than the Russians and had more opportunity.'[193]

Abler, shrewder, more self-controlled and technically more advanced than the natives, they had the additional advantage of knowing what they intended to do and how they intended to do it. The Czechs, Knox wrote afterwards, 'meant to get out and would stop at no measures to ensure this result.'[194] And they saw no point in leaving Siberia empty-handed. They had ample rolling-stock and sound engines which were well looked after. Their trains—the trucks often gaily painted with nostalgic Bohemian scenes—were really mobile cantonments, with decent, well-ordered living quarters for the men, many of whom had wives or sweethearts with them. Besides the normal amenities of life—bakeries, laundries, canteens, blacksmiths' forges—the Legion ran a bank, a postal service to Vladivostok, several printing-presses and a daily newspaper.

The men's pay was transmitted from Paris to Tokyo in francs, and there changed into roubles. When the value of the rouble began to drop steeply they were encouraged to leave most of their pay in the bank, which used the substantial credits thus built up to trade on the Legion's behalf. Instead of worthless roubles, a demi-official annalist pointed out, 'it would be infinitely better to have those articles, such as copper, rubber, cotton and groceries, that would be at a premium in Czecho-slovakia.'[195] So the trains filled up with raw materials and commodities of all kinds. Part of this valuable freight, no doubt, was paid for; but much of it, though classed by its owners as war booty, appeared to the Russians to be loot.

It was inevitable that during the retreat feeling should harden against the Czechs. Their long, well-provided, typhus-free trains carried only a fraction of the human burden with which the Russian rolling-stock was overloaded. Although only a small minority of their critics had been within a hundred miles of the front, the Czechs were reviled (behind their backs) as deserters who had fled from the fighting to build up a privileged and affluent position in the rear. They were sus-pected, moreover, of Bolshevik sympathies, and colour was lent to this view by the fact that in some places they concluded non-aggression pacts with the Partisans and in others distri-buted arms to railway-workers who undertook to guard the bridges.

To the Czechs the resentment they inspired was a matter of almost complete indifference. As far as Irkutsk they were in effective control of the stations, the workshops, the coal-supplies and the telephone and telegraph lines which served the railway. They made full use of this control to achieve their sole object, which was to transport all their personnel and all their property to Vladivostok with the least possible delay. This was a sensible object, they could have had no other; and if it needed to be justified on legalistic grounds, they had only to call in evidence the repeated injunctions of their political leaders to avoid getting involved in Russian domestic conflicts.

Unfortunately the only sure way of carrying out either their real purpose (which was to get quickly to the coast) or their ostensible purpose (which was to avoid embroilment in the fighting) was to keep their trains ahead of everybody else's trains. This they were, *de facto* if not *de jure*, in a position to do, and this they did. As a result serious—to the rearmost *échelons* fatal—delays were imposed on all Russian traffic. 'Position now is,' a British officer wired to Vladivostok from somewhere near Bogotol, 'that all Russian *échelons* from the front eastwards are at a standstill and consequently are being captured by Reds at rate of about ten to twenty a day.'[196] Many of these trains carried women, children, wounded and the sick. Probably there were more survivors than seemed likely at the time, but even if all the rumours of massacres were untrue many must have perished after being evicted from their trucks.

The decision to force Kolchak to take his place in the queue (for events were to prove that the incident at Mariinsk was not caused by a subordinate's excess of zeal) was a deliberate act of policy by the Czech leadership, at which Janin connived. On the 13th (the day on which Kolchak's trains were switched) Syrový, who had been down the line but had avoided a meeting with the Supreme Ruler, telegraphed to Janin that 'to ensure the Admiral's personal safety and in view of the state of feeling among the [Czech] troops, it was better that he should take his place in the main stream of traffic.'[197]

On the next day Syrový, back at Irkutsk, made a personal report to Janin. He painted a picture of 'inextricable disorder'—frozen locomotives, a foot of ice on the rails, strikes and desertions among the railway personnel, declining morale among the rearmost Czech *échelons*. Kolchak was said to be 'half mad with anger'; his staff were drinking heavily. Feeling against him was so strong that it would be imprudent to give his trains priority, thus further enflaming the general resentment. Janin's comment betrays the satisfaction with which he received this news; 'I ordered Syrový,' he wrote, 'to draw up a report on the situation; it would be widely circulated.'[198]

Although Janin's complicity is clear, it is uncertain who bore the ultimate responsibility for the decision to side-track Kolchak's trains a month after they left Omsk. Syrový, the Czech Commander-in-Chief, was a bleak, plodding sort of man who would have been unlikely to take the initiative in a matter of this unusual kind. The likeliest guess is that the action was resolved upon by the Czech political leaders in Irkutsk; they had been bitterly hostile to Kolchak ever since the *coup d'état*, they may well have been influenced by their many friends among the local Socialist-Revolutionaries, and they would have had no difficulty in securing Syrový's co-operation. The purpose of the manoeuvre can only be surmised; but the longer Kolchak was delayed *en route* the shorter would be the life of his tottering régime in Irkutsk, and it could not be too short for his enemies there, whether Russian or Czech.

Unreasonable is the mildest of the epithets which can be applied to the decision to deny the use of the up-line to the Supreme Ruler's trains. It is true that there were seven of them (five more, as Janin was to repeat *ad nauseam* afterwards, than the Tsar used to travel with, six more than the Grand Duke Nicholas required), and it is true that it would have been troublesome for the Czechs to fit seven extra trains into their own movement-tables; but that is the most that can be said to justify their action. It cannot be seriously argued that Kolchak's convoy would have endangered, disrupted or materially delayed the Czech evacuation, or that, leaving protocol, common courtesy and even humanity out of it, the natural thing to do would not have been to give the Supreme Ruler a fair wind.

Among Kolchak's entourage all hopes that the ominous incident at Mariinsk was due to a misunderstanding were soon dispelled. Their trains, caught up in the endless traffic-jam on the down-line, made only a few miles a day. At stations the engines were uncoupled, allotted to other trains and replaced after much delay. Junior Czech staff-officers stuck to the letter of their orders, which armoured trains stood by to enforce. Nothing was done about providing a Czech liaison officer. One of Kolchak's officers was arrested. At Krasnoyarsk, which they reached on 17 December, the whole convoy was immobilised for almost a week. A stream of telegrams from the Supreme Ruler's train conveyed protests and appeals for help to Janin, who ignored them.

It was about now—the exact date is uncertain—that Kolchak made a serious mistake. In a cipher telegram to Semenov, repeated to Horvath in Harbin, he gave orders that the Czech withdrawal was to be halted at all costs, if necessary by the demolition of bridges and tunnels; this telegram fell into the hands of the Czechs and was decoded by them.

It was virtually a declaration of war. Destruction of the forty tunnels round the south of Lake Baikal, or even of a few o them, would have blocked the Trans-Siberian for an indefinite period. Semenov, within whose grasp this vital bottleneck lay, was even more cordially detested by the Czechs than was Kolchak. That the latter should seek to thwart their escape from Siberia was bad enough; that he should use Semenov as his instrument made the project doubly odious. The Czechs had provoked Kolchak into giving them a pretext for what they were already doing to him; the fact that what they were already doing to him was wrong, and did not differ in essentials from what he had ordered Semenov to do to them, was neither here nor there. From now on the Supreme Ruler could expect no mercy from the Czechs.

Strictly speaking, it was not the dispatch of the telegram

but the discovery of its contents that so adversely affected Kolchak's destinies. Yet it is worth considering Kolchak's orders to Semenov, not as evidence which was used against him by the Czechs, but as evidence of his own state of mind. If those orders had been carried out—if the tunnels had been destroyed —he would have paid the Czechs out, many times over, for the insults and delays to which they had exposed him. But he would have cut his own throat in the process. By severing rail communications with Vladivostok he would have extinguished the last faint hope of re-forming a front on which the Bolsheviks could be held, and he would have sealed the doom of his Government, of his armies and of himself. After making allowance for the appalling stresses from which he and his companions suffered as they inched their way from one humiliation to the next, Kolchak's telegram to Semenov suggests that his mind was now entirely absorbed by his ordeal, that for him, as for a bull in the arena, the only purpose left in life was to strike back at his tormentors.

The Czech monopoly of the up-line and their high-handed treatment of the Supreme Ruler aroused furious resentment all along the Trans-Siberian; even Kolchak's critics took umbrage at the insult offered, through his person, to the Russian nation. General Kappel, who had succeeded the discredited Sakharov as Commander-in-Chief and was striving with some success to keep a rearguard in being, reacted violently. The Supreme Ruler, he telegraphed to Syrový on 16 December, had been exposed to humiliations and threats which constituted an affront to the whole Russian Army. 'Your order holding up all the Russian *échelons* . . . has already caused the loss of 120 trains full of the wounded, the sick, and the wives and children of officers and soldiers who are fighting at the front.' He called upon Syrový to rescind his order and apologise to the Supreme Ruler; failing this, 'I, as Commander-in-Chief of the Russian Army whose honour it is my duty to defend, shall demand that you give me satisfaction on the duelling-ground.'[199] His telegram, couched in dignified and moving language, was repeated to most of the principal Russian and Allied authorities in Siberia. Janin told Syrový to treat it as the product of a deranged mind, and no answer was returned to the first challenge to single combat issued by one commander-in-chief to another in modern warfare.

Hardly had the furore created by Kappel's wild gesture died down when the wires hummed with a telegram, dated 20 December, from Semenov to Syrový. After expressing in flowery terms his admiration for his 'Czechoslovakian brothers,' he drew their attention to the havoc they were creating on the railway and to their inadmissible conduct towards the Supreme Ruler. 'Brothers!' he urged them. 'Stop! Pull yourselves together! What are you doing? . . . Turn with bared breasts against the enemies of humanity who, in the trains which you have caused to be abandoned, are butchering without mercy sick and wounded soldiers, women and children.' Filled though he was with brotherly love and regard for them, he must insist that they clear the line to Irkutsk for the Supreme Ruler, the non-combatants and—here he declared a genuine interest—'the valuables which represent the last assets of the Russian Government.' If they ignored these demands, 'I will compel you, with a heavy heart but with all the resources at my disposal, to fulfil your duty to humanity and to your tortured sister, Russia!'[200]

This threat, unlike Kappel's, had to be taken seriously. Textual evidence strongly suggests that Syrový's reply was drafted by Janin. Dispatched on the 22nd, it opened with a fulsome preamble in which the Ataman's professions of esteem were warmly reciprocated. It went on to assert, with due respect, that Semenov was imperfectly seized of the true situation. Lack of coal was at the root of all the trouble on the railway; measures taken by the Czechs were already relieving the congestion. As for the Supreme Ruler, the passage of seven two-engined trains over a coal-less stretch of the line was a difficult matter; he could (here the telegram lapsed into deliberate falsification) have continued his journey from Krasnoyarsk in his personal train if he had not insisted on waiting for the other six. Steps were now being taken—this again was untrue—to extricate Prime Minister Pepeliaev's train and the one containing the gold.

The peroration, gracefully combining spurious cordiality with a hollow threat, is a minor masterpiece of crooked diplomacy.

> Our tour of duty in Siberia [Janin telegraphed in Syrový's name] has been painful; not a day has passed on which we have not endured torments. One of the worst torments is to see the misunderstanding of our conduct which has misled a man whose gallantry and military prowess have not failed to earn our fraternal esteem. It would cause us very deep regret to find ourselves obliged, sword in hand, to cut our way through his territory, when our sole desire is to return in peace to our Fatherland, without expecting a word of thanks for the services we have rendered or the blood we have shed.[201]

Kolchak, meanwhile, was still held up at Krasnoyarsk, whence on Christmas Eve one of the long series of telegrams sent by his staff to Janin mentioned, as an additional argument in favour of expediting their departure, the fact that at Krasnoyarsk it was impossible to make adequate arrangements for the security of the Gold Reserve. Next day—it may well have been by coincidence—the Supreme Ruler resumed his journey eastwards. On 27 December his trains reached Nizhne Udinsk where, hemmed in by armoured trains and covered by Czech machine-guns, they were to spend the best part of two weeks. The local Czech commander, Major Hassek, would say no more than that he had orders to isolate the station from the town, which was in the hands of insurgents, and to enforce strict neutrality. Attempts to communicate by telephone with Janin at Irkutsk, now less than 300 miles away, proved vain; the general, Kolchak was told, was not available.

IRKUTSK AND ENVIRONS

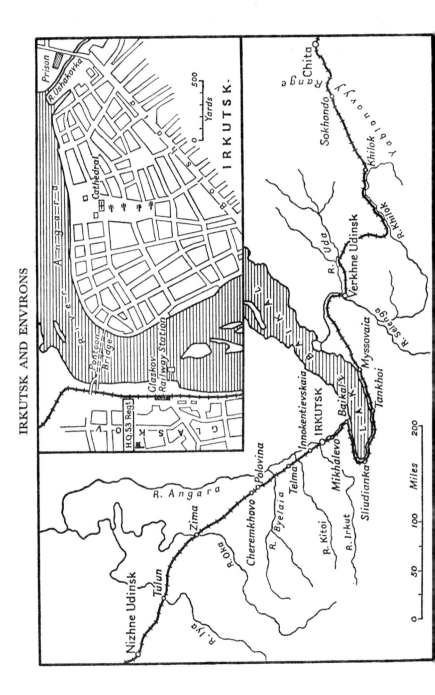

CHAPTER SEVENTEEN

Events at Irkutsk

FORTY-FOUR miles to the south-east of Irkutsk the River Angara—the sole effluent from one of the largest and easily the deepest of the world's lakes—debouches from Baikal. Irkutsk is by Siberian standards an old city; the fortified settlement from which it developed was established in 1652 on the right bank of the Angara. It is thus, as the map opposite shows, on the far side of the river from the railway which, after depositing passengers for Irkutsk at a station in the suburb of Glaskov, follows the left bank of the Angara towards the tunnels of Baikal.

In those days the station was linked to the city during the summer by a pontoon bridge. Before the river finally froze over in the winter, rendering a bridge unnecessary, huge blocks of ice, fragments of floes from the lake, were swept down by the current and disrupted the pontoons: so that for a week or two communication between the station and the city was possible only by boat. In 1919 the bridge gave way on 22 December.

At that date Irkutsk was still nominally subservient to the Supreme Ruler's Government. But the Prime Minister, Pepeliaev, was detained by the Czechs down the line, the Foreign Minister, having gone off to see Semenov on affairs of state, was continuing his journey to Paris, and the Ministers who remained behind were a gaggle of nervous nonentities. The garrison was unreliable; so was its commander, General Sychev. The régime which had so nearly been recognised by the Powers as the *de facto* Government of Russia had dwindled to a handful of agitated men confabulating about inessential matters in the bedrooms of a provincial hotel.

Their local adversaries, a coalition of Socialist-Revolutionaries and Mensheviks known as the Political Centre, went into action on the night of 23 December. In Irkutsk, after a little half-hearted fighting, the insurgents were left in control of the northern outskirts, but Sychev's forces, which included the pupils of a cadet school, still held the centre of the city. On the next day—Christmas Eve—the 53rd Siberian Regiment, quartered just behind the railway station in Glaskov and smartly dressed in British uniforms, declared for the Political Centre; and on Christmas Day Sychev announced his intention of bombarding the station, thus creating a situation of more than local interest.

In the station, which directly overlooks the half-mile-wide river, were the trains of the British, the French, and the Japanese High Commissioners; of the American Consul-General from Omsk, who for practical purposes counted as a High Commissioner; of General Janin and the French Military Mission; and of the Czech Commander-in-Chief, General Syrový, whose troop-trains packed the sidings. What was left of the Supreme Ruler's artillery was about to engage a target-area in which were concentrated what was left of his allies.

Janin took a leading part in handling this awkward situation. He declared the station and its environs a neutral zone, and after endless comings and goings across the Angara both sides were prevailed upon to accept this arrangement. The solution favoured the insurgents, for it meant that they could complete their preparations for an attack across the ice from Glaskov— the river was rapidly freezing solid—without worrying about their opponents' guns (although in reality these were too few and too poorly manned to have made any serious difference); and it looked as if the last remnants of the Supreme Ruler's power might vanish at any moment into limbo.

But on 27 December came startling news. A strong detachment of Semenov's forces, spearheaded by three armoured trains and commanded by a frightful man called Skipetrov, was reported to be advancing to the relief of Irkutsk and to have reached Mikhalevo, twenty miles down the railway from Glaskov. This development was equally unwelcome to the Political Centre, whose prospects of securing control of Irkutsk now suddenly receded, and to the neutrals in the railway station, which threatened to become the scene of hostilities more serious than those that had just been narrowly averted.

On 23 December, in the last telegram he was able to send before his trains were impounded by the Czechs at Nizhne Udinsk and he was cut off from communication—save by courtesy of his warders—with the outside world, Kolchak had appointed Semenov Supreme Commander of all armed forces in Siberia and the Far East.[202] It was under this mandate (and very probably with a view to, if possible, sequestrating the Gold Reserve) that Semenov had dispatched his expedition to Irkutsk; it was followed, discreetly, by half a battalion of Japanese infantry. Janin and the High Commissioners sent urgent messages along the line to stop it; but Colonel Skipetrov came on, and the insurgent troops in Glaskov showed signs of panic.

The situation was saved by some railway-workers, who raised steam in a locomotive and launched it down the line with the throttle wide open. It met the leading armoured train head on and derailed it. Confused fighting followed on the outskirts of Glaskov, where 168 men of Skipetrov's detachment—64 of them Chinese and Mongols—were taken prisoner; then the new-comers withdrew across the frozen river into Irkutsk, made contact with General Sychev and two days later returned whence they had come.

If, on the first day of 1920, Kolchak's cause can be said to have been still alive, the failure of Skipetrov's foray can be said to have killed it. To Kolchak personally, held virtually incommunicado at Nizhne Udinsk, it no longer made any difference whether the last vestige of his authority disappeared on a Tuesday or on a Friday. He was nevertheless to be adversely affected by one by-product of Semenov's intervention. On

2 January Sychev's Chief of Staff signed an order handing over to Skipetrov, 'for transfer to the east,' thirty male prisoners and one female prisoner from the cells reserved for 'politicals' in the Irkutsk gaol.[203] Skipetrov took these persons away with him, pinioned and roped together in pairs; they would serve as hostages if he ran into trouble.

An uneasy truce now prevailed in Irkutsk, where the failure of the municipal power-plant combined with an acute shortage of fuel to make life extremely austere. In Glaskov station the High Commissioners presided—as intermediaries, not as arbiters—over the final dissolution of the régime to which they were accredited. Its representatives refused to have any direct contact with the delegates of the Political Centre, and negotiations (if such they can be called) were carried on with the former babbling away in Janin's train and the latter, who made more sense and had better manners, installed in the British High Commissioner's. Messengers carried from one train to the other the small, rare fruits of their deliberations.

The farce lasted for two days. On the evening of 4 January firing was heard in Irkutsk, and it became known that General Sychev had absconded, after unsuccessfully attempting to requisition the contents of the State Bank. Next day the Political Centre were undisputed masters of the city. A spate of proclamations promised freedom, justice, peace with the Bolsheviks, friendship with the Allies and the convocation of a Siberian Council which would prepare the ground for a Constituent Assembly. The atmosphere of political euphoria was marred only by a growing anxiety about the thirty-one hostages removed by Skipetrov to an unknown destination.

Meanwhile Kolchak, his trains and the Gold Reserve were still held in preventive detention by the 6th Czech Regiment in the station at Nizhne Udinsk. The question of the Supreme Ruler's future had been under almost continuous discussion at Glaskov, both among the High Commissioners themselves and between the delegates of the rival factions in Irkutsk. From the first the Political Centre, although officially stigmatising

Kolchak as an enemy of the people, had been ready to grant him a safe-conduct to the east; but he was still 300 miles from the Political Centre's sphere of influence, and the intermediate territory was controlled by elements fiercely hostile to him.

On 1 January, after a long and anxious discussion, the High Commissioners resolved on a course of action which they hoped would meet the demands of a situation in which they themselves had no executive power and very little moral influence. They addressed to Janin, as Commander-in-Chief of the Allied troops in Siberia, the following directive:

> The Allied High Commissioners declare that all measures must be taken to ensure, as far as it is humanly possible to do so, the personal safety of Admiral Kolchak.
>
> If Admiral Kolchak finds himself obliged to appeal in this matter for the protection of Allied troops, it is incontestably the duty of such troops to afford him protection and to take the necessary steps to assure his conveyance to whatever place shall be designated by the Allied Governments, bearing in mind the need (should it arise) of negotiating with all parties concerned.
>
> Should Admiral Kolchak consider that circumstances are not such as compel him to seek the protection of Allied troops, it is clearly possible that a situation will arise in which it will be difficult for the Allied troops to decide what action to take. The matter then becomes a question of Russian internal politics, in which Allied troops cannot be expected to intervene. Even so, however, it will be their duty to make every effort to ensure the personal safety of Admiral Kolchak by resorting to methods of conciliation. [204]

This was the final form of the directive, which Janin accepted without demur; an earlier draft, which has not survived, was re-worded to meet his objections.

From now on Janin's attitude was to have a decisive influence on Kolchak's destiny. The French general's conduct was, to put it mildly, equivocal. On 26 December he had wired to

Paris: 'Nobody knows where Kolchak is and it will be a difficult matter to save his life.'[205] The second of these statements was perhaps, even at that stage, a fair comment on the situation; the first was disingenuous if not completely untrue. If Janin did not know exactly where Kolchak was when he sent the wire (and the chances are that he did know) he could easily have checked the location of the Supreme Ruler's trains with Syrový's staff. If Janin wanted to open the minds of the French Government—and of the Czech representatives in Paris, to whom his telegrams were repeated—to the notion that Kolchak might have to be written off, the message quoted above would have served his purpose well.

The impression that Janin—and Syrový, who was under Janin's orders—had turned their thumbs down is borne out by their refusal, despite repeated appeals from Nizhne Udinsk, to communicate on the direct line with Kolchak or with members of his staff. 'The Czechs,' one of these officers wrote in his diary, 'outwardly agreed to summon this or that person to the telephone, but when the conversation began it turned out that either communications were cut or the person wanted had not come to the instrument. The general impression was that neither the Czechs nor Irkutsk desired to hold converse with us.'[206]

On 1 January—the day on which he accepted responsibility for securing Kolchak's personal safety 'as far as it is humanly possible to do so'—Janin replied to a somewhat incoherent questionnaire which originated with the commanding officer of the 6th Czech Regiment at Nizhne Udinsk. This had been forwarded, with comments, by HQ 1 Czech Division to Syrový, who presumably asked Janin to deal with it.

The 6th Regiment reported that the insurgents at Nizhne Udinsk had demanded (among other things) that Kolchak should resign: that the Gold Reserve and the Admiral's armoured train should be handed over to them: and that the Supreme Ruler's staff and bodyguard should be disbanded. The local population was in a state of ferment, and failure to comply with these demands was liable to provoke sabotage of the railway which would prevent any further progress by the Admiral's—or anybody else's—trains. What, the 6th Regiment asked, were they to do?

Janin replied at length. He did not, as most men in his position would have done, transmit to the troops whom it most closely concerned the directive which he had accepted as binding upon them. His orders emphasised the need to observe a strict neutrality. 'We can intervene only if the Admiral seeks our protection and renounces military action'; in this event 'we have an international mandate and a strict duty to protect him,' and he would be transported in a train flying the flags of America, Great Britain, France, Japan and Czechoslovakia. There followed instructions that the Gold Reserve should be taken under close guard for eventual disposal in the best interests of the Russian people as a whole.

The telegram may have left the 6th Regiment in some doubt as to what the Allied Commander-in-Chief really wanted them to do about Kolchak; but their duties in relation to the gold were defined with precision. Its future was explained to the local revolutionary authorities, two of whom were summoned to inspect the bullion before the Czechs formally took charge of it. These simple fellows came in the expectation that the gold was to be weighed in their presence; when it was explained to them that such a process would take more than two months to complete, and that there were in any case no scales available, they peered sagely at a few ingots taken from one of the twenty-nine waggons and went back, wondering, through the silent frozen darkness into the little town.

For seven weeks Kolchak and his retinue had lived at intolerably close quarters in their crowded and generally immobile trains. Delay, frustration and a growing fear dominated their lives. They had nothing to do, nothing to discuss except the steadily fading prospects of release from the trap in which they found themselves. Tempers grew short, loyalties were eroded, nerves gave way under the strain.

At Nizhne Udinsk there was some wild talk of abandoning

the railway and making across country for Mongolia, with part of the Gold Reserve loaded on sledges. The Czechs, reasoning that once they got Kolchak off their hands their eastward progress would be smoother and more expeditious, fostered this project with the loan of maps and advice on Partisan dispositions; but nothing came of it, partly because it was realized that, whereas Kolchak could safely go on to Irkutsk under Allied protection, the hazards—great enough already—of a 250-mile trek across country would be considerably increased if he accompanied it.[207]

On 5 January orders reached Nizhne Udinsk that Kolchak could proceed to Irkutsk under Allied escort on condition that he surrendered his trains and travelled in a single coach with only such staff as could be accommodated in it. His reaction was characteristic. 'The Admiral,' his Quartermaster General telegraphed to the High Commissioners, 'has ordered me to inform you that for moral reasons he cannot abandon his subordinates to the fury of the mob and he is resolved to share their fate, however terrible it may be.' The telegram went on to demand that facilities should be provided on the railway for all those who wished to accompany the Supreme Ruler.[208]

For some days, however, it had been apparent—though possibly not to Kolchak, who rarely emerged from the *coupé* which he shared with Timireva—that his sorely-tried entourage was disintegrating. The news that the Allies regarded them as expendable brought this process to a head. 'The soldiers first timidly and then impudently began to pack their belongings and arms, and in groups left for the town, having torn off their shoulder-straps.* The band went into the town playing the Marseillaise.'[209] Kolchak formally released the officers from their duties towards him and ordered them to act as their interests and their consciences dictated. On 6 January the Quartermaster General was able to despatch a second telegram. In view of local developments, he told the High Commissioners,

* Presumably the purple-and-white shoulder-straps, described in Chapter Thirteen which identified them as members of the Supreme Ruler's household troops.

it was now possible for the Admiral and his personal staff to travel in one coach; he urged that arrangements for the journey should be expedited in view of the uncertain situation.

On the same day (6 January) Kolchak sent a cipher telegram to Janin, repeating it *en clair* to his now non-existent Government in Irkutsk. It announced his resignation of 'supreme power throughout all the Russias' (a phrase that came with sad irony from a man confined behind foreign bayonets in a second-class railway-carriage) in favour of General Denikin, commanding the Armies of the South; he would, Kolchak added, sign the formal instrument of resignation on arrival at Verkhne Udinsk in Trans-Baikalia.

This was a move that has an appearance of shrewdness and may well, therefore, have originated in some mind less impulsive than Kolchak's. Verkhne Udinsk, beyond Baikal, was in the zone of the Japanese and American garrisons. However impotent *de facto*, Kolchak was still *de jure* the Supreme Ruler; and there was a sporting chance that the Allies, of whose preoccupation with protocol Kolchak had had considerable experience, might attach importance to legitimising both his own abdication and Denikin's succession. If they did, they would want his signature; by announcing that it would be forthcoming at Verkhne Udinsk, he improved his chances of being escorted to a region where the hostile and detested Czechs would no longer be the only effective representatives of the Allied forces. The gambit was the last card in his hand. It was not a trump, it was not an ace, but it might take the trick and in any case he lost nothing by playing it.

In Glaskov station the queer little foreign colony was slowly dispersing eastwards. The trains of Consul-General Harris and of Miles Lampson, the British High Commissioner, got their long-awaited engines and, after tossing a coin to decide who should have precedence, steamed out on 4 and 5 January. Men with axes were busy freeing the trains of their colleagues, which, as always after a prolonged halt, were anchored to the permanent way by great stalactites of discoloured ice depending from lavatories and kitchens. The half-battalion of Japanese infantry who had arrived on Skipetrov's heels were enigmatically ensconced in a siding; it was given out that they had come to supervise the evacuation of their nationals.

Janin, the last of the senior Allied representatives to leave, seems to have done so on 8 January, after being invested with the Order of the Sacred Treasure by the head of the Japanese Military Mission. Although about half the troops nominally under his command were still strung out along the railway to the west of Irkutsk, it would be unfair to suggest that his departure was premature. He was, he wrote afterwards, suffering from strain and insomnia, and even for a fit man the temptation to quit the sordid, claustrophobic surroundings in which he had spent a harrowing fortnight would have been overwhelming. He may well, too, have felt that he could do more for the Czechs by ironing out difficulties in Semenov's territory than by breathing down General Syrový's neck at Glaskov; and it goes without saying that he had no wish to be anywhere near Irkutsk when Kolchak arrived there.

It was on the night of the 8th that the Supreme Ruler resumed, in greatly reduced circumstances, his progress to the east. Before the *échelons* left Nizhne Udinsk two Czech officers entered Kolchak's carriage and said that they had orders to verify his presence in it. 'The Admiral went out into the corridor and said sharply "Yes, I am here." It was evident that it was hard for the Admiral to pronounce these words and that this inspection was insulting.' [210]

Soon afterwards the 1st Battalion's train, to which Kolchak's coach was attached, pulled out of the station. Not far ahead of it, in the custody of the 3rd Battalion, the Gold Reserve was already rumbling through the night towards Irkutsk.

General Maurice Janin

General Jan Syrový

CHAPTER EIGHTEEN

Journey's End

SOMETIMES, when men privily commit an enormity, the first inklings of what has happened, however faint and indirect, seem to be tainted with the horror of the deed, are instantly recognisable as danger-signals, as evidence that something very bad has been done. It was thus in the matter of Skipetrov's hostages.

On 3 January—the day after they had been handed over—Kolchak's moribund Government in Irkutsk furnished the High Commissioners with two short declarations concerning 'the fate of personalities arrested in connection with the uprising'; all these, it was stated, 'are alive and have not been exposed to any form of violence.'[211] But the rumours multiplied as the days went by; and the enquiries, appeals and protests which reached the Allied representatives had all this same indefinable ring of doom. It was as if, although nobody knew what had happened, everybody sensed that it was something terrible. The main facts became known on the 8th.

The thirty-one political prisoners were a mixed bag of Socialist-Revolutionaries, Mensheviks and persons of vaguely Liberal sympathies; one was a young woman. None of them had been charged with an offence, let alone convicted of it. They had been arrested by Kolchak's counter-espionage service in Irkutsk merely because the town was in a state of political upheaval and they were—or had been found in the company of—the sort of people who might be expected to be against the Government; if the Bolsheviks had been in power they would have run an equal risk of being summarily imprisoned by the Tcheka.

Although they were spoken of as 'hostages,' it is not clear how

Skipetrov intended to use them in this role. He had no reason to expect that his return to Trans-Baikalia would be seriously opposed, and it is not easy to see for what advantages or concessions he proposed, at need, to barter their lives. He was, however, himself a vile man, and he was accompanied by two of the worst sadists produced by either side in the Civil War—the gangling Colonel Sipailov and Captain Grant, a renegade Englishman. The balance of probability is that, rather than return empty-handed from an operation which had cost him heavy casualties, including at least one armoured train, he decided that human booty was better than no booty at all, and prevailed on Sychev to hand over the political prisoners, who otherwise, in the precarious state of their captors' régime, might escape being brought to what passed in White Siberia for justice.

Skipetrov left Irkutsk on 3 January, and on the evening of the 5th embarked with his henchmen and their captives on the ice-breaker *Angara* on Lake Baikal.* The prisoners were herded into third-class cabins next to the engine-room, and the vessel sailed after dark.

A drinking bout continued through most of the night in the first-class saloon. Soon after dawn the prisoners were brought up there, one at a time. Each was ordered to surrender his valuables, to strip and to sign an undertaking to leave Russian territory in three days (an obviously impossible feat). It was indicated that he would be issued with prison garb, and he was in fact given a vest and drawers before being led up on deck, where there were some forty degrees of frost. Here he was immediately clubbed to death with a long-handled wooden mallet used by the crew for chipping ice off the ship's upper works.† The corpse was thrown overboard. The tireless executioner was a man called Godlevski.

Partly because this routine was sometimes varied by Sipailov,

* Although the greater part of this lake freezes over (to such good effect that in the days before the tunnels were built along its precipitous shore the Trans-Siberian trains used to cross it on rails laid upon the ice) the influence of warm springs near the point where the Angara debouches keeps a sizeable stretch of water free from ice throughout the winter.

† This implement is preserved in the Irkutsk Museum.

who when the mood took him, and with the help of some Cossacks, liked to flog a victim in the saloon after he had been stripped, the massacre took some time to complete. It had to be interrupted when the ice-breaker passed within view of, first, a lakeside village and then another ship, but was resumed with a will after these intermissions. Only one prisoner—the last of the men—offered resistance. He was thrown overboard into the freezing water and clubbed over the head when he surfaced until he went under for good. The woman, who seemed to be aged about twenty-eight, was given a thicker pair of drawers than the men, but otherwise received the same treatment; she was the last to be dispatched. At the division of the spoils afterwards Godlevski claimed her fur coat.[212]

The butchers were Semenov's men, but it was by Kolchak's underlings that their victims had been arrested and, later, given into Skipetrov's clutches. Among members of the Political Centre, now the insecure masters of Irkutsk, the revolting crime hardened feeling against Kolchak. 'It created . . . a bitter clamour for revenge. The issue became the condition of the Political Centre's further existence.'[213]

This was not destined to be prolonged. Bands of undisciplined Partisans were converging on Irkutsk, the workers were in an ugly mood, and it was daily becoming clearer that the Bolsheviks were the dominant factor in a chaotic situation. On 11 January their local leader, Krasnoshchekov, left by train to make contact with the 5th Red Army and by the 19th had found its headquarters in Tomsk. Proposals for a semi-autonomous state in Eastern Siberia, with Krasnoshchekov as a sort of Soviet High Commissioner master-minding a Government formed by the Political Centre, were forwarded to the Kremlin and approved by Lenin and Trotsky; but by the 20th the Political Centre, as impotent as the régime it had displaced, had relinquished control of Irkutsk to a Bolshevik Revolutionary Committee, known as Revkom for short.[214]

The last lap of Kolchak's last journey occupied a week. News of the total collapse of his power in Irkutsk had not reached

Nizhne Udinsk when the trains of the 6th Czech Regiment pulled out, nor was it known there that Janin and the High Commissioners had left or were on the point of leaving for Trans-Baikalia. The Allied flags prominently displayed on the second-class coach allotted to the Admiral had a reassuring look, and it was without serious misgivings that more than a hundred officers and men crowded themselves into it. Pepeliaev, the Prime Minister, was accommodated separately in a sort of small guard's van normally used by railwaymen engaged on maintenance work and similar duties. All travellers experience an intense and joyful feeling of relief when, after a period of enforced immobility, they find themselves once more on the move towards their destination; and the Russians were reasonably confident that, forming as they now did an integral part of an east-bound Allied *échelon*, they were on their way to safety and freedom.

This confidence diminished as the 300-mile journey proceeded. Czech sentries—four by day and twelve by night—stood guard in the corridor of Kolchak's coach; at many of the stations—all now in insurgent hands—there were hostile demonstrations. Angry, gesticulating mobs demanded that the Admiral should be handed over to them, and threatened that if this were not done the Czechs would get no coal; if they took the coal by force of arms, the rails would be torn up. In the end the Czechs always managed to appease the revolutionaries, but it soon got about that they did this only by giving assurances that they were taking Kolchak no further than Irkutsk, where he would be delivered to the authorities.

On 13 January his train reached Polovina (the name is the Russian word for 'half,' and the little station marks the midway point between Moscow and Vladivostok). Here a fresh engine was needed, but the local railwaymen refused to produce one unless the Czechs allowed them to place their own guards on the Admiral's coach; these guards would accompany it to Irkutsk and see that the Czechs stood by their undertaking to hand the Admiral over there.

After a long argument the Czechs gave way. Twelve armed

men wearing red rosettes took their places in the corridor, the Czech guard being reduced to one sentry at either end of it. 'We were no longer free and merely under escort—we were now prisoners,' wrote Colonel Malinovsky. Drinking-water, food and fuel for heating had been hard to come by ever since they left Nizhne Udinsk; now they were obtainable, in insufficient quantities, only by bribing the Czechs.

On the 14th, during a long halt at Innokentievskaia, a few miles short of Glaskov, Czech officers hinted to some of Kolchak's staff that they would be well advised to go for a stroll and not come back to the train. Nobody did this, but the air was heavy with forebodings and a last desperate attempt was made to establish contact with General Janin by telephoning up the line. It was, like all previous attempts, a waste of time.

Glaskov was reached in the middle of the following afternoon. A detachment of Red Guards, about a hundred strong, was drawn up in the station; but Czech sentries were posted outside Kolchak's coach, and in its occupants hope was not quite dead. They took comfort from the sight of Japanese soldiers stumping about the platform, gaping curiously up at them. As ten minutes passed, then twenty, then forty, then an hour and still nothing happened, still they were under the protection of the Allied flags, they persuaded themselves that all would yet be well. Some Austrian prisoners, in return for money, brought them bread and water.

At 6 p.m. two Czech officers entered the station, boarded Kolchak's coach and asked to see one of his personal staff-officers, Colonel Rakitin. They had, they said, orders transmitted through the headquarters of the Czechoslovak Army Corps by General Janin that Admiral Kolchak was to be handed over to the local authorities. The guard furnished by the 6th Regiment was about to stand down; the forces of the Political Centre would thereupon assume responsibility for the coach and its occupants.

Rakitin went to Kolchak's *coupé* and broke the news to him. The Admiral insisted that the unfortunate Czechs should repeat their orders to him personally, and this they did. What was being done, they said, was being done on the orders of General Janin; they themselves did not like it at all. 'So the Allies are betraying me?' said Kolchak bitterly. He appeared perfectly calm.

Elsewhere in the crowded coach panic prevailed as officers, tearing off their epaulettes, burst open windows or jumped out of doors in a last-minute bid for freedom. Several, thanks to Czech connivance, got clear away before the Red Guards closed in; others awaited arrest with fatalistic composure. There was a little random shooting at the fugitives, but nobody was hurt.

Some time after order had been restored Kolchak and Pepeliaev were brought out of the train; with them, wearing a nurse's uniform, was Madame Timireva, who refused to be parted from the Admiral. They were closely guarded by a detachment of the Political Centre's meagre forces, but the twelve men who had kept watch over their coach all the way from Polovina were reluctant to leave the centre of the stage at a moment when history was being made in Siberia. They felt a certain proprietory interest in the prisoners, they did not altogether trust the new guards and they were curious to see what would happen to Kolchak; so they deputed four of their number to attach themselves to the party and keep an eye on the proceedings.

Escort and prisoners picked their way over the rails which separate the railway station from the river-bank and set off for Irkutsk across the frozen Angara, the officers' torches casting pale, superfluous beams on the moonlit ice. This ice, formed by a jam of broken floes, was lumpy and irregular and in some places had been holed by shell-fire during the disturbances of ten days ago. Half way across Kolchak put one foot on a weak spot; his foot went through and the *valenka*—a heavy felt boot— he was wearing shipped some water. His guards helped him to take the boot off, empty it and put it on again. '*Merci*,' said Kolchak. They wondered (as indeed must we) why he chose to thank them in French.

On the far bank a staff car and a lorry were waiting, with a cavalry escort drawn up behind them. Kolchak and Pepeliaev were put in the staff car, Timireva shared the driver's cab on the lorry, and the escort piled into the back. They drove off—in low gear, so as not to outpace the cavalry—and a quarter of an hour later drew up outside a long, rectangular stone building on the north-eastern outskirts of Irkutsk. This was the gaol, where the commandant's guards took over, the prisoners were led inside, the gates locked and the escort dismissed.[215]

During the three weeks of life that now remained to him, only a handful of men were to set eyes on Kolchak. One of them was a man from Trans-Baikalia who towards the end of January arrived in Irkutsk to represent his district at a conference which had been summoned to co-ordinate Partisan activities over a wide area. For the delegates to this conference Kolchak was a figure as legendary and ogre-like as Napoleon in his day was for English peasants, and when they learnt that their arch-enemy was confined in the local gaol they asked eagerly to be allowed to have a look at him.

They were told, with a touch of doctrinaire priggishness (the Bolshevik Revkom had by now displaced the Political Centre), that the municipal gaol was 'not a Zoo'; but permission was granted for five of their number to view its most notable inmate. One of these five told me what they saw.

Kolchak and his two companions occupied three adjoining cells in a relatively modern block, which may well have been the infirmary. There was a guard at either end of the corridor, but the cell-doors were not locked and the prisoners were allowed access to one another's quarters; these moreover, though the windows were barred, were 'not like ordinary cells.' They were clean, there were blankets on the bed, chairs and a small table. From a description * of the appalling conditions in other parts of the same prison in the same year it is clear that Kolchak was treated, on the material plane, with a consideration for which the annals of either side in the Civil War can provide few precedents.

* In G. Fedotoff White: *Survival Through War and Revolution.*

Kolchak's bearing and presence made a deep impression on the five Partisans. When the NCO who was in charge of their conducted tour opened the door of his cell they noticed that he addressed the prisoner by the old honorific, *Vashoye Vuisokoye Prevoschodstvo*, meaning 'Your High Excellency.' In the cell they saw a short man with a long nose, deep-set eyes, a sallow complexion and an expression of indifference; he wore a light, sleeveless fur jacket over his uniform, and they could not tell whether the epaulettes—symbols of class-hatred at that period —had been removed. In Soviet caricatures all White leaders were depicted as bloated monsters, degenerate Falstaffs who drooled and ravened with a vodka-bottle in one hand and a pistol in the other. They were surprised, and it seems faintly awed, by the trim, lean figure who underwent dispassionately their brief, almost apologetic inspection. 'Like an Englishman' was the verdict of the five backwoodsmen; one of them had seen British officers in the streets of Vladivostok. They went back into Irkutsk and reported what they had seen to the conference.[216]

CHAPTER NINETEEN

At Bay

IT was the intention of the Soviet leaders that Kolchak should be tried publicly in Moscow, and the 5th Red Army had orders from Lenin to bring him there alive. But although the headquarters of this army had moved forward to Krasnoyarsk soon after Kolchak's arrest, its forces were still being opposed by the remnants of his rearguard under the indomitable Kappel, and he could not with safety be transported westward by rail. He had accordingly to remain in the custody of Revkom at Irkutsk, and here, on 21 January, his interrogation began.

It took place in the gaol, a *venue* chosen as much on grounds of security as of convenience, for Revkom's rule in Irkutsk had as yet little more stability than their predecessors'. It was carried out by an Extraordinary Investigating Commission of five men. This Commission had been appointed by the Political Centre on the eve of its collapse, but three of its members—two Socialist-Revolutionaries and one Menshevik—were retained by the Revkom authorities. 'The presence of these persons,' wrote Popov, the Bolshevik lawyer who was vice-chairman of the Commission, 'had the effect of loosening Kolchak's tongue. He did not see in them his determined and consistent foes.' [217] The chairman was another Bolshevik, Chudnovsky.

The interrogation was in no sense a trial. No charges were preferred, no witnesses called. It is true that, between the seventh and eighth of its nine sessions, a Revkom decree conferred on the Commission the 'function of a Court of Justice,' with powers to inflict the death penalty; but this was due to extraneous and unforeseen circumstances and produced no change in the Commission's methods. Its purposes were thus described by Popov, who wrote a foreword to the transcript of its proceedings when this was published, much later, in Moscow:

> The Commission conducted the examination according to a definite plan. It wanted to reconstruct, through this examination, not only the history of the Kolchak régime as described by its supreme head but also the autobiography of Kolchak, in order to have a more complete picture of this 'leader' of the counter-revolutionary offensive against the young Soviet Republic.

The stenographic record of this leisurely and (until the last day) curiously urbane inquisition is a remarkable document. It is dominated by the personality of the prisoner. Kolchak's bearing, wrote Popov with reluctant admiration, 'was that of the captive commander of a defeated army; and from this standpoint it was entirely dignified. . . . It must be recognised that on the whole his testimony was sufficiently frank.' Popov contrasted Kolchak's demeanour with that of his Ministers, for whose examination Popov was also responsible and in whom he found, 'with rare exceptions, cowardice, a desire to represent themselves as involuntary participants in a dirty business initiated by somebody else, even a desire to paint themselves as having opposed these others.'

The Commission began at the beginning ('*Q.* Are you Admiral Kolchak? *A.* Yes, I am Admiral Kolchak.') and went on to establish the facts that he was forty-six years old, had a wife and a nine-year-old son in France and had been the Supreme Ruler of the Russian Government at Omsk ('It was called All-Russian, but personally I did not use that designation'). Popov next asked about 'a certain Madame Timireva [who] has voluntarily caused herself to be arrested here. What is her relation to you?'

Kolchak: 'She is my good acquaintance of long standing. She lived in Omsk where she was active in my workshop for preparing underwear and distributing it to sick or wounded soldiers. She remained in Omsk until the last days; when I had to leave Omsk owing to military circumstances, she went with me in the train. She stayed in that train until the morning when I was detained by the Czechs. [*This clearly refers to the occasion of Kolchak's transfer from his own train to a second-class coach attached to a Czech échelon.*] When I came here she wished to share my fate.'

Popov then asked: 'Tell me, Admiral, is she not your common-law wife? Have we the right to set it down thus?' This question was prompted by Popov's desire to conform with Bolshevik *mores*, which at that period, with so many homes disrupted by the prevailing chaos, set little store by legal marriage and encouraged the *de facto* recognition of irregular unions. Kolchak answered curtly 'No.'

After these relatively staccato exchanges the proceedings lost the character of an interrogation. During the first day only half a dozen more questions—none of them awkward or hostile— were put as Kolchak told the Commission the story of his early life in a series of monologues which, although long, were clearly and economically worded. His father had served in the naval artillery, fought in the Crimean War, been captured by the French. His mother was of the provincial nobility and came from the Odessa region. He had two sisters, one still living but he did not know where. He himself had been married, 'here at Irkutsk,' in March 1904.

Step by step he took them through his early career in the Navy, the development of a bent for oceanography and hydrology, the growth of unfulfilled Antarctic aspirations, at last the chance to accompany Baron Toll's expedition to Taimyr and the New Siberia Islands in 1900. After three winters in the Arctic, Toll, the leader made a rash reconnaissance to Bennett Island from which he failed to return. Impossible ice-conditions frustrated attempts at rescue, and the rest of the expedition had no choice but to pack up and go home.

In Petrograd the Academy of Sciences, who had sponsored the venture, were deeply concerned about Toll's fate. Kolchak volunteered to organise a relief expedition and 'if necessary, to go to the rescue of Baron Toll even in rowboats.' The scheme, widely condemned as foolhardy, was given the Academy's approval and support; and it was in rowboats (at one stage they spent forty-two days and nights in them) that the young naval officer's party reached Bennett Island, ascertained the manner of Toll's fate and got back to Russia on the eve of the Russo–Japanese War.

By the time he reaches this point in Kolchak's testimony, it will be clear to any reader of it that the Commission was succeeding in the second of its objectives; it was eliciting, without difficulty, from Kolchak an 'autobiography,' a candid account of his career. He gave its objectively. In his narrative a proper pride and a natural modesty did not quite cancel each other out; the flavour of both remained. But the main impression produced by his long, virtually unprompted depositions is of a quest for accuracy, a desire to establish the landmarks and the milestones in a journey which was on the point of ending. 'He knew,' Popov wrote afterwards, 'what was awaiting him. He had no need of concealing anything to save himself. He did not expect and could not expect to be saved, and made no attempts to grasp at straws for that reason.' But there was more to it, one cannot help suspecting, than the grudging generosity of his (in the end) most ruthless interrogator implies.

For more than a year Kolchak had been at odds with fate and with himself, playing a part for which he was not suited in company for which he did not care. He had entertained false hopes, trusted unworthy men, made unforgivable mistakes. The last two months he had spent under restraints of the most painful and humiliating kind, cooped up in a railway-carriage like a wild animal in a cage, forced to endure belittlement, misprision and delay, with nothing to distract his mind from his predicament but the nightmare panorama of defeat unrolling endlessly along the *Trakt* below him. He had sunk swiftly from a great height into total failure, total impotence. Now he was a prisoner, facing certain death.

And yet, in this fell contingency, he seemed to grow in stature and in poise. A sense of release, almost of tranquillity, pervades —until the last day—the evidence he gave to the Commission.

There is no trace in his testimony of the nervous tension, the sudden fits of anger, so often remarked on by the Supreme Ruler's visitors at Omsk. He seems dispassionately interested in what he has to tell, genuinely concerned to get the record straight. Popov explains this frankness by suggesting that Kolchak 'intended [his evidence] not so much for the authorities who were questioning him as for the bourgeois world.' But it seems unlikely—it is indeed scarcely credible—that Kolchak had any expectation that the record of the Commission's proceedings, held *in camera*, would ever be made public; and the idea that he spoke freely in order to impress posterity is as implausible as the theory that he did so in order to facilitate the task of the Commission. The overriding impression produced by his testimony is of a man who welcomes the opportunity to put his life into focus, who does so as exactly as he can, and who finds a strange dreamy satisfaction in the process.

His interrogators never succeeded in getting him to alter or modify his statements, even when he would have lost nothing by doing so. A typical trial of strength came when they questioned him about Russia's defeat by Japan. 'You could not,' urged Alekseevsky, 'help seeing that our failures were due to political circumstances. . . . Did you not come at that time to the conclusion, as did a majority of Russia's intelligent society, that political changes were imperative, even if they had to be obtained in a struggle?'

Kolchak (who had fought, been decorated, wounded and captured in the war) would have none of this. 'In my opinion the chief cause [of our failure] was the manner in which military work was conducted in our navy. . . . The navy did not attend to its business. . . . I believe that the political régime was of secondary importance. If this [naval] work had been handled properly it would have been possible to build up, under any kind of political régime, an armed force that would do its job.'

Again and again they returned to the point. 'At the head of all armed forces was the Emperor. . . . We have a proverb: "Fish rots from the head down." Did it not occur to you that precisely from the top there came nothing but empty words

with regard to responsibilities and leadership?' Kolchak refused to recant. 'I believe the fault was not at the top,' he said,
'but that the fault was ours; we did not do any work,' and he
went on to illustrate his thesis by talking about the low standards
of naval gunnery in 1904. From the top came perfectly sound
orders that the navy should have target-practice—'there can be
no doubt of that, because you understand that it is not likely
that instructions to the contrary should possibly come from
above'—but the execution of those orders was 'horrible, thanks
to the general ignorance, the lack of knowledge among our in-
structors, and the lack of trained persons for the leadership of
the navy.' But ten years later—under the same political régime
—the navy had learnt its lesson; its gunnery in the World War
was excellent. Politics, Kolchak repeated, did not come into it.

Still they would not drop the issue. Surely the disaster of the
Russo–Japanese War had raised some doubts in his mind concerning the Imperial dynasty or the person of the Tsar? 'No,'
replied Kolchak, 'I must frankly confess that it caused me to
have no doubts with regard to the dynasty or with regard to the
person of the Emperor.' And so it went on, day after day, with
Kolchak dominating his interrogators as a bear dominates the
curs that have bayed it: too proud and too honest to trim his
testimony to meet with their doctrinaire requirements, too de-
tached (he was to all intents and purposes a dead man, beyond
their reach) to care much about the impression he created, and
yet so absorbed in the reconstruction of his own past that he
never took the easy way out, never relapsed into a contemp-
tuous fatalism, never said 'Oh, very well. Have it your own
way.'

As his questioners moved gradually forward in time and began to deal with the period of the Revolution and the Civil War,
it might have been expected that Kolchak's replies would show
traces of reserve, of wariness, of circumspection. No such traces
are discernible. Occasionally, where his evidence involved
other individuals, he denied knowledge which he may in fact
have had, or pleaded what may have been a feigned forgetful-
ness. He must of course have known that the greater part of his

Government's archives were in Soviet hands and that, if not available *in toto* to the Irkutsk Investigating Commission, they would certainly have been closely studied by the prosecution when he was eventually brought to trial; so that on some points there was little point in prevarication, and none in lying.

But he spoke freely on many matters which were outside the knowledge not only of his interrogators but of anyone else in Russia. He told them, for instance, the full facts of his connection with the British in Tokyo and Singapore; he mentioned his contacts with the Director of Naval Intelligence at the Admiralty and described his dealings with the Japanese General Staff. All these transactions, however innocent in reality, could have been made to tell against him by a Soviet state prosecutor.

Nor was he prepared to disguise his personal convictions, however abhorrent to his captors and potentially damaging to himself. At one point he confessed to the belief that 'the Bolsheviks had few worthy traits.' At another he was asked: 'What is your personal attitude towards epaulettes? This question [his interrogator added] which is in itself trifling has become a great issue in the Russian life of today.*' Kolchak replied that he personally favoured epaulettes 'on the ground that they were strictly Russian insignia existing nowhere abroad. I considered that when our army wore epaulettes it fought; and after it took them off there came the period of the greatest decline and disintegration and disgrace. I personally wondered what reasons

---

* The epaulettes worn by Russian officers are, as visitors to that country will have noted, of a more massive and elaborate design than those worn in the armed forces of other European states (see illustration facing p. 212). During the Revolution they attracted an odium vaguely comparable to, but infinitely stronger than, that felt in the British Army for the red tabs worn by staff-officers during the First World War. Captured White officers sometimes had their epaulettes nailed to their shoulders. A British witness in Krasnoyarsk after its capture by the Reds spoke of epaulettes littering the streets 'like leaves in autumn.' These insignia, after being officially proscribed as the badges of privilege and reaction, were restored to favour by the Soviet Government in 1942, when, after an unbroken series of defeats at the hands of Hitler's armies, Red Army morale was flagging dangerously. They have been perfectly *comme il faut* ever since.

there were for taking off the epaulettes. All our army always wore epaulettes.' If he had spat on the Red Flag the prisoner could hardly have proclaimed more blatantly his counter-revolutionary bias.

When the Commission ended its eighth session on 4 February it had followed, in often otiose detail, the course of Kolchak's career up to and including the *coup d'état* which had brought him to power in Omsk less than fifteen months ago; it was, in other words, about to come to the heart of the matter. But when it assembled again two days later the atmosphere of its proceedings had undergone a sharp change. The reason for this lay in developments to the west of Irkutsk.

On 15 January, when Kolchak was handed over to the Political Centre at Glaskov, there was still a large number of Czech trains on the wrong side of Irkutsk; the rearmost of them had just passed through Kansk. Their free passage to the east was in theory guaranteed by the Gold Reserve, control of which the Czech High Command had surrendered to the Revkom authorities in return for a safe-conduct; and the Czech rear was, so to speak, padded against the pursuing Bolsheviks by a buffer-force consisting of the Polish division and a Rumanian contingent, over whose *échelons* the Czech staff had been careful to ensure that their own had precedence, and who were deterred from trying to jump the queue by Czech armoured trains.

But the Czechs were not yet out of the wood. They had trouble with the Poles, who felt, with some justice, that they were being left in the lurch; and when the Poles were annihilated or captured almost to a man by the 5th Red Army, they had trouble with the Rumanians until the same fate overtook them. The Czechs were then involved in a series of sharp actions with the Bolshevik advance-guards; they met with hostility from the railway staff and the insurgents who now controlled the stations; and it was not until 7 February that they were able, at a place called Kuitun, to patch up a truce with the 5th Red Army. One article of this truce confirmed that 'the Czechoslovak forces will leave Kolchak and his adherents ar-

A Czech patrol on the River Ob

An armoured train captured from the Bolsheviks

The Irkutsk gaol and the frozen Ushakovka (February, 1961)

Kolchak

rested by Revkom in Irkutsk to the disposition of the Soviet Government under the guard of Soviet troops and will not interfere in whatever course of action the Soviet Power takes in respect of these prisoners.'[218]

The vicissitudes of the Czechs, however, affected events in Irkutsk only in so far as they increased the confusion and uncertainty of the situation along the railway, and thus the apprehension with which the Revkom authorities looked westward. The main cause of their unease, which in the first week of February began to verge on panic, was the dogged, desperate rearguard of Kolchak's armies under Generals Kappel and Voitzekhovski. When, a few weeks earlier, Kappel publicly offered to fight a duel with Syrový, Janin in a telegram to Paris commented sarcastically: 'During our retreat from Russia Marshal Ney fought shoulder to shoulder with his troops and did not bother about challenging people to duels.'[219] The gibe was grossly unfair to Kappel. His troops had no trains and too few horses, yet he kept them together as a fighting force, plodding endlessly along the *Trakt*, painfully by-passing the towns they could not take by assault, turning at bay to strike back at the Red Army when its spearheads caught up with them. Even Janin was constrained to describe their performance in his memoirs as 'an unprecedented feat of endurance,' though he went on to criticise them for not stopping to fight a pitched battle.

Kappel's men captured Nizhne Udinsk on 20 January. They had heard by now of Kolchak's imprisonment and were resolved upon his rescue. At this stage they were marching abreast of the last Czech trains, and were able to buy food from their well-stocked commissariats; payment had to be made in gold. Kappel was suffering from severe frost-bite in both legs (there were many casualties from this cause, as well as from typhus) and a Czech doctor who did what he could for him reported that his life was in danger. The Czechs offered him a place in one of their sick-berths, but Kappel would accept no favours from the men who had betrayed his leader and, mortally ill, continued to brave the pitiless cold on a sledge. He died on 27 January, after handing over command to Voitzek-hovski. The Czechs took his body with them to Chita, and there the best of Kolchak's captains was buried.[220]

His men pressed forward under Voitzekhovski. They took Zima and went on to Cheremkhovo, where the Czechs, seriously concerned about the effect on their evacuation of renewed fighting round Irkutsk and not relishing the possibility of Kolchak's liberation, attempted to deny them the use of the *Trakt* and to prevent them from requisitioning horses employed on the transport of coal to the railway from the neighbouring mines. But Voitzekhovski brushed these obstructions aside and on 2 February was in control of Innokentievskaia, the last station before Glaskov.

These developments caused growing alarm in Irkutsk. Martial law was proclaimed on 29 January, 'siege law' on 2 February. Land-mines were laid in the ice on the Angara, and a quantity of ammunition and other war-like stores was evacuated into the forests to the south of the city, presumably in case Irkutsk proved untenable. But it was physically impossible to disperse the Gold Reserve and patently unsafe to move it eastward by rail into Semenov's territory. Revkom's acute anxiety in this matter is reflected in an order issued on 6 February; this enjoined all concerned with the railway to destroy bridges, tunnels, tracks and all means of transport rather than let the gold fall into the enemy's hands.[221]

Meanwhile attempts at mediation were being made by an Allied triumvirate consisting of General Syrový, Blahos, one of the Czech political leaders, and Captain Stilling, an officer of the British Military Mission who, stranded in Irkutsk, contrived by bluff and adroitness to invest himself with the sort of diplomatic immunity which a consul would enjoy. These three were intermittently in touch with Voitzekhovski by telephone, and through them, on 2 February, the White commander transmitted the terms on which he was prepared to by-pass Irkutsk and leave its rulers unmolested. They were stiff terms, and included the following demands:

Kolchak and those imprisoned with him to be released and handed over to the Allied representatives.

An indemnity of two hundred million roubles, including fifty million in gold and silver, to be paid to the White forces.

A safe-conduct through Irkutsk to be granted for a number of Red Cross trains carrying sick and wounded.[222]

Acceptance of these terms would have exposed the members of Revkom, in due course, to severe retribution at the hands of the Soviet authorities. They accordingly rejected them; only on condition that Voitzekhovski's men handed over their arms would they be allowed to pass through Irkutsk. At this point the negotiations, such as they were, were broken off, and on 4 and 5 February the Whites resumed an advance which brought them into the outskirts of Glaskov. Revkom's position was unenviable. Its own forces were of poor quality, Irkutsk was full of discontent and destitution, there was believed to be a White underground movement in the city, and the attitude of the Czechs in a crisis would be guided solely by their own interests. But in this uncertain situation (closely resembling that which in July 1918 had faced the Tsar's custodians at Ekaterinburg) there was one duty which Revkom must and could perform; on the night of 4–5 February they decided to execute Kolchak and Pepeliaev, subject to the 5th Red Army's approval. This was forthcoming on the evening of the 6th.

CHAPTER TWENTY

A Hole in the Ice

On the morning of 6 February Kolchak appeared before the Extraordinary Investigating Commission for the last time. He had a fair idea of what was in the wind. He knew of Voitzek-hovski's ultimatum, had noted the strengthening of the prison guard, could hear, intermittently, the distant sound of gunfire from across the Angara. Popov recorded the interception—'precisely during those last days, in the course of a search of the prison'—of a note to Timireva in which Kolchak foresaw that Voitzekhovski's intervention 'would only hasten the inevitable end'; this evidence suggests that the prisoners were now more straitly confined and were no longer permitted access to one another's cells.

Kolchak, according to Popov, was nervous on this last day. 'The calm and self-control which marked his previous conduct during questioning left him. The examiners themselves were somewhat nervous and hurried.' They were no longer after a full-length 'autobiography'; they needed damaging admissions about the Omsk régime, they had only a day to get them in, and they set about getting them (as Popov admits) 'in a very haphazard manner.'

At the first eight hearings the average number of questions addressed to Kolchak by his interrogators was twenty-four; at the ninth they asked nearly six times that number. All traces of urbanity had vanished from their manner. They no longer began with 'Tell us, Admiral' or 'Is it permissible to ask?' They themselves were frightened men, and this combined with the necessarily stepped-up tempo of the interrogation to make them hectoring and exigent. But Kolchak, under pressure, held the only part of an indefensible position which it was essential that he should hold. 'Although very nervous,' wrote Popov, 'he nevertheless showed great caution in testifying. He steered clear of even the least chance of supplying material for the indictment of persons who had already fallen, or might fall, into the power of the re-established Soviet rule.'

They began with a series of questions, all asked by Alekseevsky, on matters of marginal importance. Had he met Prince Lvov? Savinkov? General Aprelev? Kolchak was unable to identify Aprelev. What had been his relations with Regnault, the French High Commissioner, to whom he had made an obscure reference in a letter to Timireva? Textually there is not a great deal to distinguish the transcript of the Commission's last hearing from its predecessors until Popov, the lawyer, begins to take a hand in the questioning.

Popov was not interested in abstract matters—in Kolchak's relations with the Allies or his reactions to the Armistice; Popov was interested in arrests and executions, tortures and the taking of hostages, and he knew a great deal about these things. Before long the interrogation, like a kestrel which after swinging and soaring inconsequently over a twenty-acre field suddenly hovers motionless and prepares to swoop, was concentrating its attention on the Kulomzino rising of December 1918 and its brutal repression. Popov had asked few questions during the earlier hearings; this was the occasion for which he had been waiting, and he rose to it.

Popov, as it happened, had been a prisoner in the Omsk gaol at the time of the Kulomzino revolt, and his name had been on the list of those selected for execution in the subsequent reprisals. But he was suffering from typhus, the staff of the gaol refused to hand him over, and Bartoshevski and his fellow-executioners were not prepared to face the risks of entering the ward reserved for typhus-patients and dragging Popov out of it. So Popov survived.

He thus knew at first hand most of what there was to know about the proceedings of the so-called 'field courts martial' and the wholesale shootings which followed or in some cases preceded them ('As Supreme Ruler, you ought to have known that in reality no trials of any sort took place, that two or three officers sat somewhere, and parties of fifty men were brought in and were shot.') He knew about the mass floggings. He knew about the torture-chambers in the counter-espionage department of the Stavka ('I personally saw people sent to the Alexandrovsk Prison who were literally covered with wounds and their flesh torn with iron rods—did you know of it?') And he had studied with diligence the captured records of the ineffective judicial enquiries which the Supreme Ruler had instituted into the more notorious of these atrocities.

To his barbed questions Kolchak could return only lame answers. He had been seriously ill at the time of these incidents. 'I do not remember. . . . I had no such information. . . . Nobody reported to me on that. . . . This is the first time I have heard this.' In hard fact it no longer made the slightest difference what answers he gave. He had nothing to lose, his interrogators nothing to win. But both sides had been playing the same strange game in the same stuffy room for nine days, and although the result was no longer in doubt they were still obedient to the rules, still absorbed in the play. It must have been painful for Kolchak to find himself, for the first time, at a serious disadvantage.

At the end of the hearing he was fighting back, gaining a little ground. From the ethics of shooting hostages the Commission had passed to the question of burning down villages by way of reprisal. Kolchak said that he had never formally sanctioned such action, 'but I believe that during fighting and suppression of rebellions, such a measure is inevitable and one is compelled to have recourse to it.' He knew of three cases of villages being razed, 'but these cases, so far as I understood, were of a military nature, as they were fortified points which became destroyed in battle.'

Garrisons, they suggested, could have been left in such places: upon which Kolchak tried, in the last words he addressed to the Commission, to recall them to the harsh realities of civil war.

In the Urals, he said, a captured revolutionary had told him of finding people in one village whose ears and noses had been cut off by the White troops. Kolchak did not deny that this was possible, whereupon the man described his reaction; he had amputated a prisoner's foot, tied it to him with string and sent him back to the White lines. 'To this I could only say to him: "Next time, possibly, people, on seeing one of their own with a foot hacked off, will burn down a village and massacre its people. This is usually done in war and in a struggle." '

While these words were being taken down by the stenographers the Commission rose and Kolchak was escorted back to his cell.

Some time that evening Revkom were notified that the Revolutionary Military Soviet of the 5th Red Army had approved their proposal to liquidate Kolchak and Pepeliaev, and they set about preparing a proclamation announcing that the sentences had been carried out. Self-justificatory in tone, it recorded that there was a secret White organisation in Irkutsk; arms had been hidden, mysterious movements were going on, portraits of the Admiral were being circulated in the town; Kolchak had already been declared an outlaw; to prevent unnecessary casualties involving harmless people he and Pepeliaev had been shot. It was better that two prisoners should be killed than that hundreds of innocent persons should lose their lives.[223]

In the small hours of 7 February 1920 a firing squad arrived by lorry at the prison. They were accompanied by the Town Commandant of Irkutsk and by Chudnovsky, the Chairman of the Extraordinary Investigating Commission. Chudnovsky (whose evidence cannot be regarded as wholly reliable) claims that he found Kolchak shaved and fully dressed to go out, wearing a fur coat and a fur hat, and that, although his bearing was calm and dignified, he made an unsuccessful attempt to swallow poison when told that he was to be taken for execution. This last detail is inherently implausible since, if Kolchak had poison on him, it would have been as easy to take it in good time as it was to put on his fur coat by way of preparation; from a topo-graphical error in his account of the events that followed it seems possible that Chudnovsky's memories of the occasion were blurred, perhaps by alcohol.

The wretched Pepeliaev had broken down and begged on his knees for mercy. A tall, paunchy Siberian (*'fait comme un sac,'* said Janin) of mediocre attainments, he had spent virtually the whole of his Premiership confined in railway-carriages from which it was impossible to carry out any of the functions of his office, and it is hard to see on what grounds—save those of protocol—he was held to have deserved the death penalty. It is not known whether, before the two men were led out, Kolchak was allowed to say goodbye to Timireva in the adjoining cell.

The prison stood, and indeed still stands, on the bank of a tributary of the Angara called the Ushakovka. Roughly a hundred yards downstream, under a slight escarpment, a hole had been cut in the ice below the bank; it was the responsibility of the prison staff to keep it from freezing over. The lip of the escarpment was illuminated by the headlamps of the lorry that had brought the firing squad; its members were drawn up on either side of the bonnet, so as not to obscure the headlamps. In the still, freezing night desultory shooting could be heard to the westward as guards under the prison commandant led Kolchak into the funnel of yellow light. Pepeliaev had to be dragged. Both men were handcuffed.

Kolchak was offered, but refused, a bandage for his eyes. There are various accounts of his last words, none reliable. Only one has, for me, the ring of truth. In this version Chudnovsky asked whether he had a last request to make. 'Would you be so good,' said Kolchak, 'as to get a message sent to my wife in Paris, to say that I bless my son?' 'I'll see what can be done,' replied Chudnovsky, 'if I don't forget about it.'[224] Nothing was done.

A priest was there. Both prisoners said their prayers aloud. Then they were placed, side by side, on the spot where many men, and some women, had looked for the last time on the stars. Pepeliaev's eyes were shut, his face livid. Kolchak was entirely master of himself: 'like an Englishman'—the analogy oddly recurs in an official Soviet account of the execution.[225]

The order was given, the soldiers fired raggedly, both men fell. There was a second and perhaps—visibility was poor—superfluous volley. (Timireva, alone in her cell, could hear the detonations.) The corpses were kicked or prodded over the edge of the escarpment, down the short *piste* of frozen snow discoloured by the transit of their predecessors, into the water and under the ice. Chudnovsky, the Chairman of the Extraordinary Investigating Commission, remained under the impression that they had been committed to the Angara.

Then the firing squad formed up again; while they were about it, there was a third victim to be dispatched. He was a Chinese called Cheng Ting-fan, who had been employed by the Supreme Ruler's security services to do the dirtiest of their work for them in the gaol; he possessed various techniques which had been of great value during interrogations. This horrible creature was frog-marched into position, another volley rang out, and Cheng Ting-fan left this world by a route down which he had supervised many previous departures. The lorry-driver cranked his engine, the soldiers climbed aboard and the vehicle jolted back past the prison, across the bridge just beyond it, over the Ushakovka and into Irkutsk. Behind them dawn was breaking.

CHAPTER TWENTY-ONE

Rights and Wrongs

THE Intervention had failed ignominiously. The last Allied troops had sailed from Archangel on 27 September 1919; the 6th Red Army, unopposed, entered the city five months later, the leading troops being well received by the inhabitants. Denikin, who in the autumn seemed to be almost within striking distance of Moscow, had been decisively routed; in March 1920, with the remnants of his armies pent up in the Crimea, he resigned command of them to Baron Wrangel.

All was not quite over bar the shouting, for the Poles launched a successful offensive deep into the territory of their former overlords, and the French, who were warm supporters of the Polish cause, encouraged Wrangel to break out of the Crimea and create at least a diversion. Wrangel's dash and his enemy's distractions produced a sort of epilogue—as bloody and futile as the chapters preceding it—to the main history of the Civil War; he reconquered a sizeable bridgehead in South Russia, and in August 1920 his administration was given *de facto* diplomatic recognition by the French Government.

But Poland and Soviet Russia made peace in October, the Red Army was able to concentrate against the last bastion of counter-revolution, and Wrangel, throwing in his hand, carried out a remarkably successful evacuation of the Crimea, 100,000 troops and nearly half as many civilians being carried in 126 ships—mostly French and Russian—to Turkey.[226] Wrangel, like Kolchak, was not always well served; and perhaps the picture he drew of his senior army commander in the final crisis may serve as a memorial effigy to the twilight of the White cause.

General Slachtov, earlier described by Wrangel as 'a slave to morphia and a confirmed drunkard, quite incapable of holding a responsible position, however small it might be,' was nevertheless defending the vital Perekop Isthmus, the gateway to the Crimea. To his Commander-in-Chief, visiting the front, he presented

> a terrible spectacle. His face was deadly pale and his mouth never ceased to tremble, while tears streamed from his eyes. . . . Incredible disorder reigned in his railway carriage. The table was covered with bottles and dishes of *hors d'oeuvres*; on the bunks were clothes, playing-cards and weapons, all lying about anyhow. Amidst all this confusion was Slachtov, clad in a fantastic white dolman, gold-laced and befurred. He was surrounded by all kinds of birds; he had a crane there, and also a raven, a swallow and a jay; they were hopping about on the table and the bunks, fluttering round and perching on their master's head and shoulders . . . I insisted on General Slachtov undergoing a medical examination.[227]

In Siberia the shipwreck of all Allied projects—save those of Japan—had been tacitly acknowledged ever since the fall of Omsk, though vague hopes persisted that the gold might be salvaged. The last of the two British battalions, the 1st/9th Hampshires, had sailed from Vladivostok on 1 November 1919. Several of the officers and men were in, or near to, tears as the troopship drew away from the shore; their grief was not due to remorse, or to compassion for the martyred country they were leaving, but to the fact that quarantine regulations, enforced at the last moment, obliged them to leave behind the dogs they had adopted. These poor beasts had thus to be abandoned on the quayside, where they ran to and fro in a frenzy of distress or sat on their haunches, howling.[228]

The French, too, had left: also the Italians. Washington's counsels on the question of withdrawal were so divided, and so confused, as almost to defy analysis. Provocative acts committed by Japanese troops and their Russian *protégés* against

American soldiers and American railway engineers had become increasingly frequent, until 'by the end of August 1919 affairs had reached a crisis.'[229] A note of protest to Tokyo, threatening the withdrawal of all United States troops if this sort of thing did not stop, upset the Omsk Government but failed to elicit a reply from the Japanese for two months. In October General Graves was receiving intelligence reports that Semenov and his lesser fellow-puppets, Kalmykov and Rozanov, were planning an attack on his widely scattered forces; and further diplomatic pressure was applied in Tokyo with inconclusive but vaguely encouraging results.

By now the Omsk régime had collapsed, the Red Army was approaching Lake Baikal and it became obvious that, if the Americans held their ground, they could hardly avoid being embroiled with the Bolsheviks. At this point it was opportunely realised that their original purpose—the rescue of the Czechoslovak Legion—was within sight of accomplishment. In circumstances which for a variety of reasons gravely offended Japan and seriously perturbed China, General Graves was ordered, early in January, to concentrate his force in Vladivostok for evacuation.

The State Department and the War Department, who had been at loggerheads throughout these transactions, now found cause for further disagreement. The State Department contended that if the American garrisons guarding the railway in Trans-Baikalia left for Vladivostok before the Czechs had passed through their zone, the Czechs would have no one to defend them if Semenov turned nasty. The War Department pointed out that there were in Siberia 72,000 Czechs and only about 5000 Americans, and recalled the opinion, hitherto unchallenged, of an expert that if the small American detachments along the railway found themselves in danger, they could always rely on the protection of the Czechs. After this the evacuation was completed without incident, the last American contingent sailing from Vladivostok on 1 April 1920.[230] It was not until two and a half years later that the last Japanese troops were withdrawn.

RIGHTS AND WRONGS

Defeat always breeds recrimination. The Russians accused the Allies of bad faith, the Allies no longer had any need to conceal their conviction that the Whites were corrupt, incompetent and often cowardly. But in Siberia there was one matter which provoked bitter controversy and concerning which the indignation felt by the Russians was widely shared throughout the Allied camp. This was the manner in which Kolchak had been delivered into the hands of his enemies.

In so far as it lay in their power to do so, the Allied High Commissioners had formally guaranteed Kolchak's personal safety. General Janin, as Commander-in-Chief of all Allied troops in the theatre, had accepted from them a directive which made their intentions perfectly clear and which laid on him responsibility for protecting the person of the Admiral if he appealed for protection. By depriving Kolchak of his trains and restricting his communications with the outside world, the forces under Janin's command had left Kolchak with no alternative but to fall in with the arrangements which they made for guarding and transporting him; and in doing so, on 6 January, he asked in so many words to be placed *'sous la garde des Puissances Alliés.'* Although the Czechs had treated him in a high-handed way, their obligations towards him were not in doubt; 'we have,' Janin reminded them, 'an international mandate and a strict duty to protect him.' The Allied flags displayed on his coach were intended to advertise its status as an asylum. Against this background the surrendering of Kolchak—without protest and apparently by pre-arrangement—to the insurgents in Irkutsk was not a pretty deed to contemplate.

It profoundly shocked the High Commissioners, and from Harbin, where news of the affair overtook them, Lampson in Great Britain's name, Kato in Japan's, and even de Maugras in France's, addressed to General Janin a joint protest couched in the strongest terms. They saw in the action of the Czechs the dereliction of a plain duty, and they called on their Commander-in-Chief to account for it. It is evident that they were taken by surprise, that it had never occurred to them that Janin (who did not even notify them of Kolchak's arrest) would allow the Czechs to betray their trust. 'General Janin's action,' Lampson wired to the Foreign Office on 23 January, 'is all the more incomprehensible seeing that above arrangement [the High Commissioners' directive] was drafted in his presence and with his full concurrence; wording was even specially modified to meet his wishes in view of known sentiments of Czech troops to whom its execution had perforce to be entrusted.'[231]

Janin, whose conscience was not clear, had been expecting trouble. After leaving Irkutsk on 8 January he travelled slowly eastwards, compiling as he went voluminous telegraphic reports to Paris. In these the pretence was for a time kept up that his absence from Irkutsk was intended to be temporary only. 'In order to spend a few days outside the city' he had first gone to Sliudianka, at the southern extremity of Lake Baikal, but the railway-sidings there were overcrowded and he moved on a hundred kilometres to Tankhoi; here lack of adequate communications dictated a further retreat to Myssovaia. 'Circumstances will decide,' he told Paris on 12 January, 'whether I return to Irkutsk or continue my journey eastwards.'[232] If Janin had gone back to Irkutsk his arrival there would have roughly coincided with Kolchak's; his memoirs, strongly supported by probability, suggest that he never entertained the project.

On 14 January he was at Verkhne Udinsk, where the American garrison under Colonel Morrow were holding in detention one of Semenov's generals, six officers and forty-eight men. These formed the crew of an armoured train which had been captured by the Americans after firing, by night, into one of their stationary troop-trains. Interrogation of the prisoners revealed that in the last ten days they had murdered more than forty men and (after raping them) three women; they were perforce released when Morrow's contingent left for Vladivostok on 23 January.[233] Skipetrov and his associates also went scot-free, for Janin found himself obliged to yield to Japanese pressure, applied on behalf of Semenov, and the Czechs, in whose custody they were, were ordered to set these butchers at liberty. East of Lake Baikal, an atmosphere of tragedy had been replaced by one of Grand Guignol.

RIGHTS AND WRONGS

On the afternoon of the 14th Janin was called to the telephone by Syrový from Irkutsk. The Czech Commander-in-Chief gave an alarmist report on the prospects facing the Czech rearguard. The miners and the railway-workers were on strike; preparations for armed resistance were being made at Glaskov station (other evidence suggests that this statement was unfounded); popular feeling against Kolchak had been further enflamed by the *Angara* massacre. 'The Czech army was in peril and Syrový apprehended that it would be impossible to escort the Admiral further than Irkutsk,' Janin wrote in his memoirs.

He went on: 'I had been expecting this development for several days and had often thought about it, especially during bouts of insomnia.' He continued however to display, if not indifference to, at any rate a marked lack of curiosity about, the fate of Kolchak. It was only at the end of a long session with a delegation from the Political Centre, which came to see him at Verkhne Udinsk on 16 January, that he asked: 'Can you give me any news of the Admiral?' When they told him that the Czechs had handed Kolchak over to their own forces on the previous day, he dropped the subject, and the meeting almost immediately closed.[234] The delegation was composed of humble, deferential men to whom Janin's attitude was throughout seignorial; it seems strange that he did not do what, surely, anyone else would have done—ask what they proposed to do with Kolchak, or express the hope that he would be humanely treated.

Within a week a deluge of indignant protests was pouring into the train of the French Military Mission, and Janin found that he was widely held responsible for 'betraying' the Supreme Ruler. The vehemence, the promptitude and the sheer volume of his replies suggest that he was not unprepared for the accusation. To former pillars of the Omsk régime, telegraphing their florid denunciations from Harbin or Vladivostok, he ordered his chief of staff to send '*quelques mots sévères*'; their purport was that no Russian who was himself in a place of safety could reproach Janin for not ordering foreign troops to lay down their lives for Kolchak.

But the telegrams of the High Commissioners touched him more nearly, and to them he sent what were intended to be reasoned replies. Lampson described them as 'of immense length' and suggested to the Foreign Office that in view of their tone 'it seems unwise to have any further dealings with General Janin.'[235] The General had (as will be shown below) a stronger case than is apparent from his barely coherent attempts at self-justification.

In these he complains that the High Commissioners ordered him to protect Kolchak but failed to provide him with any of their own national forces with which to accomplish this task. He criticises them for departing precipitately from Irkutsk. He blames the small Japanese detachment at Glaskov for shirking a task—the rescue of Kolchak—which (he repeatedly asserts) it would have been suicidal for the Czechoslovak Army Corps to attempt. He harks back, again and again, to 'a precedent concerning the late Tsar which governed my action,' claiming that, when the Imperial family were arrested, he and some of the other heads of Allied Military Missions in Petrograd had volunteered to undertake their rescue and had earned severe rebukes from their Ambassadors. He argues that, although Kolchak had announced his resignation, he had not actually resigned: that therefore he was still Supreme Ruler when he reached Irkutsk: and that consequently any attempt by the Czechs to protect his person would have been a breach of their strict orders not to intervene in Russian politics. And finally, in the versions of these telegrams which he transmitted to Paris, he makes clear his conviction that 'many men have been shot who have done less harm to Siberia and to Russia than the Admiral, his Ministers and his entourage.'[236]

There are two sides to every question; and, although Janin's apologias make a lamentable impression, Churchill's opinion, recorded nine years later, that 'every allowance must be made for the difficulties of this officer's position'[237] should not be disregarded. Let us look at the matter from Janin's and Syrový's point of view.

Janin contended, with some justice, that he had no right to hazard the Czech rearguard in an attempt to save Kolchak's life; and Syrový, from Irkutsk, represented the consequences of such an attempt as dangerous and perhaps fatal to their prospects of evacuation. It is an undoubted fact that the Czechs had been meeting with hostility, that their eastward progress had been incommoded by strikes (or the threat of strikes) and by an unco-operative attitude on the part of railway personnel and local authorities, and that this was due in some measure to the fact that they appeared to be transporting Kolchak—and the gold—out of reach of the Revolution.

It was also true that Kolchak had given the Czechs every reason to regard him as their enemy, and that they had been particularly incensed by his action in ordering Semenov to prevent their evacuation by blowing up the Baikal tunnels. Parfenov, a Soviet historian of the Civil War, suggests that 'the Czech troops were demanding the handing over of Kolchak,' and Syrový himself wrote afterwards that 'the maintenance of discipline in the Czechoslovak Army made it necessary to relinquish the task of escorting Kolchak.'[238] Although this last statement can hardly be taken at its face value, it remains doubtful whether Syrový could have relied on his orders being obeyed had those orders committed his men to energetic and necessarily risky measures aimed at the transport of Kolchak further than Irkutsk. Had they come from Janin, whose authority over the Legion was never more than titular, any such orders would certainly have been disregarded.

Thus a strong, or anyhow a specious case can be made out in defence of the action taken by Janin and Syrový. 'In spite of the difficulties and dangers threatening our evacuation,' wrote the latter in an official report, 'we actually protected Kolchak for longer than we could afford to';[239] and he further pointed out that in any case Kolchak was not handed over to the Bolsheviks, but only to the relatively moderate Political Centre.

The protestations of Janin and Syrový that the betrayal of Kolchak was a necessity would carry more weight if either of them had ever said, or even implied, that it was a regrettable necessity. Neither did so. 'A good riddance' is the theme which underlies all their attempts at self-exculpation, and this dismissive, this almost vindictive attitude to the man for whose summary execution they must bear some responsibility, is a reminder of the manner in which they had treated Kolchak ever since the fall of Omsk. For two months the Allied Commander-in-Chief in Siberia—who, whatever he thought of the Supreme Ruler, was not totally devoid of obligations towards him—had studiously avoided all contact with him, even over the telephone. For two months General Syrový had delayed, when necessary at gunpoint, the eastward movement of his trains and staff. It is difficult to see in what ways, during that period, these two senior Allied representatives could have done more damage than they did do to the man whose cause it was their duty to support.

Viewed in this perspective, the surrender of Kolchak presents itself, not as the only way out of a critical situation which had suddenly arisen at Irkutsk, but as the logical culmination of a long-term plan for his destruction or abandonment. Who were the authors of this plan, or to what extent it was consciously formulated, it is impossible to determine; all that, on the evidence of the facts, can be said with certainty is that it was successfully carried out. Janin and Syrový assert that they had no alternative but to hand Kolchak over; but neither they nor anybody else made the slightest effort to find out whether there was an alternative, and the evidence that they acted under *force majeure* is unconvincing.

The Political Centre was a moribund administration. Its troops were few and unreliable. The advance-guards of the Red Army were several hundred miles away. Kappel's forces still stood between them and Irkutsk. Although the Czechs alleged that popular feeling along the railway was so inflamed against Kolchak that it was impossible for their trains to convey him any further, they had in fact, without firing a shot or breaking a head, escorted him through 300 miles of territory whose hostile population constantly demanded his surrender. If they needed to buy a safe-conduct, they had the Gold Reserve to buy it with: tamely to surrender (as they did) Kolchak *and* the bullion to a weakling régime argues a lack of resource as well as a cynical disregard of the international mandates which charged them with the custody of both. The position was realistically summed up a few weeks later by Robert Hodgson, the quondam British Consul in Omsk. After rehearsing what may be called the *non possumus* arguments of apologists who maintained that the Czechs had no alternative but to hand Kolchak over, he wrote:

> It is unlikely that these considerations would have weighed seriously with the Czechoslovaks had they had at heart the safety of Kolchak. They had in their hands an ample supply of rolling stock, capable railway personnel among their own people and sufficient force to secure the working of the Cheremkhovo mines if necessary. That it was physically possible for them to get through is sufficiently demonstrated by the passage of Kappel's army, which was close to them, had not the use of the railway, was dragging with it a multitude of sick, wounded, women and children and yet, fighting the whole way, crossed Siberia from Novonikolaevsk to Chita. [240]

Kolchak, somebody once said, 'dug his own grave,' meaning by this that his conduct towards the Czechs was a main cause of his arrest and execution. On the face of it this thesis is valid, and it is supported by evidence which belongs, not to the subsequent polemics but to the immediate aftermath of his surrender. A Czech announcement issued in Irkutsk early in February gives a succinct statement of the Legion's case against Kolchak. It reads:

> We handed over to the Political Centre Admiral Kolchak, who, like every Russian citizen, is subject to trial by a court of law for his actions. Admiral Kolchak could not reckon on receiving sanctuary with the Czechoslovaks, against whom he had committed a criminal offence in giving his orders to Semenov to prevent by all possible

means our movement to the East, and not even to stop at the destruction of bridges and tunnels.[241]

Two points need to be brought out here. The first is that, although Kolchak's order to Semenov was an insensate act of folly, it was not issued until after, and would not have been issued unless, the Czechs had arbitrarily and without warrant prevented *his* 'movement to the East.' The second is that, by the time Kolchak was handed over, the threat to the Legion's interests which his order originally conjured up had been revealed as hollow. By mid-January Czech *échelons* had passed and were passing through the long bottleneck of the Baikal tunnels. Skipetrov (whom Janin believed, or affected to believe, had been charged with their demolition) was in Czech custody; and although he was supposed to have a quantity of high explosive with him, his small, motley force included no trained engineers and was in no way qualified to tackle the formidable task involved in demolishing a series of tunnels cut through the living rock.

It was natural that the Czechs should feel indignant with Kolchak, whose attitude towards them had been consistently ungracious and whose politics they violently disliked. It was natural that their animus should be increased by his order to Semenov, natural that they should overlook the fact that their own treatment of him had provoked it. It was natural, too, that they should want to disembarrass themselves of the responsibility for guarding him, since his presence in one of their trains was complicating, and might jeopardise, their evacuation.

'Do your best,' Janin says he told Syrový on the day before Kolchak reached Irkutsk. 'Preserve the honour of Czechoslovakia. I shall back you up.' It seems almost certain that both men had tacitly agreed, some time before this, that Kolchak was to be handed over. There was no attempt to stall, to delay matters, to argue the toss. The High Commissioners' directive was not invoked, although it was binding on Syrový and on Janin, and could not have been totally disregarded by the Political Centre, who were well aware of its terms. Nothing was done, nothing was said, to obstruct the smooth progress of an amicable transaction; the Czechs were even given a receipt for Kolchak.

An historian never knows *all* the facts, let alone all the fallacies which, working on men's minds, play their part in shaping events. But concerning the circumstances in which (to quote an official announcement) 'at 2155 hours on 15 January 1920 the representatives of the Political Centre . . . received from the hands of the Czechoslovak High Command the former Supreme Ruler Admiral Kolchak and the former Prime Minister Pepeliaev' the evidence that survives is, in essentials, complete. The gaps in it are not the sort of gaps that provoke doubts about its general tenor, about the authenticity of the picture that emerges. We know what was done, how it was done, why it was done. General Janin and General Syrový were responsible; and history, after making due allowance for their difficulties, must arraign them as the sponsors of an odious deed.

CHAPTER TWENTY-TWO

Mopping Up

'So ends a │ not very │creditable enterprise.'
│ highly dis│ H
C

THIS *envoi* closes a Foreign Office file dealing, in early March 1920, with the abolition of the post of British High Commissioner in Siberia. 'H,' who wrote the minute, was the Permanent Under-Secretary of State, Lord Hardinge; 'C,' who amended it, was Lord Curzon, the Foreign Secretary.[242]

None of the Interventionist Powers could with honesty have passed a more favourable verdict on their own activities in Siberia. It is true that their original object was achieved. The troopships carrying the last units of the Czechoslovak Legion sailed from Vladivostok on 30 November 1920. Altogether some 90,000 souls, including an unspecified number of women, children and old people were repatriated; with them went much valuable freight. But although the Czechs, like the White Russians, received material assistance from the Allies, it would be difficult to maintain that Intervention made a decisive contribution to the Legion's successful withdrawal from Siberia. Events proved that the Czechs were perfectly capable of extricating themselves, and would indeed have done so more expeditiously if no Allied forces had been present. The influence of these forces on their fortunes was in practice almost wholly detrimental; for although the Japanese and American garrisons east of Lake Baikal protected the railway against the Partisans, it was their presence that provoked Partisan activity because it outraged national feeling and stimulated revolutionary fervour in a way that the transient Czechs never did; and the heavy demands made by these foreign detachments on rolling stock and other railway facilities inevitably delayed the movement of the Legion towards the coast.

Apart from all this, the only direct threat to a successful Czech withdrawal from Siberia was exerted by Semenov; and the only reason why Semenov had to be taken seriously was because he had the Japanese behind him. Without them he would have had little more significance than a recalcitrant station-master; and without them he would not have pressed recalcitrance beyond the point of risk.

In the whole theatre the Czechs had only one essential requirement: a secure base at Vladivostok. They seized control of the port with a small part of their forces before a single Allied soldier was in sight; nothing happened afterwards to prevent them from holding it unaided, and if an internal or external threat to the security of Vladivostok had developed, the Allied warships lying in the harbour were a sufficient guarantee that nothing serious could come of it. The Czechs, in short, gained almost nothing from the cumbrous, controversial apparatus of Intervention, and would have been better off without it.

The liquidation of the Kolchak régime produced in Eastern Siberia conditions bordering on anarchy. But early in April 1920 the foundations were laid of a sort of buffer-state, known as the Far Eastern Republic, which gradually asserted its authority over most of the territory between Lake Baikal and the Pacific. Although it abolished the private ownership of land, the Far Eastern Republic was a radical democracy rather than an authoritarian state on Soviet lines, and for the two and a half years of its existence it remained nominally independent of Moscow. It was in effect a satellite, owing its viability less to Siberian aspirations for autonomy than to the Soviet Government's desire to insulate its eastern marches from direct contact with the Japanese. Its headquarters were at Chita, whence

Semenov was extruded in October; he fled in an aeroplane to Manchuria, where the least predictable of fates overtook him a quarter of a century later.

The departure of the last Americans (in April 1920) and the last Czechs eight months later left Japan with no valid excuse for retaining a large expeditionary force on Russian territory. But in March the Japanese garrison of Nikolaevsk, at the mouth of the Amur, and all the Japanese civilians in the town were massacred by Partisans.* Public opinion in Japan was profoundly shocked, and just before the last American troopship sailed Tokyo issued a statement alleging that the disturbed situation in the Russian Far East threatened not only the lives of Japanese residents in Siberia but also 'the general peace' in Korea and Manchuria; it was therefore impossible for the Japanese forces to be withdrawn 'immediately.' They finally left (after contracting their zone of occupation to a coastal enclave covering Vladivostok) in October 1922. In the following month the Far Eastern Republic responded to a jerk on the puppet-strings which linked it to Moscow by voting itself out of existence; and the Bolsheviks moved in.

The tragedy ended, the actors dispersed: some to obscurity, some to oblivion, many—from the White Russian camp—to a barbaric fate. Not all faded from the world's view. General

---

* The Japanese—numbering in all some 700—were by no means the only victims. At least 6000 men, women and children—more than a third of the population—were slaughtered on the orders of Triapitsyn, the Partisan leader. One of his orders prescribed the killing of all children over the age of five, who would otherwise remember what they had seen and might in later years harbour thoughts of revenge. Triapitsyn's Chief of Staff, and also his mistress, was Nina Lebedeva, a 25-year-old Communist who was supposed to see that the Nikolaevsk Partisans conformed to Soviet policy; showily mounted, armed to the teeth and habitually clad in dark red leather, she was a melodramatic figure. When a Japanese punitive expedition appeared, Triapitsyn razed Nikolaevsk to the ground and withdrew into the interior, where his followers, belatedly sickened by his monstrous deeds, arrested him. He, Nina and some of their viler associates were executed after a summary trial. There were few more gruesome episodes in the Civil War than the Nikolaevsk affair.[243]

Sirový was Minister of War in the Czechoslovak Government at the time of Munich; after the war he was sentenced to life imprisonment for collaborating with the Germans and died in 1953. General Gajda, after being tried for treason and acquitted in 1926, joined the Fascist party and for this offence (although he refused to have anything to do with the Nazis during the German occupation of his country) found himself in the same prison as Sirový in 1945. He was later amnestied, and is now dead. General Sir Alfred Knox, after retiring from the Army, had a distingushed Parliamentary career and is still alive. So, more surprisingly, is Anna Vasilievna Timireva.

But there were two men who, because each in his own way had a decisive influence on Kolchak's downfall, deserve a less cursory dismissal from these pages: Ataman Semenov and General Janin.

Semenov's flight to Manchuria was a direct consequence of the Japanese withdrawal towards the coast. In the early months of 1920 the advance-guards of the Red Army were still far away beyond Lake Baikal; but to the west and the east of Chita the Partisans were growing in strength and audacity, indiscipline was rife in the Ataman's small swashbuckling army, and his administration (if such it could be called) was rapidly losing the last vestiges of authority. So while the going was good he went, abandoning his little kingdom and its people to the encroaching chaos. Before his aircraft took off from Chita, his great hoard of bullion and other loot had already been transported, by courtesy of the Japanese, to Manchuria.

This remained his base for the rest of his career, though he once made an excursion to America, whence after a scandal and a lawsuit he was deported. As the Japanese hold on Manchuria tightened, Semenov's dependence on them became more complete; and he may be assumed to have figured in many of their nebulous plots and projects directed against his spiritual home, Mongolia.

All his life he had been a successful predator, making trouble, feathering his nest and then skipping when things got too hot. There was thus a certain irony in the fact that at the last he fell tamely into the hands of the régime which for twenty-five years he had strenuously opposed by words if not by deeds. When at the end of the Second World War the Red Army defeated Japan's Manchurian forces in a campaign lasting barely a week, Semenov was arrested by the Russian security services in Dairen.

In August 1946, with seven other White Russians of whom the most notable was Prince Ukhtomski, he was tried in Moscow by the Military Collegium of the Supreme Court of the USSR; all eight defendants were charged with carrying on anti-Soviet activities over a long period, throughout which they had been in Japanese pay. Evidence against them was given, with apparent alacrity, by senior Japanese officers who had been taken prisoner. Little was said about Semenov's record in the Civil War, but it was alleged that in the spring of 1917 he had tried to organise a plot to murder Lenin and other Soviet leaders.

All the accused were found guilty. Two were given long prison sentences with hard labour, five were condemned to death by shooting; Semenov was hanged. Justice, improbably personified by a Stalinist tribunal, thus overtook a man whose perversions of it had killed, maimed or ruined countless innocent people.

When news of what had happened at Irkutsk reached Paris, the French Government relieved General Janin of his command and ordered him to return to France, without, however, making their action public. He left Harbin in April, but before doing so accepted from General Dieterichs the custody of three suitcases and a chest containing a number—311, to be exact—of Imperial relics from Ekaterinburg. Besides a dossier of documents and photographs, his precious burden contained 'about thirty fragments of bone, a little human fat which had dripped off the logs [on which the bodies were burnt], some hair, an amputated finger which expert knowledge identified as one of the Empress's ring-fingers, charred remains of jewellery, small ikons, scraps of clothing and of shoes, such metal accessories as buttons, shoe-buckles, the buckle of the Tsarevitch's belt, bits of blood-stained carpet, revolver bullets, etc.' (The fact that this sad necrology included no teeth Janin attributed to the fact that the corpses had been decapitated and the heads, packed in sawdust, removed by a man with the sinister name of Apfelbaum; Janin believed firmly that the Tsar's execution was engineered by German agents.)[244]

These Romanov remains had been collected during a judicial enquiry into the massacre, and various people in Harbin—among them Robert Wilton, one of *The Times's* correspondents in Siberia, and Pierre Gilliard, a French tutor attached to the Imperial household—were trying to arrange for their delivery to the Grand Duke Nicholas, the senior surviving member of the family, who was then in France. For some reason Janin chose to surround his own part in the transaction with a cloak-and-dagger atmosphere.

After recalling his own close links with the Tsar (who had once, in conversation with a French politician, referred to him as 'my friend General Janin'), he described how the British authorities were asked to take responsibility for transporting the relics to Europe but refused; behind this unco-operative attitude Janin implausibly detected the influence of the wife— 'said to be a relation of Trotsky's'—of the British Consul in Harbin.

Janin leapt with alacrity into the breach thus created. The three suitcases and the chest were brought to his train after dark by Dieterichs and Gilliard; they reported being followed by '*des silhouettes inquiétantes*' which melted away when confronted by the Czech sentries. It is impossible to deduce from Janin's account who he supposed to have designs on the Imperial relics, what form those designs took, or what motives lay behind them. Nevertheless at Peking he took the precaution of having diplomatic seals affixed to the boxes, and when he embarked on a French warship at Shanghai her officers '*me facilitèrent la garde des valises durant la traversée.*' Against whom they were being guarded on board the cruiser is beyond conjecture; nor do we know how the more perishable relics withstood a voyage across the Indian Ocean at the hottest time of the year.

On arrival at Marseilles Janin was chagrined, and claims to have been surprised, to find that no official reception had been prepared for the dynastic débris of which, in France's name, he had assumed the curatorship. A local functionary suggested that he should transfer his responsibilities to the Ministry of Foreign Affairs, who would see that the cases reached the Grand Duke Nicholas; but Janin felt that such a course was incompatible with the obligations he had personally assumed, and he deposited the relics at his villa near Grenoble before going to Paris to report his return from service in the Far East. Reading between the lines of his account, one senses behind Janin's fussy attitudinising over the relics a pathetic anxiety to justify himself, to distract attention from his dubious performance in Siberia, to assert, with the help of a few bones and buttons, his claim to recognition as a pall-bearer at the funeral of the alliance with Russia which had once meant so much to France.

The gambit failed. Janin had a cool reception in Paris. The Minister of War warned him that at the Quai d'Orsay he was in bad odour. This was confirmed by the Minister of Foreign Affairs at an interview which, since Janin described its atmosphere as '*assez vive*,' must have involved plain speaking; there was talk of a commission of inquiry into his conduct towards Kolchak. Nothing came of this, but Janin was dropped—with many expressions of their esteem—by the Czechs, and as a result of '*des démarches diverses*' failed to get the appointment of head of the French Military Mission in Prague for which he should have been the obvious choice. He was given leave, and served thereafter in positions of obscurity.

It was not until October 1920, six months after taking charge of them, that Janin was able to disencumber himself of the Imperial relics. Nobody seemed to want them. The Grand Duke Nicholas declined their custody on the grounds that he was now only a private citizen. The former Russian naval attaché in Paris, who somehow became involved in the problem of their disposal, had nowhere to store them; '*un coffre de banque n'eût pas été décent*,' explained Janin, who seemed to feel that the suitcases ought to lie, as it were, in state.

In the end Janin received instructions from the Grand Duke to transmit the relics to a senior member of the Russian diplomatic service and was given a receipt for them, in triplicate. He was told that they would be sent to Wrangel's headquarters in the Crimea, but shortly after this Wrangel collapsed, and Janin never heard what finally became of the strange cargo which he had been at pains to salvage from Harbin. It was ironical, he reflected, that all that was left of the Imperial family should travel across the world in the care of a foreigner with a faithful heart and should finish up in France—where once the person of the Tsar had been enthusiastically acclaimed—without anyone knowing whether the sad remains had found a worthy resting-place.

His reference to irony will serve as a cue on which to take leave of the 'foreigner with a faithful heart,' who spared no effort to preserve the Tsarina's finger, her son's belt-buckle and many other small, charred, hallowable objects. If Janin had shown an equal solicitude for the brave man to whose interests duty and honour bound him, Kolchak would have found a worthier resting-place than the bed of the frozen Ushakovka.

FINIS

NOTES

CHAPTER ONE

1. My account of the Chelyabinsk Incident is based on documents quoted in *Za Svobodu* (*Towards Freedom*), Vol. II (Prague, 1926). Swollen though they are by rodomontade and trivialities, the four volumes of *Za Svobodu* contain—like even the most incoherent regimental histories—much detailed evidence which is of value to the historian. A circumstantial account of the same incident, which appeared in the *Daily Telegraph* of 27 May 1919 and is extensively quoted by W. P. and Zelda K. Coates in *Armed Intervention in Russia, 1918–1922*, tells roughly the same story but is disfigured by inaccuracies.

2. W. H. Chamberlin: *The Russian Revolution, 1917–1921*. Vol. II.

3. Karl Baedeker: *Russia (with Teheran, Port Arthur and Peking)*.

4. Quoted in A. L. P. Dennis: *The Foreign Policies of Soviet Russia*.

5. *Ibid.*

CHAPTER TWO

6. George F. Kennan: *Russia and the West*.

7. Quoted in Richard H. Ullman: *Intervention and the War*.

8. *The Testimony of Kolchak*. Ed. Varneck and Fisher. This source will hereafter be referred to as *Testimony*.

9. *Ibid.*

10. Testimony of Lt. I. E. Vuich, one of Kolchak's two companions.

11. Kolchak MSS.

12. Vuich.

13. *Testimony.*

CHAPTER THREE

14. Ullman.

15. *The Russian Revolution*. Vol. II.

16. Ullman.

CHAPTER FOUR

17. Wrangel: *Memoirs.*

18. Quoted from Semenov's memoirs in *Ataman Semenov* by D. J. Footman (St Antony's Papers on Soviet Affairs: unpublished MS). To this source I am indebted for many details concerning Semenov's activities in 1917–18.

19. Quoted in Ullman.

20. *The Decision to Intervene.*

21. Colonel John Ward: *With the 'Diehards' in Siberia.*

22. Quoted in Footman. *Op. cit.*

23. Baring's Diary.

24. C. G. F. Channing: *Siberia's Untouched Treasure.*

25. *Documents on British Foreign Policy, 1919–1939*. First Series, Vol. III. (Hereafter D.B.F.P.)

26. Britmis MSS.

27. *Testimony.*

28. *Ibid.*

29. Kolchak MSS.

30. *Ibid.*

31. Ward.

32. Kolchak MSS.

33. *Testimony.*

CHAPTER FIVE

34. John W. Wheeler-Bennett: *Brest Litovsk: the Forgotten Peace.*

35. *Ibid.*

36. Kennan: *Russia and the West.*

NOTES

37. Jane Degras: *Soviet Documents on Foreign Policy.*
38. Elsa Brändström: *Among Prisoners of War in Russia and Siberia.*
39. R. H. Bruce Lockhart: *Memoirs of a British Agent.*
40. Cumming and Pettit: *Russian–American Relations, 1917–1920: Documents and Papers.*
41. Kennan: *The Decision to Intervene.*
42. *Ibid.*
43. T. G. Masaryk: *The Making of a State.*
44. *Souvenirs de Guerre et de Révolution.* (Hereafter *Souvenirs.*)
45. Colonel A. Vergé: *Avec les Tchécoslovaques.*
46. *Ibid.*
47. *The Decision to Intervene.*
48. *Ibid.*
49. *Ibid.*
50. Maj.-Gen. W. S. Graves: *America's Siberian Adventure.*
51. *Ibid.*

CHAPTER SIX

52. T. Takeuchi: *War and Diplomacy in the Japanese Empire.*
53. B. M. Unterberger: *America's Siberian Expedition, 1918–1920.* (Hereafter Unterberger.)
54. Maj.-Gen. Sir C. E. Callwell: *Field-Marshal Sir Henry Wilson.*
55. *The Decision to Intervene.*
56. *Russia and the West.*
57. J. A. White: *The Siberian Intervention.*
58. Peter Fleming: *The Siege at Peking.*
59. Graves.
60. *Testimony.*
61. *Ibid.*
62. *Ibid.*
63. *Ibid.*
64. Britmis MSS.

CHAPTER SEVEN

65. Masaryk.
66. Beneš.
67. Masaryk.
68. Beneš.
69. Kennan: *The Decision to Intervene.*
70. Beneš.
71. Kennan: *Op. cit.*
72. Beneš.
73. Chamberlin.
73ᵃ. Sokoloff: *Enquête Judiciaire sur l'Assassinat de la Famille Impériale Russe.*
74. W. J. Novitsky: *The Russian Gold Reserve* (unpublished MS.).

CHAPTER EIGHT

75. Quoted in Ullman.
76. *Ibid.*
77. *Ibid.*
78. Howgrave-Graham's Diary.
79. Cazalet's Diary.
80. Unterberger.
81. Graves.
82. Britmis MSS.
83. *Ibid.*
84. *Ibid.*
85. Kolchak MSS.

CHAPTER NINE

86. Sir Bernard Pares: *My Russian Memoirs.*
87. *The Aftermath.*
88. Britmis MSS.
89. Janin: *Ma Mission en Sibérie.*
90. Footman: *Civil War in Russia.*
91. Bečvar: *The Lost Legion.*
92. Footman: *Op. cit.*
93. *Testimony.*
94. *Ibid.*
95. D.B.F.P.
96. Bečvar.
97. Britmis MSS.

NOTES

CHAPTER TEN

98. Ward
99. Footman: *Civil War in Russia.*
100. *Testimony.*
101. Chamberlin.
102. *Testimony.*
103. *Ibid.*
104. Kolchak MSS.
105. L. H. Grondijs: *Le Cas-Koltchak.*
106. Britmis MSS. My italics.
107. *Ibid.*
108. *Ibid.*
109. *Ibid.*
110. *Ibid.*
111. *Ibid.*
112. Information from a retired member of the Foreign Service.
113. Ward.
114. *Testimony.*
115. Kolchak MSS.

CHAPTER ELEVEN

116. Kolchak MSS.
117. Cazalet's Diary.
118. Beneš.
119. Janin.
120. Britmis MSS.
121. *Ibid.*
122. C. Nabokoff: *Ordeal of a Diplomat.*
123. Howgrave-Graham's Diary.

CHAPTER TWELVE

124. *The Aftermath.*
125. Janin.
126. *The Aftermath.*
127. *Ibid.*
128. Britmis MSS.
129. Cazalet's Diary.
130. D.B.F.P.
131. Ward.
132. Britmis MSS.
133. Kolchak MSS.
134. Britmis MSS.

135. Grondijs: *La Guerre en Russie.*
136. G. Fedotoff White: *Survival through War and Revolution.*
137. Grondijs: *Op. cit.*
138. Footman: *Civil War in Russia.*
139. *Ibid.*
140. D.B.F.P.
141. Britmis MSS.

CHAPTER THIRTEEN

142. G. F. White.
143. Kolchak MSS.
144. Baring's Diary.
145. Kolchak MSS.
146. Howgrave-Graham's Diary.
147. Baring's Diary.
148. Britmis MSS.
149. G. F. White.
150. *Ibid.*
151. HMSO: *Eastern Siberia.* M. A. Novomeysky: *My Siberian Life.*
152. Britmis MSS.
153. Grondijs: *La Guerre en Russie.*
154. Chamberlin.
155. Novomeysky.
156. *My Russian Memoirs.*
157. *With the Russian Army.*
158. Howgrave-Graham's Diary.
159. *Krasnii Arkhiv.* Vol. 49.
160. Britmis MSS.

CHAPTER FOURTEEN

161. D.B.F.P.
162. *Ibid.*
163. Quoted in Chamberlin.
164. Kolchak MSS.
165. D.B.F.P.
166. Grondijs: *La Guerre en Russie.*
167. A. I. Denikin: *The Russian Turmoil.*
168. Britmis MSS.
169. Janin.
170. Britmis MSS.

NOTES

171. *Ibid.*
172. *Ibid.*
173. *Ibid.*
174. D.B.F.P.
175. *Manchester Guardian*, 20 July 1920.
176. *Ibid.*

CHAPTER FIFTEEN

177. Footman: *Civil War in Russia.*
178. Private Information.
179. Britmis MSS.
180. Grondijs: *La Guerre en Russie.*
181. F. McCullagh: *A Prisoner of the Reds.*
182. George Stewart: *The White Armies of Russia.*
183. McCullagh: *Op. cit.*
184. L. E. Vining: *Held by the Bolsheviks.*
185. McCullagh: *Op. cit.*
186. Footman: *Op. cit.*
187. Grondijs: *Le Cas-Koltchak.*
188. Janin.
189. *Ibid.*
190. Footman: *Op. cit.*
191. Grondijs: *Op. cit.*

CHAPTER SIXTEEN

192. *The Aftermath.*
193. Footman: *Civil War in Russia.*
194. Britmis MSS.
195. H. Baerlein: *The March of the Seventy Thousand.*
196. Britmis MSS.
197. Janin.
198. *Ibid.*
199. Grondijs: *Le Cas-Koltchak.*
200. *Ibid.*
201. *Ibid.*

CHAPTER SEVENTEEN

202. Footman: *Civil War in Russia.*
203. Irkutsk Municipal Archives.
204. Grondijs: *Le Cas-Koltchak.*
205. Grondijs: *Op. cit.*

206. Britmis MSS. Diary of Lt.-Col. Malinovsky.
207. Footman: *Civil War in Russia.*
208. Grondijs: *Op. cit.*
209. Malinovsky.
210. *Ibid.*

CHAPTER EIGHTEEN

211. Grondijs: *Le Cas-Koltchak.*
212. Grondijs: *La Guerre en Russie.*
213. Footman: *Civil War in Russia.*
214. *Ibid.*
215. Testimony of I.D.S., a citizen of Irkutsk, who was one of the four men from Polovina accompanying the escort.*
216. Testimony of I.S.P., a citizen of Irkutsk, who was one of the five Partisans.*

* Experience has taught me that, unless their stories are supported by documentary evidence, only a very limited reliance, and often no reliance at all, can be placed on men's recollections of distant events in which they took part. But the testimony of the two eyewitnesses quoted here struck me as having unusual claims to authenticity. Each was in effect a member of a small delegation whose members all saw the same things at the same time and had the duty of reporting back to their comrades what they had seen immediately after they saw it; thus the accounts of their experiences were crystallised at an early stage, before the moths of time and human fallibility could begin to erode the fabric of truth. Both men spoke as private individuals, eager to talk about what had possibly been 'their finest hour.' I do not think that the accuracy of their small contributions to history needs to be called in question.

CHAPTER NINETEEN

217. *Testimony:* No further references to this source will be

given, since extracts from the proceedings of the Commission are readily identifiable as such and can have no other provenance.

218. Gutmann-Gan: *Beloe Delo.* Vol. III.

219. Grondijs: *Le Cas-Koltchak.*

220. Footman: *Civil War in Russia.*

221. Irkutsk Municipal Archives.

222. Britmis MSS.

CHAPTER TWENTY

223. Irkutsk Municipal Archives.

224. Grondijs: *Le Cas-Koltchak.*

225. *Ibid.*

CHAPTER TWENTY-ONE

226. Stewart: *The White Armies of Russia.*

227. Wrangel: *Memoirs.*

228. Howgrave-Graham's Diary.

229. Unterberger.

230. *Ibid.*

231. Britmis MSS.

232. Grondijs: *Le Cas-Koltchak.*

233. Graves.

234. Grondijs: *Op. cit.*

235. Britmis MSS.

236. Grondijs: *Op. cit.*

237. *The Aftermath.*

238. Grondijs: *Op. cit.*

239. *Ibid.*

240. Britmis MSS.

241. *Ibid.*

CHAPTER TWENTY-TWO

242. D.B.F.P.

243. The story of the Nikolaevsk Massacre, admirably pieced together, is to be found in *Testimony.*

244. Janin.

BIBLIOGRAPHY

[Unpublished sources are described and acknowledged on pp. xv–xvi.]

BAEDEKER, Karl. *Russia (with Teheran, Port Arthur and Peking)* (London, 1914)

BAERLEIN, Henry. *The March of the Seventy Thousand* (London, 1926)

BARING, Maurice. *What I saw in Russia* (London, 1939)

BEČVAR, Gustave. *The Lost Legion* (London, 1939)

BENEŠ, Edouard. *Souvenirs de Guerre et de Révolution, 1914–1918* (Paris, 1929)

BRÄNDSTRÖM, Elsa. *Among Prisoners of War in Russia and Siberia* (London, 1929)

BUNYAN, James. *Intervention, Civil War and Communism in Russia, April–December 1918* (Baltimore, 1936)

CALLWELL, Maj.-Gen. Sir C. E. *Field-Marshal Sir Henry Wilson, Bart., G.C.B., D.S.O., His Life and Diaries.* 2 vols. (London, 1927)

CARR, E. H. *The Bolshevik Revolution, 1917–1923.* Vol. III. (London, 1953)

CHAMBERLIN, W. H. *The Russian Revolution, 1917–1921.* 2 vols. (London, 1935)

CHANNING, C. G. F. *Siberia's Untouched Treasure* (New York, 1923)

CHURCHILL, Winston S. *The World Crisis, V, The Aftermath.* (London, 1929)

COATES, W. P. and Z. K. *Armed Intervention in Russia, 1918–1922* (London, 1935)

CUMMING, C. K. and PETTIT, W. W. *Russian-American Relations, 1917–1920: Documents and Papers* (New York, 1920)

DEGRAS, Jane. (Ed.) *Soviet Documents on Foreign Policy.* Vol. I (London, 1951)

DENIKIN, General A. I. *The Russian Turmoil* (London, 1922)

DENNIS, Alfred L. P. *The Foreign Policies of Soviet Russia* (New York, 1924)

DUNSTERVILLE, Maj.-Gen. L. D. *The Adventures of Dunsterforce* (London, 1920)

FISCHER, Louis. *The Soviets in World Affairs.* 2 vols. (London, 1930)

FOOTMAN, David. *Civil War in Russia* (London, 1961)

Ataman Semenov (Unpublished MS.)

BIBLIOGRAPHY

GRAVES, General W. S. *America's Siberian Adventure, 1918–1920* (New York, 1931)

GRONDIJS, L. H. *La Guerre en Russie et en Sibérie* (Paris, 1926) *Le Cas-Koltchak* (Leiden, 1939)

GUINS, G. K. *Sibir, Soyuzniki i Kolchak.* 2 vols. (Peking, 1921)

HALLIDAY, E. M. *The Ignorant Armies* (London, 1961)

HODGES, Phelps. *Britmis* (London, 1931)

HOFFMANN, Maj.-Gen. Max. *The War of Lost Opportunities* (London, 1929)

IRONSIDE, Field-Marshal Lord. *Archangel 1918–1919* (London, 1953)

JANIN, General Maurice. *Ma Mission en Sibérie, 1918–1920* (Paris, 1933)

KENNAN, George F. *Soviet-American Relations, 1917–1920.*
        Vol. I. *Russia Leaves the War* (London, 1956)
        Vol. II. *The Decision to Intervene* (London, 1958)
        Russia and the West under Lenin and Stalin (London, 1961)

KNOX, Maj.-Gen. Sir Alfred. *With the Russian Army, 1914–1917* (London, 1921)

KRIST, Gustav. *Prisoner in the Forbidden Land* (London, 1938)

LLOYD GEORGE, David. *War Memoirs.* Vol. VI. (London, 1926)

LOCKHART, Robert Bruce. *Memoirs of a British Agent* (London, 1932)

McCULLAGH, F. *A Prisoner of the Reds* (London, 1921)

MASARYK, T. G. *The Making of a State* (London, 1927)

MEDEK, Rudolf. *The Czechoslovak Anabasis across Russia and Siberia* (London, 1929)

MELGUNOV, S. P. *Tragediia Admirala Kolchaka.* 3 vols. (Belgrade, 1931)

MONTANDON, G. *Deux Ans chez Koltchak et chez les Bolchéviques* (Paris, 1928)

NABOKOFF, C. *Ordeal of a Diplomat* (London, 1921)

NORTON, H. K. *The Far Eastern Republic of Siberia* (London, 1923)

NOULENS, Joseph. *Mon Ambassade en Russie Soviétique, 1917–1919* (Paris, 1933)

NOVITSKY, W. J. *The Russian Gold Reserve* (Unpublished MS.)

NOVOMEYSKY, M. A. *My Siberian Life* (London, 1956)

PARES, Sir Bernard. *My Russian Memoirs* (London, 1931)

PHILIPS PRICE, M. *My Reminiscences of the Russian Revolution* (London, 1921)

SADOUL, Jacques. *Notes sur la Révolution Bolchévique* (Paris, 1920)

BIBLIOGRAPHY

SOKOLOFF, Nicholas. *Enquête Judiciaire sur l'Assassinat de le Famille Impériale Russe* (Paris, 1924)

STEWART, George. *The White Armies of Russia* (New York, 1933)

TAKEUCHI, Tatsuji. *War and Diplomacy in the Japanese Empire* (London, 1936)

ULLMAN, Richard H. *Intervention and the War* (London, 1961)

UNTERBERGER, B. M. *America's Siberian Expedition, 1918–1920* (London, 1956)

VARNECK, Elena and FISHER, H. H. (Ed.). *The Testimony of Kolchak and other Siberian Materials* (London, 1935)

VERGÉ, Col. A. *Avec les Tchécoslovaques* (Paris, 1926)

VINING, L. E. *Held by the Bolsheviks* (London, 1924)

WARD, Col. John. *With the 'Diehards' in Siberia* (London, 1920)

WHEELER-BENNETT, John W. *Brest-Litovsk: The Forgotten Peace,* (London, 1935)

WHITE, G. Fedotoff. *Survival through War and Revolution in Russia* (London, 1939)

WHITE, J. A. *The Siberian Intervention* (Princeton, 1950)

WRANGEL, General Baron Peter. *Memoirs* (1929)

Official Publications

Eastern Siberia (H.M.S.O., 1920)

The Evacuation of North Russia, 1919. Cmd. 818 (H.M.S.O., 1920)

Documents on British Foreign Policy, 1919–1939. First Series. Vol. III. Ed. E. L. WOODWARD and Rohan BUTLER (H.M.S.O., 1949)

History of the Great War. Naval Operations. Vol. V. Sir Henry NEWBOLT (London, 1931)

The Campaign in Mesopotamia. Vol. IV. Brig.-Gen. F. J. Moberly. (H.M.S.O., 1927)

Krasnii Arkhiv. Vol. XLIX (Moscow, 1931)

Index

249

INDEX

INDEX

Kolchak, Admiral A. V.: desire to serve British govt., 32–4; and Chinese Eastern Railway, 35–6, 54–5, 73; and Mme Timireva 56, 140–1, 163, 190, 198, 202–3, 216; at Irkutsk, 56, 195–208, 211; at Harbin, 68, 72–5; at Tokyo, 32–3, 75–6, 95–6; at Omsk, 99–127 *passim*, 134–6, 138, 139, 140–4, 154, 155, 157; appointed 'Supreme Ruler of All Russia', 111; aiming for Moscow, 147–8; eastwards from Omsk, 163–5, 170–3, 177–81, 185, 186–92; surrendered by Allies, 221–9, 237

Kotlas, 42 n., 120

Kraevsk, 105

Krasilnikov, 109–10, 112, 120–1

Krasnoshchekov, 195

Krasnoyarsk, 81, 123, 136, 165, 168, 178, 181, 201

Kudashev, Prince, 34, 35, 36, 54, 55

Kuitun, 208

Kulomzino revolt, 121–2, 213–14

Kuroki, Capt., 49

Lampson, Miles, 52, 191, 221, 224

Lansing, 65, 66

Latvia, 45 n., 133, 135, 155

Lazo, 48

League of Nations, 135

Lebedev, Col., 136, 158

Lebedeva, Nina, 232 n.

Lenin, 29, 57, 195, 234

Lithuania, 45 n., 133, 135, 155

Lloyd George, D., 24, 38, 91, 124, 125, 135

Lockhart, R. Bruce, 38, 39, 51, 60

Malinovsky, Col., 197

Malleson, Gen., 45

Manchuli, 48, 49, 50, 74

Mannerheim, 44, 155

Marianovka, 24

Mariinsk, 148, 172–3

Masaryk, Dr., 61, 65, 79

Maxa, 23

Mensheviks, 133, 163, 184, 193

Mesopotamia, 34, 35, 36

Middlesex Regt, 92–3, 101, 104–5, 108, 117

Mikhalevo, 184

Milner, Lord, 38

Mirbach, Count, 82, 87

Morrow, Col., 222

Mukden, 50, 53

Murmansk, 43, 44, 46, 64, 134

Myssovaia, 222

Nakajima, Gen., 73–4, 75, 95

Nicholas II, Emperor, and family, 84–8, 206

Nielson, Col. J. F., 113–16, 117

Nikolaevsk, 232

Nizhne Udinsk, 181, 184, 188

Novonikolaevsk, 24, 168, 169, 171, 227

Odessa, 131–2

Omsk, 23, 24, 62, 88–9, 98, 105, 123, 126, 136–7, 140–2; West Siberian Commissariat, 63, 81, 82; Directory, 97, 99–101, 108–11, 116; Kolchak at, 99–104, 108–22, 139, 140–2, 145, 154–64 *passim*, 220

Orel, 161

Orenburg, 84, 120, 148

Orlov, Col., 68

Otani, Gen., 93

Pasternak, Boris, 157

Payne, Capt., 22, 101

Peking, 34, 36, 41, 54, 55, 72

Penza, 24, 62, 63, 81, 83

Pepeliaev, Victor, 172, 181, 183, 196, 198, 215–16

INDEX

INDEX